AIR BABYLON

AIR BABYLON

IMOGEN EDWARDS-JONES
& Anonymous

BANTAM PRESS

LONDON · TORONTO · SYDNEY · AUCKLAND · JOHANNESBURG

TRANSWORLD PUBLISHERS
61–63 Uxbridge Road, London W5 5SA
a division of The Random House Group Ltd

RANDOM HOUSE AUSTRALIA (PTY) LTD
20 Alfred Street, Milsons Point, Sydney,
New South Wales 2061, Australia

RANDOM HOUSE NEW ZEALAND LTD
18 Poland Road, Glenfield, Auckland 10, New Zealand

RANDOM HOUSE SOUTH AFRICA (PTY) LTD
Endulini, 5a Jubilee Road, Parktown 2193, South Africa

Published 2005 by Bantam Press
a division of Transworld Publishers

A catalogue record for this book is available
from the British Library.
ISBNs 0593 054563 (cased)
0593 054571 (tpb)

Typeset in 11.5/16pt Sabon by
Falcon Oast Graphic Art Ltd.

Printed in Great Britain by
Clays Ltd, Bungay, Suffolk.

7 9 10 8 6

Papers used by Transworld Publishers are natural, recyclable products
made from wood grown in sustainable forests. The manufacturing
processes conform to the environmental regulations of the country of origin.

For The Passenger –
whoever you may be

ACKNOWLEDGEMENTS

With very grateful thanks to the wonderful Eugenie Furniss and Stephanie Cabot, the industrious Jenny Dare, the handsome Doug Young, and all of Transworld for their fabulousness.

And to all the people whose time and patience I called upon during the hours and days I spent interviewing them in cafés, offices, warehouses and cold damp corridors: I am extremely thankful as I could not have done this without your humour, trust and kind cooperation.

AUTHOR'S NOTE

All of the following is true. Only the names have been changed to protect the guilty. The anecdotes, stories, situations, highs, lows, scams, drugs, love, death and insanity are all as told to me by Anonymous – a wide and varied collection of people who work at the heart of the airline industry. The airport is fictionalized but the incidents are real, the celebrities play themselves, but the stories now all take place within a single fictitious airline known as Air Babylon. Narrated by Anonymous, the stories have been condensed into twenty-four hours, but everything else is as it should be. The rich scam up-grades, the poor smuggle themselves into the country, and the greedy spin a profit wherever they can. It's just another twenty-four hours in the life of the airline industry.

5-6 AM

Having spent the past ten years working for this airline, you'd have thought I'd have a better parking spot by now. Somewhere within the airport, at least, where I could park up in the short-term multi-storey and walk across without getting bloody rained on. But no. As duty manager, I'm one of the most senior employees my airline has working over here in the UK; I'm in charge of all that goes on in the airport and I am still parking my car at the bloody north perimeter fence along with all the other riff-raff.

And I've got a rubbish car. Well, everyone has a rubbish car if you compare them to the hardware the baggage handlers drive to work. It's like the forecourt of Jack Barclay out here. It's known as Jag row, although they aren't obviously all Jags. I can see a couple of shiny Audis, a BMW, a Lexus and a brand-new Merc glistening in the rain. Quite how baggage handlers manage to afford such glamorous transport on their wages is anyone's guess. But one thing's for sure: I won't be doing the asking.

I had a run-in with those boys a couple of years back. I found out they were watching the soap opera *Neighbours* on the TV instead of processing my lunchtime bags onto the carousel. They were causing chaos. I had irate passengers waiting for over an hour for their luggage. It was a nightmare. So I got their TV stopped and had my tyres slashed in return. A similar thing happened to a mate of mine. She was trying to broker a deal with baggage, knock down the quadruple overtime they get paid, change their working conditions a bit. She had her brake lines cut, she received threatening phone calls, and eventually she ended up being driven to and collected from work for her own protection. They are blokes not to be messed with. So now I know to keep my head down and not to ask too many questions.

It's still dark as I make my way to the bus stop and wait for the British Airport Authority courtesy transport to take me to the terminal. It's drizzling slightly. It's not enough to penetrate my clothes, but it sits on my shoulders like a dank cloak and makes my back feel cold. I stamp my feet slightly and scan the horizon for a glimpse of the dawn. In my job I can go for days at a time without seeing daylight. No wonder I have skin the colour of an avocado and red-rimmed eyes like a smack addict. I am supposed to do a five a.m. to three p.m. shift, but planes get delayed and passengers go crazy, and I'm not often out of the place until well after six p.m., when for half the year the sun has well and truly gone. Some days I don't even make it home. I check into a nearby hotel for a couple of hours, along with all the other aviation staff, then stumble back across the road to the airport. So you can understand why I am keen to spot just one ray of sunshine to get me through the day. That is, after all, why most us of got into the flying business in the first place. Sun, sand, sea and, of course, the glamour. It all seems rather ironic now, standing here, in the drizzle, waiting for the bus.

The queue is long. There are at least fifty of us waiting in a quiet, neat line. No-one is talking to anyone. Everyone is avoiding eye contact. I scan the group for anyone I recognize. I don't often find anyone. Well, there are some seventy thousand of us employed here and the whole airport has to drive to work. The public transport connections to this place are non-existent at this time of day/night, so none of us has much choice. A few of the locals manage to get here, catching the odd passing night bus, but other than that it's motors all the way.

I've got an old-school air hostess, or more correctly a flight attendant, standing in front of me. She's in her navy uniform, carrying her hat. She must be in her early forties but she is still slim and ramrod straight, sporting the hair-in-a-bun-and-pearl-earrings combination that used to be regulation some years back. You can always tell the old school from the new school by the way they are turned out. The old school wear pearls, tie their hair up and pile on the make-up. There used to be this rule that eyes and lips had to be visible six rows back, and they all still adhere to it. This one is wearing her high-heeled walking-through-the-airport shoes that make her hips swing as she whisks past the check-in. I suspect her flatter onboard shoes are in her wheeled bag.

The bus turns up and we all file in in an orderly fashion. It's weird, but on this journey, which I do every day, no-one ever barges past anyone else. The bus always fills up from the back and everyone takes their orderly place. It's like the most well-behaved school trip you've ever seen.

We travel to the terminals in silence. Our damp coats and warm breath quickly steam up the inside of the bus. I press my nose against the glass and try to look out. There isn't much of a view – giant warehouses, the Royal Mail sorting office, rows and rows of parked cars, the catering building that produces some ten thousand non-identifiable chicken dishes a day. The bus does the circuit of the terminals and my stop is last. By the end it's just me and the old-school hostess. We wander through the revolving doors into the building, into the glare of neon strip-lighting. She places her pillbox hat on her brushed and lacquered head and sashays off in the direction of some Far Eastern airline. I turn left, towards the five check-in desks that have been my domain for as long as I can remember.

Having been closed all night – there are no flights out of the airport after eleven p.m., and no flights coming in before six a.m. – the terminal is just beginning to come to life. Devoid of the usual throng of milling passengers, the place seems strangely empty. There are few signs of life. Two cleaners polish the floors, swinging their humming, hovering machines in ever more jaded circles, and various corpses stir on the seats and benches as I walk past. Tramps, alcoholics, Tube passengers who have fallen asleep and missed the last train home, airline passengers who have missed their flights and can't afford to stay in any of the nearby hotels – they've all bedded down together. Some are more semi-permanent residents: drug addicts who survive by selling discarded Underground tickets, students who have run out of money and need somewhere to crash for a few weeks, and petty thieves who dodge the police and pick pockets for a living. They say that an airport is like a shopping centre with runways, but I always think it's more like a city. It has the same facilities – its own police, its own ambulance crews, its own church – and it has exactly the same social problems.

The young shop assistant in WHSmith is struggling under the weight of the morning papers. His face is puffed pink and sweaty as he looks around for someone to help. He is on his own. None of the other shops is quite open yet, although there seems to be someone in Boots, striding around inside the shop, preparing to lift the metal grille and get the show on the road.

Just as I am walking over to give the poor bloke a hand, I feel a tap on my shoulder.

'Oi, where are you off to?' comes a familiar voice.

'Andy,' I say, turning around to smile.

'Morning,' he declares.

'Morning,' I reply.

'How's tricks?'

'Good. You know, the usual.'

'You don't sound too good,' he teases. 'Little bit grumpy.' He turns down the corners of his mouth.

'No? What? I'm fine. It's early.'

'Early for some,' he says with a grin, 'or late for others. It depends which way you look at it.'

'Right,' I say, stopping on the concourse and looking him up and down. 'Have you been out all night again?'

'Not *all* night,' he corrects.

'Oh, good,' I say, a rather large amount of sarcasm creeping into my voice.

'Just most of it.'

'What does that mean?'

'Well, I had a disco nap till midnight and I've come straight from Trade. Can you tell?'

I have to say, I can't. For a man who abuses his body and pumps it full of chemicals on a regular basis, Andy looks remarkably well. His permanent tan, acquired on the electric beaches of Sunbury, does much to cover a multitude of sins and heavy nights out. His white blond hair is gelled immaculately into place. His bleached teeth show no signs of nicotine. The only place where last night's decadence really tells is around the eyes. But Andy's always slathering on the Clinique eye gel that he gets at a 10 per cent discount at Boots. As airport employees, we all get 10 per cent off in the shops, but Andy's the only one who really takes advantage of this perk. Once you've had a few cheap burgers, bought your mother a scarf from Accessorize and shelled out on some cufflinks in Gucci the thrill tends to wear off. Unless, of course, you are Andy. He loves to shop almost as much as he loves to dance and take drugs.

And Andy does quite a lot of dancing and taking drugs. You would have thought his drug-taking would be a problem for the management, but I am the management and I don't really have a problem with it. Well, I can't really afford to have a problem with it. If I did have a problem with drugs then I'm afraid I'd lose half my check-in staff, particularly at the week-end. Come Saturday or Sunday morning, most of them arrive for work slightly the worse for wear, having spent the night knocking back vodka, Red Bull and Es on a podium in some club, somewhere. But just so long as they are pleasant to customers and do their jobs correctly, I don't care what they do in their spare time. They get a basic £11,000 a year, and I think we don't pay people enough to start dictating what they do after hours. Anyway, at least they pop their pills and snort their lines on their own time, which is more than I can say for some flight attendants I could mention.

'I don't think you look too bad at all,' I say, inspecting Andy's proffered-up face. His fingers stretch the skin under his eyes in an attempt to look younger.

'Not bad for an OAP?' he asks.

'An OAP?'

'Aren't you forgetting something?'

'Oh, happy birthday,' I say.

'Oh, happy birthday,' he mimics. 'Can't you say it with a bit more gusto? It's not every day that a man says goodbye to his youth and embraces middle age.'

'Middle age?' I laugh. 'You're only thirty.'

'Oh, don't,' he says, covering his ears and closing his eyes. 'Don't tell everyone. D'you have any idea how old that is in gay years?'

'No?'

'I'm practically dead!' he declares. 'Gay men age more quickly than dogs.'

'Oh,' I say. 'Bad luck.'

'Bad luck!' he repeats. 'I'll be lucky if I ever get laid again.'

'Chance would be a fine thing,' I say.

'What's that supposed to mean?'

'Nothing.' I smile. 'Absolutely nothing.'

'Is that all you're taking?' he asks, pointing to the small leather rucksack on my back.

'What else do I need?'

'Well, what have you got in there?'

'Toothbrush, trunks, clean underwear. I'm not going for long.'

'Straight men,' says Andy, and rolls his eyes. 'You've got no idea.'

I look down at the large, heavy-looking suitcase he is wheeling along beside him. 'What have you got in there?'

'Outfits,' he says. 'Just a few outfits.'

'But we're not even staying the night.'

'Who's the birthday boy?'

'You are.'

'Well, what's wrong with wanting to look your best?'

'Nothing,' I say. 'Absolutely nothing.'

We walk into the small office to the side of the check-in desks. Reserved for check-in staff, it smells of cheap coffee, sweet perfume and sweaty trainers. Lit by familiar neon strips, two of the white Artex walls are lined with pegs and it is a dumping ground for coats, bags and shoes. The scene of many a bitching session or crying fit, it is where all members of staff start and end their day.

Andy and I hang up our coats on our respective pegs and put

8

on our luminous yellow BAA gilets. I put my airside pass on its silver chain around my neck and switch on my black two-way radio. Andy does the same. He is my deputy and as such has to be in contact with me at all times. Working, as we do, both land- and airside, it's important that each of us knows where the other is at various stages of the day.

I think about making a cup of coffee using the small plastic kettle in the corner. But I can see there's no milk, so I decide against it. Anyway, I've got such a caffeine and nicotine problem that most of the time my hands shake. I really should cut down, but it's difficult. That's one of the problems working here: the hours are so long and anti-social, we all need a little something to get us through the day.

Andy blows his nose. It sounds like he has a heavy cold.

'Urgh,' he says, wiping his nostrils. 'I've got a bad case of cocktail flu.'

'I'm off to check the rosters,' I say. 'Do you want me to look at anything for you?'

'Oh,' he says, looking over his handkerchief. 'Can you just make sure they've got me on till seven p.m. tonight. Don't want to do all those extra hours and not get paid for it.'

'Especially on your birthday,' I say.

'Especially on my birthday,' he echoes with a grin.

It's because of Andy's birthday that we are both working so hard and pulling a near double shift. Instead of knocking off at the usual time, we are working through right up until we get on the 2015 flight to Dubai. Nine of us are going from the UK. Andy and I are the only ground staff who have made the effort; the rest of them are flight attendants, five of whom have requested to work the trip. For someone who doesn't fly, Andy seems to possess an unnatural number of flying friends. But that is probably because he shares a flat with Craig, a straight flight attendant and the only other person I know who is more badly behaved than Andy. In Dubai we are, supposedly, joining up with more flight attendants who are meeting us there from Thailand, Singapore or Australia. We are arriving early in the morning, partying the whole day and evening, and taking the 0140 flight back, landing at 0445 BST just about in time to start another shift.

To be honest with you, I am slightly dreading the whole thing. I'm the wrong side of thirty-five, and I feel a bit too old to be gallivanting halfway across the world on a giant piss-up. Don't get me wrong, I can booze and fly with the best of them. It's just that I have done rather a lot of it – New York, Rio, Miami – and I thought my day-tripping or weekend-tripping days were behind me. But I was extremely flattered to be asked and I suppose that is the reason I accepted. Andy's a nice fun guy and I didn't want to appear to be the dullard boss who was too boring to make it. So now I am pulling a double shift, doing an eight-hour flight, indulging in a day-long drinking binge, followed by another eight-hour flight, and all in the pursuit of fun and the celebration of Andy turning thirty. How on earth did he manage to persuade me that this was a good idea?

As I walk back out through the airport on my way to the roster office I notice that life is returning to the building. The WHSmith assistant must have found someone else to help because his newspapers are now all face out on their stands and he is managing the small queue that has already gathered at his till. Boots is open, and a powerful waft of caffeine tells me the guys from Costa's have already got the cappuccino machine up and running. I keep an eye out for the Benedictine monks who sometimes stalk the terminal looking after the homeless and the distressed. Mostly they do the evening shift from about seven p.m. till one a.m. but sometimes you can see their black robes flowing about the place in the early hours.

I walk past the arrivals gate and I can't help smiling. There is always some prat dressed up in something to delight and amuse. It strikes me as odd that people think they need to put on a costume to meet their loved one off a long-haul flight. It's just what you want when you get off a plane after a twenty-hour flight, to meet your family dressed as a bunch of kangaroos. There's normally some granny being welcomed home with a homemade banner stuck on a couple of broom handles. Or a collection of drunks with corks swinging off their broad-brimmed hats. Today, there are two young blokes in cork hats, some old bloke dressed as the Statue of Liberty complete with crown and torch, and a young woman still in her pyjamas. I know it's early, but you can't help thinking she might have made the effort to get dressed, especially as those PJs have certainly seen better days. Who beyond the age of ten still sleeps in Snoopy nightwear?

I finally arrive at the roster office, a large room not far away from the main concourse, next to a bureau de change, which we share with three other airlines. Walking in, you might be forgiven for thinking that you had entered maternity world, for every woman working in the roster office is up the duff. There are about twenty of them in here, all in various stages of pregnancy from the very slim to the huffing enormous. Some of them are so big you wonder how or why they came to work.

It is airline policy that as soon as any flight attendant falls pregnant, she is grounded and found an admin job of some description. Not that there is any medical evidence that flying is bad for you, or at all dangerous for your unborn child, or so they say. But there were incidences of attendants miscarrying at five and six months. Common sense suggests that all you really need to do is consider how cabin pressure crushes an empty water bottle to understand what it might be doing to the womb. Plus the flight attendant unions are powerful negotiators. Anyway, the uniforms don't contain enough Lycra to stretch over a bump. So what better place to put them than on rosters?

Janet is one of the girls who does our rosters. She is blonde, model-pretty and six months pregnant. She used to fly long haul out of London, but since her affair with a married pilot ended in pregnancy and tears she has been grounded and he hasn't had to see her in twenty weeks. Still, she seems to be remarkably stoical about the whole thing. Other girls would be in tears most of the time, but she apparently has a supportive mum who is only too thrilled that she is having a baby.

'Oh, hiya,' she says, as I come in. She always sounds a bit surprised.

'You're definitely showing these days,' I say, for lack of anything else.

'Oh, I know,' she groans, stroking her stomach. 'And I've got so much longer to go.'

'Oh, yes.' I nod.

'Don't say that,' she says.

'Oh, no,' I quickly reply, shaking my head.

'Anyway,' she says.

'Yes, right, well,' I say. 'I'm just here to check that you have both Andy and me on a double shift today.'

'Right,' she says, picking up a pen and clicking the end. 'Both of you?'

'Yes, both of us.'

'On a double?

'Yes, that's right.'

'No.'

'No, what?'

'No I haven't,' she says.

'Oh.'

'I've just got you,' she adds, flicking through her papers, licking the tip of her index finger as she does so.

'Oh,' I say again. 'But you should have Andy as well.'

'Right,' she says. 'Did he put it in writing?'

'Oh, I don't think he knew he had to.'

'It's the new rules,' she says. 'Since September eleventh—'

'But September eleventh was years ago.'

They're always doing this, introducing new rules whenever they feel like it and then blaming them on 9/11. It drives the industry mad. The pilots hate being locked into their flight decks, not being able to speak to anyone other than their number two for hours at a time. The hosties, or hostesses, hate having to remember ridiculous passwords, like 'mojo', in order to speak to the pilots. The ground staff find the no-nail-scissors, no-nail-files rules ridiculous, especially as there are glass bottles on the plane and sharper plastic knives in the air than there are penknives on the ground. And the flight crew find it pointless silver-serving bread rolls and salmon en croute only to have the first-class passengers tuck in using plastic.

And everyone finds the five-year security background check that we all have to go through these days in order to get an airside pass the most annoying thing of all. Not only was there a seven-month backlog when the new rule was introduced, despite the government claiming that it would only ever take six weeks, but now everyone, no matter how menial, has to be vetted. So, in order for Accessorize to employ a school leaver they have to write to their primary school to check they actually went there. Only last week I had to try to get a reference from a language school in China where one of my prospective employees worked during their year off. Anyone who's chopped and changed a bit, had more than two jobs a year or moved about doesn't get a look-in these days. Simple reason is, no-one can be arsed to check their employment records. Who wants to make thirteen phone calls when a couple will do? Talk to anyone who works in airport security and they'll tell you that the whole thing is pointless anyway. Anyone who wants to put a bomb on a plane can put a bomb on a plane. The only reason we haven't had another 9/11 in this country is because so far the terrorists have chosen not to.

'Well, that's what they said,' Janet says.

'When?'

'At the meeting last week.'

'So they actually mentioned nine-eleven?'

'Yeah.' She nods. 'That's the reason.'

'God.' I exhale loudly. 'So now we have to write everything down?'

'Or have it approved by your supervisor.'

'Well, I am Andy's supervisor, and I am also your supervisor, and I approve it all.'

'Do you?' she says, her voice rising up an octave. 'Well, that's OK then.' She writes Andy's name down on the roster.

'So that's all OK now?'

'Yeah.' She nods. 'Just so long as you say so.'

'Well, I say so.'

'Then it's OK.' She beams at me and leans towards a pack of biscuits. 'Hobnob?'

'No thanks.' I smile. 'You tuck in. You're eating for two.'

'Not these days you aren't,' she declares. 'You're not really supposed to put any weight on at all.'

Fortunately, before I can be drawn any further into this fascinating conversation, my radio crackles into life. It's Andy.

'Mate,' he says. 'You there?' He never uses the correct form of address.

'Yup, um, roger,' I reply down the receiver, as neither do I.

'The zero-zero-five is about to land,' he says.

'Yup, I was on my way to the gate.'

'Well, we've got a corpse,' he says.

'Oh, no. Roger that.'

'No thanks,' declares Andy.

'Not funny,' I say.

'Yeah, well. Will you deal?'

'Roger.'

'Careful,' he adds with a snigger, 'I've informed all the right authorities.'

'Thanks.'

'No worries,' he replies. 'See you over there.'

I sigh as I put my radio back in my pocket. A corpse. That's all I need at this hour of the morning.

6-7 AM

As I approach gate 56C, flight 005 is already docking. Being one of the more shitty airlines here at the airport, we've been allocated one of the more shitty gates. Airport gates are awarded on the basis of money and clout. The more the airline pays the BAA for landing rights at the airport, the more planes it has and the longer it's been flying in and out of the airport, the better the gate. So a small-time, impoverished parvenu like us tends to get the gates at the far reaches of the terminal, far from the lounges, where our passengers are more likely to get lost, go missing and not make their flights. It is also a nightmare for the wheelies, or wheelchair users. Not only is it hard enough to find a bloody wheelchair in the airport these days, but to push them to this back-of-beyond gate is a job in itself. Fortunately, as far as I know, we've had no call for wheelchairs on this flight.

I can see Andy is already on site and the ramp rats are attaching the finger – or, to put it more plainly, the blokes on the ground are hooking the plane up to the concertinaed end of the gate. This can cost precious seconds, and some of the low-cost airlines, namely Ryanair, who like to turn a plane around in forty minutes flat, choose to refrain from such customer luxuries as delivering passengers to the terminal. Hence most Ryanair flights dump you on the tarmac and make you walk the rest of the way, shaving whole minutes off their turnaround time.

'Sorry I'm a bit late,' I say when I finally reach Andy's side. I am sweating and slightly out of breath, having jogged past the last three gates.

'You're not.' He smiles, turning to face me. 'And I see you've brought your own entourage with you.'

I turn round to find a whole troop of policemen arriving in my wake. Shit, I think. What the hell is going on? We don't normally have this many bobbies for a body. I'm the one supposed to be in charge here and I'm clearly not abreast of anything.

'What are they here for?' I whisper into Andy's ear.

'Fuck knows,' he shrugs.

'You're no bloody help,' I mutter. 'Hi there,' I say, striding confidently towards the group of twelve rapidly approaching policemen. 'You all seem to be going somewhere in a hurry.'

'We're here for the incident,' says the more senior-looking of the bunch.

'Good,' I say, nodding away, using my most assured, most in-the-know voice. 'Very good. Um, there are quite a lot of you . . .'

'Yes, well,' sniffs the policeman, 'the man was reported to be violent.'

'He was?'

'Yes,' agrees Andy, with over-egged enthusiasm. He's a terrible actor. 'Quite violent indeed. Especially when he went for the, um, pilot . . .' His voice peters out.

'His wife, actually,' corrects the policeman. 'Quite a violent attack, or so I'm told. He's been in handcuffs since Singapore. Or at least that's the information we have from the captain when he radioed in this morning.'

'Oh, that man!' I say, rather weakly, convincing no-one. 'This radio's been on the blink all morning.' I smile and pat the top pocket of my blue suit. 'Never got the full story.' I never got any story at all. I feel like a total prat and shall be speaking to the captain about it as soon as I see him.

'Right,' sniffs the copper, looking towards the door of the plane.

Andy is clearly finding the whole situation hilarious. He is staring straight ahead, sucking on his cheeks and digging his right thumbnail into the flesh of his left hand. He always does this when he is trying to stop himself from laughing.

'All right, you guys? Where's the stiff?'

I turn around and peer through the mêlée of policemen to see Terry and Derek, the ambulance guys, walking towards us. Dressed in yellow jackets and green boiler suits, they look like two elderly members of an eighties boy band. Both in their late forties, they've been working in the airport for as long as I can remember. Grey-haired, florid-skinned, with fast-food bellies; they have the gentlest of demeanours and the most cynical senses of humour. They've seen it all, dealt with it all and packed it all off home in a bandage.

'It's always you long-haul lot who ruin our day with a stiff,' says Terry, the older and redder-faced of the two. 'Not enough air, that's my theory. You whack up the heating to twenty-six degrees to make the bastards fall asleep. Then you cut down the oxygen to save on fuel and you wonder why some of them cop it and the others end up kicking the shit out of one another.'

'Morning, Terry,' I say. 'Lovely to have you with us.'

'Morning, mate,' he says, slapping me on the back. 'So what have we got this time? A customer service director dead in the toilet?'

Both he and Derek laugh. Andy pretends to look shocked.

'You two,' he says. 'You're all heart.'

They might all snigger now, but at the time it was no laughing matter. A month ago one of our customer service directors died on a return flight from Thailand. It was a heart attack, apparently. The rest of the crew didn't know what to do with the body. The plane was full and there were no seats available, so they shoved him into the toilet. What else were they supposed to do with him? Pop him on a jump seat in front of all the passengers? All was fine until the plane landed and we had to try to get the body out of the loo. Rigor mortis had set in and it was impossible to move him. Terry, Derek, Andy and I were in there for hours, tugging and pushing, back and forth. It was worse than trying to get a great big sofa into a small sitting room. Eventually we had to break down the toilet. We pulled the whole thing apart. It grounded the plane for a whole forty-eight hours. The airline wasn't best pleased to say the least.

But, you know, any death on a plane is a nightmare. For a start, what do you do with the body? Leave it there? Move it? Do you have anywhere to move it to? Does someone have to fly next to the corpse? Is the neighbour the dead person's travelling companion? Wife? Daughter? Husband? Or do you put a blanket over the body and an oxygen mask on its face, pretend to the other passengers that they are just a bit under the weather and not, in fact, dead? Have they crapped themselves? Pissed on the seat? Everything comes out when you're dead. It can be quite disgusting. We have to ground the plane and change the seat covers immediately after someone's died. It's not much fun.

There are ways around it, though. I remember Andy telling me about a Filipino maid who died in economy on some continental airline only to be placed into a waterproof ski bag and filed on a seat in first class. Made the whole thing much easier. 'It was the only way she was ever going to be up-graded,' he said. 'Poor old bird.'

You'd be amazed how often it happens. Not upgrading corpses, but airline deaths. It's not a rare occurrence at all. In fact, it is so common that Singapore Airlines have just introduced a corpse cupboard into their new extra-long seventeen-hour Singapore to Los Angeles route. Some say there are so many air deaths because it is so stressful negotiating your way through an airport that by the time you actually make it to the plane your body is ready to collapse. Others, like Terry, think that it's the conditions on the plane itself – the lack of space and fresh air, combined with the cabin pressure – that lead to the number of heart attacks and embolisms we witness. Either that or there are so many elderly people doing long-haul 'trips-of-a-lifetime' to places like Australia when normally they barely get to the end of their street that some of them are bound to meet their maker before they touch down. Only the other day the BA208 from Miami had two deaths on the plane. The first was a grandmother who died of a heart attack, and the second was a man who more obscurely died of viral meningitis. Those seated next to him had to get written information on the virus before they were allowed to disembark.

There's a noise coming from inside the plane. It's the sound of doors going to manual. Suddenly they open and a dark-haired, rather attractive flight attendant appears. It's Shirley, who's in her late twenties and has principally been doing the Sydney run for the last three years.

'Morning, gentlemen,' she says.

We all take a step back as the fetid, foul air created by 378 people eating, breathing, farting, sweating and taking off their shoes escapes from the plane. The air is heavy and thick and the aroma is cloyingly stale. It's hard to believe that all these people have survived the stench and so little oxygen. Some flights are obviously worse than others, depending on what the passengers have been eating and how long they've been cooped up together. Sometimes the smell of body odour is so overpowering the last thing on earth you want to do is get on board. Fortunately for us, it's the police who have to go in first.

'He's right at the front of economy,' explains Shirley. 'The captain's on his way. He assaulted his wife and one of our members of staff. Slapped her across the face.'

'Leave it to us, miss,' says the senior officer. 'Just point out the wife because we'll need her to make a statement.'

The senior officer and three attending officers all board the plane, the other eight stand around looking official and important. Andy and I wait our turn. It's better to keep out of their way when it comes to arresting someone as there's no telling what might happen. And anyway, our passenger is hardly going anywhere.

No sooner do the police go through the door than some woman comes out. She has very short, very dyed blonde hair; she is wearing a denim mini skirt and a bright pink vest that matches the tanning stripes she has down both her shins. In her late thirties, she has the lines of a heavy smoker, the broken veins of a drinker and a red welt across her right cheek. She is being chased by Shirley.

'Hang on a second, madam, wait there,' she says.

'You can all fuck off,' yells the blonde as she strops towards us. 'The whole fucking lot of you.'

'There's no need for that, madam,' replies Shirley.

The blonde is standing right next to me. I brace myself. In my experience, telling someone off for swearing only ever leads to more.

'Don't you fucking tell me what I can and I can't fucking do,' the blonde continues. 'I'm on fucking land now. I'm nothing to do with you any more.'

'It's just that we need you to make a statement about your husband,' Shirley persists.

'A statement?' says the blonde. 'Fuck off! All I want is a fag.'

'If you could make a statement first,' tries Shirley, her voice growing weak.

'I want a fucking fag,' says the woman. 'I've been seventy fucking hours without one.' She starts rattling around in her handbag.

23

'Perhaps I could help you, madam?' I ask, trying to back Shirley up.

'Not unless you've got a fucking light,' she replies.

'We do need you to make a statement otherwise we can't charge your husband with the assault,' I explain as pleasantly as I can.

'What?' she says, looking up from her handbag, a cigarette balanced on her bottom lip.

'We can't charge him otherwise,' I say, with a smile.

'Like I fucking give a shit,' she says, the cigarette moving in time with her speech. 'I don't care what happens to him. I'm having a fag and I'm out of here. As far as I'm concerned he's your fucking problem.' She sparks up her cigarette with a Sydney Opera House lighter.

'Excuse me, madam,' says one of the policemen. 'You can't smoke here.'

'Oh Jesus Christ!' she exclaims, hurling the cigarette to the floor and stubbing it out with her white high-heeled sandal. 'I'm fucking out of here.'

And with that, she marches off along the corridor towards the terminal. No-one tries to stop her. We all just turn and watch her go.

'I think I might've punched her,' concludes Andy, 'if I had to sit next to her all the way from Sydney to London. No wonder he lost it in Singapore.'

At that moment the brawling husband in question is escorted out of the plane. He has a policeman at each armpit and his hands are tied in front of him with the same plastic handcuffs they used to restrain him on the plane. Red-faced and dry-mouthed, he smells like a pub carpet and looks slept in. Behind him comes a small, mousey flight attendant with an obvious slap mark across her face.

This man is in serious trouble. Air rage incidents are viewed dimly by the courts. I remember an Essex man who was recently sentenced to four years for slashing an attendant with a vodka bottle across the face, leaving her needing eighteen stitches. Also there was this extended Irish family who started a brawl on a Jamaica flight and were given twelve months and six months for endangering the flight and affray. So this bloke will get something like six months in prison with or without his wife's testimony, after his trip to Uxbridge Magistrates Court.

You have to feel sorry for the flight attendants who have to deal with it all. Air rage is on the rise: incidents increased by a factor of six worldwide between 1994 and 2002, from 1,132 to 6,500, and over half the incidents involved alcohol. Even celebrities aren't immune. I remember hearing about REM guitarist Peter Buck who was accused of attacking a member of the British Airways staff with a yoghurt pot, but was acquitted at trial. Then there's the more horrific story of the Stone Roses singer Ian Brown, who threatened to cut off a flight attendant's hands and was sentenced to four months in jail as a result. *Coronation Street*'s Tracy Shaw was an apparent victim of tiredness and lack of nicotine when she fought with her husband during a flight to the Cayman Islands. And a mate of mine had to deal with a northern rock band when they were threatened with handcuffing after they started throwing fruit at the air hostess on the plane. Fortunately the captain and the first officer managed to calm down the situation and prevent anything too unpleasant from happening.

But any air rage situation is enough to make you shit scared. Fights in confined places are no laughing matter, which is why the courts hand out such stiff penalties. Our flight attendants are now trained in how to restrain difficult passengers, and we supposedly have what is known as a 'sensible drinking' policy. Although no-one knows if that applies to the staff or the passengers. Having said that, judging by their appearance, I bet half the people coming off this flight have a hangover of some description. They all look a bit dishevelled.

'Morning,' says Andy, with amazing breeziness.

'Morning,' they mutter back as they file past.

If you've been in this business as long as I have you can begin to predict which passengers are going on to or coming off which flights. Affluent couples with Louis Vuitton weekend luggage go to Paris or Rome. Families with children and bright pink inflatables go to Spain. Backpackers and elderly trip-of-a-lifetime couples go to Australia. And this flight, so far, seems to be proving the point.

'Morning.'

A blue-rinse granny in pistachio slacks and yellow jumper who walks at a snail's pace.

'Hello.'

A flushed-looking middle-aged couple who've gone to either a wedding or the christening of their first grandchild.

'Morning.'

A young bloke the colour of mahogany, with sun-bleached hair, open-toed sandals and a didgeridoo.

'Morning.'

Another young bloke with a scarlet face and a didgeridoo.

'Hello.'

Yet another honey-tinged chap and a didgeridoo.

We must get about fifteen to twenty didgeridoos coming off any one Australia flight. I have no idea what you are supposed to do with them once you get them home. Leave them to gather dust in your bedroom? You could just leave them to travel round and round on the carousel, which is how at least two or three of them per flight end their lives when they get to the UK.

'Hello there,' says a young freckled flight attendant carrying a clipboard. 'Which one of you two is here for the un-accompanied minor?'

Both Andy and I look at each other and I can see his shoulders slump slightly. He knows that if he doesn't offer to take the minor then I'm quite likely to pull rank. Given a choice between a dead body and an unaccompanied minor, the body wins every time. Unaccompanied minors are a right pain in the backside. Not only do you have to sign for them at every stage of the game, like some very expensive parcel, making absolutely sure that you hand them over to the correct parents/guardians in arrivals, but they also seem to want to make it their business to run away from you. Just as you are looking out for their luggage, making sure you get their passport back or sorting out a visa, they piss off. They hide in the shops, squirrel themselves away in the toilets; they make it their business to give you a full coronary by the time you get to Customs. I've had my fair share of minors; quite honestly, give me a corpse every time.

'I'll swap you the stiff for the child,' mutters Andy out of the side of his mouth, knowing he is on the road to nowhere.

'No way,' I say.

'Come on,' says the attendant. 'He's not that bad.'

'Yeah, right,' Andy and I say at the same time.

'No,' she insists, 'he's really very sweet. Aren't you?' she adds, looking down at this short, rotund boy, squeezed into a pair of navy shorts. He has a rucksack on his back and a large plastic killing toy in each hand.

'Yes, Kathy,' says the child, smiling sweetly at Kathy before turning to look at Andy. 'I'm Jamie,' he says, his expression hardening, his eyes narrowing as a pair of horns seem to spring from the top of his head. 'Bet you my dad's richer than yours.'

'Probably,' says Andy, brusquely taking Jamie's dimpled hand. 'But I had mine killed.'

As Andy walks towards the terminal with his now mute charge, Terry, Derek and I get the nod to go aboard the plane.

Inside, the place is a mess. There are newspapers all over the floor, magazines lie curled up on the seats, and hundreds of bits of plastic ripped off complimentary terry socks or warm face flannels litter the length of the two aisles. It is amazing how much chaos nearly 400 people can create when flying from the other side of the world.

Terry and Derek go ahead of me. It's up to them actually to check that the passenger is really dead. I walk up the aisle behind Shirley, as she checks for anything left behind on the plane. You would be amazed by the sort of stuff they find. Dentures, spectacles and for some reason panties are the things most left behind on a plane, plus, of course, the odd coat, bag, book, magazine and stash of duty free. Shirley already has a coat over one arm and a child's brace in her hand and we're only halfway through economy.

Another couple of rows back and we reach the corpse. Terry and Derek are both nodding their heads, confirming that the man is dead; meanwhile a woman I presume to be his wife is still sitting next to the body. Her face is as white as a sheet and she is mincing her hands as she stares ahead, muttering under her breath. You can't help but feel for her sitting there, next to her dead husband. She must be in terrible shock.

I have to admit I don't feel that great myself. I know Andy and I sound quite blasé about these things, but you never quite get used to having to deal with the dead. The body has a blanket tucked around it and an oxygen mask pushed to the top of its bald head. The man's face is white and waxy, his mouth is slightly open, and his eyes don't appear to be totally closed. He looks as if he was in his late sixties. His wife appears to be about ten years younger.

'It happened so quickly, it happened so quickly,' she says over and over. 'One minute he was fine and the next he was dead. It happened so quickly . . .'

'Don't worry, madam,' says Derek, 'there is nothing you could have done. He wouldn't have suffered a thing.'

The captain arrives behind me.

'Heart attack?' he asks, in what sounds like a pseudo-concerned voice.

'Looks like it,' says Derek. 'It would have been very quick,' he adds, catching the widow's eye.

'That's what Shirley said,' says the captain with a nod, his

29

tight, dark curls shining with some sort of hair product. He leans forward towards the widow and pats her on the shoulder. 'I am terribly sorry for your loss.'

'Thank you,' she whispers.

'I know the hostesses did what they could.' He smiles and pats some more.

'They have been amazing,' confirms the widow.

'So, he died just as we landed,' he says quickly, turning to Terry, who is beginning to fill in the paperwork. Jesus, this man moves fast.

'No,' says the widow. 'It was somewhere over India.'

'Yes, of course,' agrees the captain, all smiles. 'Just as we landed? Mate?' he says to Terry.

'Don't worry,' confirms Terry. 'On touching down.'

Officially, when a passenger is taken ill or dies the captain is supposed to put down at the nearest available airport. But this almost never happens. Captains hate doing it as it ruins their schedules and costs the airline thousands in fuel and delays. This is also the reason behind the airlines' reluctance to fly anyone who looks a bit peaky, as if they might peg it halfway across the Atlantic. Captains like their passengers to die on terra firma in the UK, as getting a death certificate out of, say, the Indian authorities is often more trouble than it is worth.

'How long for the coroner and the undertakers?' asks the captain, checking his watch. He is supposed to be the last person off his plane, and this one is obviously keen to get the corpse shifted so that he can get off home.

'Not long now,' says Terry.

'Right,' says the captain. 'Tell me when they're here. I'll be on the ramp talking to the engineers. Goodbye, um, Mrs . . . ?'

'Mrs Fletcher,' says Mrs Fletcher.

'I am terribly sorry for your loss, Mrs Fletcher,' he says again, giving her shoulder another squeeze before disappearing up the aisle.

'Um, madam,' I say to Mrs Fletcher, who is watching the captain walk away. 'Would you like to come with me?'

'What?' she says, looking vacantly around to see who's speaking to her.

'Would you like to come with me?'

'Oh, right,' she says.

'Do you have anyone to call?' I ask, as she gets out of her seat.

'Oh,' she says, fumbling about in her handbag. 'Um, our daughter lives in Hammersmith.'

'Let's get you out of here, give you a cup of tea and call your daughter,' I suggest.

'I don't want to leave Albert,' she says.

'I know,' I say, 'but let's just let these guys get on with their job and you'll see your husband in a minute. It is for the best, I promise you.'

It really is for the best. The last thing she needs to see is her husband's corpse being hauled out of his dirty seat, placed on top of a drinks/dinner trolley and wheeled out of the plane. It is not the most dignified of exits and certainly not something that a wife should witness. But it is usually the only way to get a corpse out of a plane, especially when they've died this far back. If they're in first, club or further up the front you can put them on a stretcher, but this far back it's too heavy and difficult to get them out without using the drinks trolley.

I walk Mrs Fletcher very slowly through the terminal. She doesn't say a word as I take her through passport control and Customs. I tell her not to worry about her bags, saying that they'll be collected off the carousel and delivered to where she wants them to go. It is an odd feeling taking somebody so shrouded in grief through an airport of holidaymakers. The noise, the lights, the laughter and the music seem so wholly inappropriate. I only hope that she doesn't really notice. She is quite unsteady on her feet by the time I get her to the Quiet Room. It's a place where we take the bereaved and distressed so they can calm down and be alone.

Just as I settle her down into a comfortable chair and explain that I am about to get her a cup of tea and phone her daughter, my radio goes again.

'Hi, it's me,' says Andy.

'Sorry, I'm going to have to take this,' I say to Mrs Fletcher, whose eyes only vaguely seem to register the interruption. 'Go ahead, Andy.'

'Houston, we've got a problem,' says Andy.

'Can't you deal with it?'

'No, not really, mate,' he says. 'I'm waiting for my minor's parents to arrive.'

'I'm still with Mrs Fletcher.'

'We've got an illegal,' he says.

'Oh no,' I say. My heart sinks. 'Really?'

'Really.'

I tell you, now we're in the shit.

7-8 AM

I leave Mrs Fletcher in the hopefully capable hands of Janet. Well, there is no-one else to call on this early in the morning and, as a grounded flight attendant, she is sort of trained for trauma. I suppose I could call up Barry, the chaplain, on his mobile, but he doesn't come in until eight a.m. and it seems a bit unfair to call him in just to hold someone's hand for an hour, until their daughter arrives. Although, Barry's such a lovely bloke he'll probably be a bit pissed off I haven't disturbed him. Grief counselling is one of his fortes. He's the first person any of us calls in a disaster. I remember when they flew seven bodies home from the Australian hostel fire a few years ago, he was there, counselling all the relatives, making sure all the coffins came off the flights OK. He's a great bloke, but I do think Janet can manage the catatonic Mrs Fletcher until her daughter gets here from Hammersmith. All she really has to do is help her decide where to send her husband's body once the coroner has signed it off on the plane. There are funeral directors here in the airport to help her if she needs them.

Having settled Mrs Fletcher into Janet's care, I have to admit I'm hardly rushing towards passport control. Truth be told, I am rather steeling myself for an encounter with Immigration. I don't really like the bastards at the best of times. They're surly jobsworths. Employed by the Home Office, they are as unionized as the baggage boys and just as uncooperative. Woe betide any airline whose plane lands early before the beginning of Immigration's shift because their passengers will be left standing in passport control until those clock-watchers decide it is time to start work. They also blame the arrival of illegals on the airlines, like it's our fault that someone decides to rip up their passport, shove it down the toilet and claim political asylum. We're charged £2,000 for every illegal who makes it into the country and it is up to each airline to shell out for their deportation.

As I approach passport control my heart sinks further. All my hopes for one of those elderly customs officials who has seen it all before and cares a little less are dashed. Over in the far corner of the area, underneath the yellow sign, stand two rather lonely-looking figures. The first, in baggy, beige cotton trousers and a thin checked short-sleeved shirt, appearing all stooped and defeated, is my illegal. The second is equally slim but waspish, young and exuding so much officious authority that I can smell it from here.

'You took your time,' he says.

'I had a corpse to deal with,' I explain, irritatedly.

'Yes, well,' he bristles. You can tell this man went into Immigration because no-one was nice to him at school. 'Next time . . .'

Next time what? I feel like saying, but I don't. Things are bad enough for this illegal guy without me winding up the passport Nazi.

'Of course,' I smile instead. 'Anyway, who have we here?'

I nod in the direction of the illegal and try to catch his eye, but his head is lowered, his eyes fixed on his shiny new shoes. They look a little large for him. We get that a lot – illegals arriving in big new shoes. They come inappropriately dressed in summer clothes, their only concession to the inclement UK a pair of lace-up shoes. There can't be that many on sale in the Far East because they never seem to fit.

'No idea,' says the immigration officer, 'but my guess is he's from Indonesia.'

'Right,' I say. 'Has he said anything?'

'Not a word.'

'Right.'

'Except "political asylum",' he adds. 'They all know how to say that as soon as they step off the plane.'

'OK,' I say. 'Are you sure he's one of ours?'

'Don't try that one on me,' sniffs the officer.

'It's just that Qantas and BA have flights coming in at the same time as us—'

'We've got a video of him coming off your plane,' he says. 'Flight zero zero five, gate fifty-six C. You can't get out of it that easily.'

'Right,' I say. It was worth a go. I'm just trying to save

myself some time and the airline some cash. 'Any document-
ation at all?'

'Sweet FA,' says the officer.

'OK.' I sigh. 'Luggage?' The officer shakes his head. 'Great.
Nothing at all?'

'Nothing.'

His thin lips break into a smile as he knows exactly what I
have to do next. We both have visions of me in rubber gloves
shifting through shit in the aircraft toilet as I search for a
ripped-up passport.

'I'd better go and have a rummage and see what I can come
up with,' I say.

'Yes, you had,' he smiles.

'Right,' I say.

'In the meantime, I'll see if I can get hold of an Indonesian
translator.'

'Good. And I'll get Andy to check through the passenger list.
Someone must know who this man is.' I turn to the illegal and
tap him on the shoulder. 'OK?'

He looks up. His large dark eyes are haunted. They look
straight into mine. His misery sends a jolt right through my
whole body. Jesus Christ. Why do they put themselves through
this? Is it really worth it? Where must he have come from
for this to sound like a good idea? I really want to tell him to
get on a plane and go home. His admin hell has only really just
begun. He has months of limbo ahead of him. And for what?
Some shit, poorly paid job? Life's not that brilliant over here.

'I'll be back in a while,' I say to him. I'm not sure if he speaks
English. Sometimes you enunciate away like a moron only to

find out later that the man you presumed to be some dumb farmhand is in fact an emeritus professor of mathematics at some far-flung university with a perfect grasp of four languages, including English. He takes hold of my hand in both of his and squeezes it, like I might be able to help. It makes me feel even worse. 'I'll see you later.' I smile and nod at him. This has to be one of my least favourite aspects of the job.

Walking along one of the many corridors back towards the gate, I console myself that I might at least be able to slip off and have a cheeky cigarette before having to don my rubber gloves. We're not allowed to smoke at all in the terminal these days. We used to be able to puff away at will, or at least in the smoking areas along with the rest of the general public. But now it's a disciplinary offence to be seen with a fag in hand – they confiscate your airside pass. So if I can, I always find a route that takes me outside and out of view. I have a sixty-a-day habit. Fortunately I get them cheap. But that's mainly half-cigarettes snatched en route, rather than whole fags languidly enjoyed over a coffee.

I put a call through to Andy, just to keep him up to date with what's happening.

'Andy, mate, it's me. What are you up to?'

'Jesus bloody Christ,' he comes back. 'I've only just got rid of that little fucker.'

'What? The minor?'

'Honestly, mate, if I had my way, all kids would be shot at birth. Or born as adults. Thank God I'm fucking gay and I'll never have to deal with them. He was a right pain in the arse.

His parents were forty minutes late. It's a wonder they turned up at all. I wouldn't have, if that had been my child. I thought ten-year-olds were supposed to be sweet. This one was a right fucker.'

'What did he do?'

'What didn't he fucking do? He ran off, demanded sweets, hit a granny, attacked me with his plastic fucking toys. And he wouldn't stop talking. With the hangover I'm developing, it was a nightmare.'

'Having a happy birthday?' I ask.

'Bloody marvellous,' he replies. 'Anyway' – he lets out a long, loud sigh – 'I've delivered the little shit.'

'Yes,' I reply. 'And could you now have a look through the passenger list to see if we have anyone who might be our illegal.'

'OK.'

'My guess is he's Indonesian and got on at Singapore.'

'OK. Travelling alone?'

'Looks like it.'

'Anything else?'

'No, nothing I can help you with. Oh, male, obviously, and in his thirties.'

'Don't mention the "T" word,' moans Andy.

'Oh, sorry,' I say. 'Think of me, sifting through shit,' I add.

'It's an image I shall treasure,' says Andy.

'Good.' I laugh. 'Oh, will you check on Mrs Fletcher for me?'

'Done,' says Andy. 'Janet seemed to be doing fine. The daughter's yet to show.'

'OK, keep me up to date.'

'Will do, over and out.'

'Speak later.'

Just before my gate I spot a handy emergency staircase and slip off for a cigarette. It's been quite a morning and I need to gird myself before I get the gloves on and go passport fishing. At the bottom of the stairwell I find a Styrofoam cup packed to the brim with cold coffee and slowly biodegrading butts; plenty of people have clearly had this idea before me. I stand outside by the door and watch the ramp rats going about their business, unloading the baggage cartons, sorting out cargo, hooking the plane up to the electricity in the terminal, and attaching a tug cart to trawl it around the airport.

They are a real mixture of people. Some of them are full time, like the ex-dockers who took up jobs just as the ports were in decline and the airports were on the rise. The others are part-time plumbers and builders who need to put something down on their tax forms before accepting all those cash-in-hand jobs. Those are the guys who tend to call in sick when the World Cup is on; they are struck down with some terrible disease every time England play. They are similarly afflicted during major rugby games and on festive dates such as New Year's Day. They get paid when they call in sick – you only need a doctor's certificate after seven days – so what do they care?

A bloke in a bright yellow protective suit drives past on the honey wagon. His job is to empty the plane toilets. He attaches a hose to the side of the aircraft and pumps out the contents. It's not the most pleasant of jobs, and I swear to God the bloke who does it has smelt of shit every time I've stood behind him in the canteen.

Despite the conditions on the ramp, the noise, the rain, the cold, and the gales of freezing air every time a plane screams past, the atmosphere is jokey and packed with blokeish banter. There are some legendary nicknames that circulate. There's Kitkat, the bloke with only four fingers – he lost one while attaching a luggage trolley to a tug and was well compensated for his loss. There's also the Burglar, a bloke whose nose is so flat he looks like he is wearing a stocking.

But it is also a dangerous place. Accidents, such as Kitkat's finger, are more frequent than you'd think. The worst ramp story I ever heard was when a baggage handler got locked into the hold of a plane. It can happen quite easily if you are loading at the back of the plane and someone closes the hold door. Anyway, the plane was about to take off when a colleague realized he was missing. They ran across and stopped the plane on the runway. When they managed to get the hold door open, the baggage handler hurled himself out of the plane onto the tarmac, shattering his ankle, and ran and ran. Eventually they found him near the perimeter fence and he was a gibbering wreck. He had only been in there for half an hour but it had been long enough to send him crazy. Being locked in the hold is the baggage handler's equivalent of Room 101. It is pitch black in there and, when in the air, the temperature gets as low as minus forty. Apparently all the baggage handler could say was, 'It was cold, it was cold.' He had also undone some of the suitcases in there and had wrapped himself in clothes. Needless to say, he never worked again.

'All right?' I nod at one of the ramp guys as he walks past. I think I recognize him. He's called Kevin or Ken, or something like that.

'All right,' he sniffs back.

'Having a good day?' I ask in the special bloke voice I usually reserve for London cabbies or the ramp.

'What?' he says, turning to look at me. He's not the bloke I thought he was at all.

'Um, having a good day?' I ask again, rapidly losing confidence in my question.

'All right,' he sniffs again, and walks off, putting on his earphones, terminating our witty banter.

I take one last drag on my cigarette. The nicotine rush is making me feel a bit better. If only I could combine it with a cup of coffee, the alchemy would be complete. I throw the butt to the floor and stamp on it with my shoe.

'Excuse me,' comes this rather well-spoken female voice. I look up. Standing in front of me in a bright yellow coat over what looks like a navy puffer jacket is a woman *d'un certain âge*, or possibly older. She is wearing a calf-length navy skirt and flat, sensible shoes. 'Can I have a look at your pass, please?'

'Sorry?' I say, rather taken aback.

'Can I look at your pass?' she repeats.

'Um, sorry, who are you?'

'I'm one of the plane guards,' she replies, sounding put out.

'Oh!' I say. 'I'm terribly sorry.' I hand over the pass that was swinging around my neck. 'I'm just on my way to that plane.' I point over her shoulder. 'Looking for a passport, or a bit of one.'

This is one of the few times I've come across the new plane guards. A post-9/11 precaution, they are usually deployed in twos – one to stand at the entrance to the plane checking who comes in and out while the other circles on the ramp. They tend to swap over when the circling one gets too chilly. Anyone who thinks these new guards are CIA lookalikes with earpieces and guns will be sorely disappointed, as most of them are retired pillars of the community or housewives earning pin money. This one could be either. Their training, or so Andy says, runs along the lines of a two-day course during which they are shown the plane and the ramp and told not to get run over. I'm sure they'd scare the shit out of any al-Qaeda operative.

'Right,' she says, squinting slightly as she takes a closer look at my card. I want to hold it up to the light so that she can see it more easily. 'That all looks OK to me.'

'Thanks.' I smile. 'Seen anyone dangerous today?'

'Not so far,' she replies as she walks away. Humour is clearly not part of the job description.

I walk back up the stairs and along the corridor towards the gate. I am just in time to see Mr Fletcher coming off the aircraft on top of the drinks trolley surrounded by Terry, Derek, the coroner and a couple of blokes in smart dark suits who I presume to be the undertakers. They have covered the corpse in a blanket but it is still a deeply undignified exit. I'm glad Mrs Fletcher is at the other end of the terminal. Terry catches my eye and gives me a wink.

'Only the best for your airline,' he grins. 'No expense spared.'

They transfer the body into a black bag and on to another

more dignified trolley not usually reserved for drinks and snacks. They then wheel it off in the direction of the ramp and a waiting van. This comes as something of a relief as it's perhaps not the best advert for our airline to have the corpse wheeled through the terminal.

I watch Mr Fletcher's body turn the corner before boarding the plane. Poor bloke, I think, I bet he never thought it would end this way.

Onboard the place is a hive of activity. There are about six or seven cleaners scouring up and down the plane. Sporting industrial-strength pink rubber gloves, they are spraying and polishing away like they mean it. Unlike the cleaners in the airport who are mainly from Africa or the Eastern bloc, plane cleaners are all from the Indian subcontinent. The job is contracted out and each of the terminals has its own clique or group. Some say that they divided up by religions, Terminal 1 being Sikh and 4 being Hindu. Our terminal is mixed, but the guys who do our planes are mainly from north-west India, mainly Sikh, and mainly called Singh. In the good old days this used to work to their advantage. Paid around £250 a week, they used to split the job between a few of them so that any day of the week there was always someone who turned up, and they were always called Singh. They might look nothing like the guy on the pass, but no-one seemed to mind very much. These days, however, it is different. The rules have really tightened up. Only the real Mr Singh gets through. But sometimes I wonder, who is kidding whom?

I pick up a spare pair of pink rubber gloves from the cleaning trolley parked in club class. They go very well with the blue suit. Walking back into economy, I start picking my way through the rubbish on the floor. It's back-breaking work. Searching through biscuit crumbs, odd socks, glasses cases and curled-up newspapers is not my idea of fun.

But someone's got to do it, I suppose. Civil Aviation Authority regulations dictate that all planes have to be searched when they touch down, following some case in the eighties when a bomb was left on a plane after two passengers disembarked. But then again, plane searches don't always seem to happen. The other day a mate of mine found Shirley Bassey's passport, two days after she had flown. The plane had been to the States and back twice, and still no-one had spotted it. Quite how she made it through passport control without it is anyone's guess.

'Has anyone seen a passport? Or any bits of a passport?' I ask, standing in the aisle. Only two of the cleaners bother to look up and acknowledge my question. 'No? Anything?'

'No,' says one of them, a large smile on his face.

I'm not sure whether to believe him or not. There are a certain number of perks that go along with the cleaning job – a sort of finders-keepers unwritten rule. Although an airline will always insist that you'll be able to get your wallet back if you leave it on a plane, it isn't always the case. The same goes for any alcohol that's left unlocked, or bar that is left unbonded, or unsecured. But perhaps a passport is pushing it a bit. After all, how much is an Indonesian passport worth on the black market?

I make my way to the toilets. I don't know why I didn't go for them straight away – they are the most likely place. There is piss and toilet paper all over each of the floors. The stench is quite overpowering. I go through the bins underneath the basin, hoping that our illegal might have dumped the documents in there. The contents are quite unpleasant. I hold my breath so as not to have to inhale too much. Used sanitary towels, filthy tissues, a diabetic's syringe, the packaging for some anal pessaries – it is all in there. But no passport.

I don't know what to do. I'm not about to go through the contents of the actual toilet; Immigration can do that if they really want to. I've got another flight to deal with. The 0810 is about to land from Sydney via Bangkok and I have to be gateside for that.

Andy calls me on the radio. He sounds hassled.

'Where are you?' he asks.

'Elbow deep in shit.'

'Get your arse over to gate 54A. The flight's come in early.'

I peel off my pink gloves and sprint down the plane. If I hurry, I can go via passport control, inform the officer about the passport or lack of it, and still make it for the Bangkok flight. I need to be there on time. There is always no end of problems coming off that flight.

8–9 AM

By the time I arrive at gate 54A, via passport control, I am pink, puffed and have run so hard that I can feel the sweat snaking its way down my sides. This is turning out to be quite an exhausting morning. It's amazing how one corpse and an illegal can put the rest of your day totally out of whack. So far I've only managed one cigarette and a whiff of coffee each time I've sprinted past Costa's, and I'm really beginning to feel it. My stomach is rumbling. What the hell am I doing? I'm pouring sweat, my stomach is doing somersaults, and to be honest, my suit is looking a bit worse for wear. I'm hardly a good look for the airline at the moment. The glamorous face of the service industry. Exactly what the customers want to see when they disembark the plane.

There are a couple of ramp rats standing by the gate, but Andy's not here. They tell me he's off sourcing wheelchairs – the bane of our lives. Not only is there always a shortage of the things, but the people who request them often don't need them at all. I've lost count of the number of times I have wheeled someone through the airport, taken them through customs and passport control, and got a porter to pick up their bags, only for them to get out of the wheelchair in arrivals and sprint towards their waiting relatives. It is one of the oldest scams in the book. If you're in a wheelchair you get taken to the front of every queue and get given the same treatment as a visiting VIP. So you can understand its appeal. If you don't fancy waiting around it is the quickest way through the airport. It drives one of my flight attendant mates, Lynne, so crazy that as soon as the passenger gets out of the chair she shouts, 'Ladies and gentlemen! I give you another miracle courtesy of the airline industry! After decades in a chair, he walks again! Look how good he is on his feet! Look how fast he is!' They are normally so embarrassed by her outburst that they end up sprinting off as quickly as possible. Some passengers have no shame at all and use the wheelchair for their hand luggage when they get off the plane. It is extraordinary. Sometimes, and I don't say this very often, I think Ryanair had the right idea when it charged their passengers for use of wheelchairs. Perhaps it would sort those in real need from the fakes.

Andy finally arrives with three chairs. Two have Derek and Terry at the helm.

'Back again?' I say to Terry, who is looking even redder-faced than before.

'Yup.' He smiles. 'Seen your stiff off.'

'Good. Any problems?'

'No,' says Derek. 'The daughter turned up from Hammersmith and they all seemed to be OK when we left.'

'That's good.'

'We left them dealing with the paperwork,' Derek continues.

'Yuk.' Andy shivers, his skin looking grey despite his electric tan.

'What?' I say.

'Paperwork,' he says. 'Can't abide the stuff.'

'What are you expecting off here?' I ask Terry.

'Not sure. Just so long as it's not some old bird covered in shit like we had the other week.'

'What?' I say, taken aback.

'Jesus,' says Derek, bowing his head, 'that was a bloody nightmare.'

'It was,' agrees Terry.

It turns out some woman had come off an Air India or Air Pakistan flight on a stretcher and her colostomy bag had burst. Not only was she covered in its contents but she was shaking and sweating at the same time. All that sweat and shit looked like it might be catching so they called the Port Health Authority, which is what they are obliged to do if they think they have come across anything that might be contagious. The man from the Port Health Authority arrived slightly the worse for a few drinks and told them they were panicking over nothing. Terry and Derek refused to budge. They've seen enough shit, so to speak, to know when something doesn't look right. They didn't have the right equipment to deal with her and they weren't going to. Eventually, they got permission for a couple of Devonshire ambulancemen to come airside and collect her, taking her back to Devon where she lived.

'And do you know what?' says Derek.

'What?' I ask.

'We got a call yesterday to say that the blokes who took her down south were so ill with exactly what she had they had to fumigate the ambulance and boil all their clothes.'

'Really?'

'I know.' He nods. 'We know our shit.'

'Well, that's a nice story,' says Andy, running his hands through his bleach-blond hair. 'I'm glad you could share that with the group. Perhaps you would like to share it with those nice Customs boys coming up our rear ... all right, boys?' Andy looks the pair of them up and down. One of them is quite good-looking.

'All right.' They both nod.

'Here for any reason?' I ask.

It is quite unusual to have Customs meeting our Sydney–Bangkok flight. Thailand is obviously a drugs-producing country, but they have a death penalty in place for drug smuggling, which does tend to put people off somewhat. Jamaica, Nigeria, Pakistan and Turkey are their favourite flights to meet and they usually have a couple of money-sniffer dogs checking the flights out to Switzerland, as it's one of the favourite money-laundering routes for drug smugglers and gangsters. I never knew they had dogs that could sniff out cash until I started to work here. Apparently they can be trained to sniff out almost anything.

Then again, Customs have to be on their toes at all times. Only the other day they busted this smack-smuggling ring where the bags were coming through actually soaked in heroin. The drugs had been suspended in an ethanol solution and the bags had been soaked in the solution and then dried off. When they reached the UK they were re-soaked, the heroin was washed out and then dried. It was ingenious. But unfortunately for them one of the dogs got hold of the bags, and once you get picked out by the dogs, Customs won't let you go. Out come the Marigolds, and then it's a question of bend over and where's my torch? Or sit on the transparent toilet for the next couple of days and let's see what happens.

They do get quite a few swallowers coming through. They usually get spotted and flagged up on the plane, as a belly full of coke-packed condoms tends to put you off your lunch. And as soon as you don't eat anything, your card is marked by the flight attendant and they point you out to customs. You'd be amazed how much people can get inside them. Hauls of up to two hundred condoms at a time are not uncommon. Women, especially, seem to manage to smuggle quite large quantities. They caught a woman with a thermos full of cocaine inside her just the other day. She was walking rather strangely, which is what gave the game away. As was the guy they grabbed last week who had a whole load of diamonds up his backside. On his way to Uxbridge Magistrates Court, he managed to get out of the car and scale a wall, not realizing there was a thirty-foot drop the other side. He broke both his legs and ended up in hospital.

But it's not just the funny walkers they notice. Girls on their own are also on the list. Known as 'naive travellers', they are apparently what the mule-hunting smuggler is looking for in

Thailand, Turkey and Jamaica; as a result, lone females are often picked on over here. Sometimes it is just people who stick out – white people on predominantly black or Indian flights, or vice versa. Unless you fit the norm, the prototype for the flight, you scream something to Customs and they will pick on you no matter how innocent you may actually be. They spend their lives watching people, so they know what normal behaviour is, and as soon as you deviate from the norm they will pick you up.

And they are watching everywhere. From the moment you walk off the plane, while you are standing waiting for your bag, and most especially as you come out the other side of Customs, which is when most people finally let their guard down. The Customs mirror itself is supposedly designed to shift that process along a bit. It stretches you slightly, so you feel better about yourself, a little bit taller and thinner, as you go through, and you let your guard down just that bit more. They're full of little tricks and ploys. And they almost never tell you anything.

'No reason,' says the young, dark-haired bloke.

'You don't have a tip-off or anything?' asks Andy.

Neither of them bothers to say anything.

Finally, the plane door opens.

'Here we go,' says Derek, rubbing his hands together. 'Bring on the sick, the lame and the lazy.'

'Hi, hi, hi everyone,' says a rather round-faced attendant called Susan, who I have known for years and rather inexplicably started to fancy in the last six months. It is all rather worrying. I really must get out a bit more. I can't remember the last time I had dinner with a woman, let alone went to bed with one.

'Hello there, Sue.' I smile pathetically as I step back slightly, letting the foul inflight air out. 'Good trip?' I'm sure she knows I like her.

'Not too bad.' She smiles, fiddling with her small blue hat that is part of the new uniform. 'Only a few people misbehaved.'

'Right.' I can feel my cheeks growing hot under her gaze.

'Only a few,' says Andy, sounding disappointed.

'Although I do have a character for you today,' she adds.

'Me?' I ask.

'No, Andy.' She smiles.

'Oh yes?' he says, suddenly perking up.

'Don't get too excited. He's in his eighties but he's hilarious. Broke his leg trying to get it on with some lady on a cruise. He went back to her cabin and missed the bunk bed. He fell and broke his leg, and now all he can moan about is how he never got his end away.'

'I know how he feels,' mutters Andy. I look the other way.

'I thought as much,' says Sue. 'So, shall I give him to you?'

'Fine,' Andy replies. 'We can be two born-again virgins together.'

'What about last week?' I ask Andy.

'What about it?' He shrugs.

'Come on,' beckons Sue. 'He's right at the front.'

'What about us?' says Derek.

'Oh, an old biddy and some woman who broke her arm falling off a barstool.'

'Oh God,' moans Derek. 'Not another cocktail fracture.' Sue just smiles. It is wide and perfect. She always looks like she's just brushed her teeth. 'I bloody hate bloody drinking injuries,' Derek continues. 'It's always the bloody elbow. They fall off the stool and, in an attempt not to spill their drink, they land bloody elbow first.'

'Is that right?' asks Andy, clearly thinking it a good idea.

'At least it's better than another case of Venice bloody ankle,' says Terry, turning his wheelchair towards the plane door.

I've often heard them complain about 'Venice ankle'. In fact, I've often heard them complain about most things. But Venice ankle is a particular favourite. So many elderly Americans visit Venice and don't realize that the floors are made of marble. They slip over and twist or break their ankles, then their insurance companies end up paying for one of the boys to escort them home. Derek and Terry don't spend all their time at the airport, you see. They spend quite a lot of it actually on flights escorting patients home. There are thirteen regular staff in their unit but there are also a few who work part time, so they aren't always in the air. But more often than not they are. And the majority of the time is spent escorting Americans. Terry's favourite rant is that the Americans think that no part of the world is closed to them: 'The fact that they're ninety-three, on permanent oxygen, on their fifth coronary and they weigh fifty-four stone apparently doesn't bar them from sub-zero trekking in Iceland.'

But it's not all Americans with broken ankles. They get transplant patients arriving, with accompanying boxed-up livers purchased from somewhere where labour is cheap and body parts even cheaper, who need to be taken to a London hospital. They collect patients with terminal illnesses, transport premature babies in incubators and escort families where one or more have been involved in car accidents. They sometimes have to do incredibly long trips such as Kathmandu–Singapore–Amsterdam–Newark, which means that they have to travel in pairs so one can sleep while the other is awake. Terry's longest trip, as far as I know, was to the Falkland Islands. Apparently, by the time he got down there the patient had taken a turn for the worse and was unable to fly. So Terry sat on his backside for two weeks, checking out the penguins, looking at the views, contemplating his navel. Then, just when he was about to leave, patient on board and everything stowed, they found out there was no oxygen on the flight, and the poor bugger had to be disembarked again. Eventually the insurance company got so pissed off they threatened to sue the airline, and the airline, fearing a lawsuit, chartered a 747 just for Terry and his patient. They flew them to Cuba and the US in immense style.

'Oh, one other thing,' says Sue with a special smile as she makes to go back inside the plane.

'What?' I smile right back.

'We think we have a snake on board.'

'What?'

'I know.' She laughs. 'Bit of a nightmare for you, but' – she winks at me – 'I'm sure a big man like you can cope.'

'Of course.' I smile again, my chest involuntarily puffing itself out. God, do I hate snakes. 'Do you know what sort it is?'

'No. Some Thai guy brought it on in his rucksack and I think it has escaped into one of the lockers. It's right down the other end of the plane. Rachel's dealing with it.'

'Rachel . . .' I repeat, like I don't know who she is.

'Yes, you know, Rachel. Blonde, blue eyes, long legs.'

Sue is being generous. Rachel is nowhere near as lovely as she sounds. Sue has omitted to mention that Rachel is carrying more than the recommended hostess weight around her hips, and the fact that I once kissed her on the staff outing to Alton Towers three years ago. It was one of those mad drunken days when we all tucked into the warm white wine on the way back in the coach and one thing led to another. I tried to keep it a secret because I did rather like her. But she told everyone, adding that I kissed like a washing machine and that she'd only done it because she was drunk. As a result most of the flight attendants now give me a wide romantic birth, most probably Sue included. So, Rachel is the perfect person to be in charge of poisonous snakes, you may think. (Did Sue say the snake was poisonous? Or did my imagination just make that up?)

'I know Rachel,' I say eventually.

'Course you do,' says Sue. 'Well, she's waiting at the back. Oh, by the way. Don't mention the snake out loud. The only person who knows about it is the Thai guy who brought it on board, the passengers in his row and the crew, and we'd like to keep it that way.'

'OK,' I say. 'I'll get on to Animal Welfare straight away.'

'Hang on a sec,' says one of the Customs guys. 'I think we should have a look at it first. He may well be trying to smuggle it into the country.'

'I don't think so,' says Sue. 'I think he's got the paperwork, he just didn't want to put it in the hold.'

'You're welcome to have a look first,' I say – anything to

stop me from having to deal with the thing. It's something about the way they slither that makes my skin crawl.

'Um . . .' The young, dark-haired officer hesitates. 'I don't know one end of a snake from another.'

'No,' agrees the other.

'Whatever,' says Sue as she turns to go back inside the plane. 'I've got passengers to disembark. And you know how much they like to be kept waiting.'

'I think we should leave it to the professionals,' says the dark-haired officer.

'Yeah,' agrees the other. 'Get it caught and identified correctly and then we'll deal with it.'

'Anyway, we've got bigger fish to fry.'

'Yeah, absolutely.'

'So I'll call the Animal Reception Centre?' I suggest.

'Yes,' they both reply.

I walk back up the corridor to the gate to use the phone. I get hold of Jeremy from the Reception centre who seems thrilled to get my call. The youngest and newest of the Welfare guys, I've only done a couple of jobs with him, but he is always enthusiastic.

'A snake?' he says.

'That's correct.'

'Great! Do you know what type?'

'No, but it's from Thailand.'

'Great, Thailand,' he repeats. 'Reptiles are really my thing, you know. I've always loved them. Ever since I was at school. I've got a few at home, including a chameleon that eats flies and changes colour all the time. Oh great, a snake . . .'

'That's good.'

'I know, isn't it? Oh great!' he says again. 'I'll see you in ten minutes. Gate fifty-four?'

'That's the one. See you in a bit.'

As I stand by the telephone, the passenger stampede begins. I can see them all sprinting along the corridor the other side of the glass. I never know why people bother to rush off an aircraft. I suppose it's because they've been cooped up for hours, fed and watered at someone else's whim, and now, suddenly, they are allowed free will. But it doesn't make a blind bit of difference. If they are not held up by passport control, Baggage will get them in the end. They'll all end up standing next to one another in the taxi queue at the other end no matter how speedily they exit the plane.

Andy walks past wheeling his eightysomething sexpot. He points at the old boy's head and makes some sort of oo-er racy bloke gesture; he then gives me a little wave and blows me a kiss through the glass. Terry is not far behind. His old biddy is the colour of putty and looks like she's either been exhumed or is, in fact, not long for this world. He gives me a discreet finger as he pushes her along. Derek's too busy not being furious to do anything other than push his injured boozer along. I can see his determined face from here. And you can hardly blame him. Slouched in her chair with her tight yellow perm and sun-blasted face, shouting to someone on her mobile phone, she looks perfectly capable of walking.

I wander slowly back down to the plane to wait for Jeremy to turn up. He doesn't take long; clearly his reptilian enthusiasm makes him drive the ten minutes from the centre a whole lot faster. Skinny, mousey-haired and in his late twenties, he beams and waves as he walks towards me, bag and stick in tow. I tell him the little I know as we walk past the waiting Customs officers, who seem disappointingly short of smugglers. We board the aircraft together, but I hang back a bit. Well, there's no real point in getting involved, is there? I'm only here to see if the passenger is all right. Long, slithering reptiles don't know how to fill in customer satisfaction forms.

'You took your time,' says Rachel, clearly not relishing her proximity to the snake.

'I'm very sorry,' says Jeremy, apologizing for no reason. 'It takes me a while to get here from the centre. Now, what have we here?'

'I don't know,' says Rachel, stepping closer to the toilets.

'Hello,' says Jeremy, smiling at the Thai passenger. 'What sort of snake is it?'

The Thai shrugs and, smiling, points to the closed locker above his head. He clearly doesn't understand much English. 'Is it in there?' asks Jeremy rather slowly. The Thai guy smiles and nods again. 'Is the snake large or small?' he asks Rachel.

'I don't bloody know,' she babbles. 'I saw its head just when we were about to take off and I managed not to scream. I thought of taking the passenger and the snake off the flight, but you know how expensive that would have been, so I took all the other bags slowly out of the locker and asked the passengers to put them elsewhere. Told them there was a slight leak in the aircon and that locker was wet, and then I sealed the thing with some Sellotape.'

'So it has been in the locker the entire flight?' asks Jeremy.

'Yes,' she replies.

'Are you sure about that?'

'What?' says Rachel.

'Has anyone checked that it is still in there?'

'Um, no,' she says.

'What did its head look like?'

'What?' asks Rachel, not really listening. Instead she is slowly looking around the plane as if the snake could appear from anywhere. I have to admit I take an unchivalrous step backwards as well.

It has happened before. Last year a mate of mine had five African snakes escape from the hold. No-one knew how it happened, but they made it out of their boxes and into the passenger section of the plane. They were poisonous snakes and the airline spent a good two hours trying to find them. Eventually they gave up and the plane flew for weeks and weeks with them on board. The flight attendants were instructed to keep their eyes open for any reptilian stowaways. But they were never discovered. The theory is they escaped during a maintenance check.

It's a nightmare flying livestock. There are so many rules. Animals aren't allowed to fly with food for hygiene reasons, or coffins because the smell sends them mad. They also cause endless amounts of damage to the planes. Their urine is corrosive and their crap always ends up all over the hold. And they are always dying during flights because the captain forgets to flick on the hold heating switch on the flight deck and the temperature plunges to minus forty. I have seen so many dogs and cats arrive as stiff as boards it doesn't bear thinking about.

Some airlines will let animals fly with passengers. Household pets, for instance, are allowed to fly in kennels or cages. But anything like a snake or a lizard or a ferret is not. You'd be surprised to know how many people actually think they can get away with putting their lizard in their handbag, or travelling with a goldfish on their lap. We've had ferrets in rucksacks, guinea pigs in holdalls and tarantulas in jars. In the States, however, they do make an exception for 'celebrity pets', which are apparently allowed to travel just like any well paparazzi-ed human being. Regulations state that 'cats/dogs that are seen on popular TV programmes/commercials usually travel in the first-class cabin'. They may also travel in a seat provided that it is 'a celebrity animal' and does not just have 'a celebrity owner'. Also 'the animal companion must provide own seat cushion and seat belt adaptor for animal to be strapped in seat'. So I suppose the Dulux dog must be a regular up front from New York to LA along with Tom Cruise and Brad Pitt.

'What did its head look like?' asks Jeremy again.

'It was big and pale,' says Rachel through curled lips.

'OK,' says Jeremy. 'Sounds like a python to me.'

'A python!' says Rachel, edging ever closer to the toilets. 'You're kidding! D'you mean we've done a full service with a python on board?'

'Possibly,' mumbles Jeremy.

He is already standing on one of the chairs, peeling back the Sellotape from around the overhead locker. His thick rubber-gloved hand and forked stick are poised and he is looking to open the hatch.

'Um, do you really need me standing right here?' I ask.

'What?' he says.

'Do you mind if I step back a bit?'

'That would be right,' says Rachel. 'You take a step back.'

I ignore her, like I rather wish I had done three years ago.

'No, be my guest,' says Jeremy, slowly opening the locker. 'Anyway, by my reckoning the snake's not poisonous.'

'It's not?' My shoulders come down from around my ears; my heart flutters a little less.

'No, it's a constrictor,' he says, poking his head over the parapet.

The relief is short-lived. I take rather a large step back.

'Ahh,' says Jeremy. 'Sweet . . .' Since when has a snake been sweet? 'It's asleep.'

'It is?' I take a step forward.

'Oh, no,' he says. 'I've just woken it up.'

A couple of swift, deft stick-and-glove movements later and Jeremy has the albino snake out of the locker and into a waiting bag. He knots the top and starts to move up the aisle towards me. I give him a wide berth.

'OK if you come back to the centre with me, mate?' he asks me.

'Yeah sure,' I reply, trying to sound as relaxed as I can about travelling in a car with a bloody python.

'I need to go through your passenger's import and export papers, check to see if the snake is OK, if it needs some food, and make sure it's not a rare breed or anything like that. And work out if we need to fine the airline for bringing it in.'

'Right,' I say. 'I'm right behind you.'

That's not strictly speaking true. It's more like a good ten yards, but he gets my drift.

9–10 AM

I sit so rigidly quiet in the front of Jeremy's van that by the time we arrive at the Animal Reception Centre my whole body is stiff and immobile. I have tried to explain in sign language exactly what is going on to my Thai passenger who, according to his passport, turns out to be called Mr Narkpreecha, a thirty-eight-year-old textile dealer from Bangkok. But I'm not sure how much he understands. Judging by his well-tailored suit and pale blue Ralph Lauren shirt he clearly has plenty of money and does not seem perturbed or unduly worried about being carted off to the ARC. Indeed, he seems much more interested in the welfare of his snake, which is curled up in a sack in the back of the van. I've radioed through to Andy to track down a Thai speaker and send him or her along to the ARC pronto.

I have been to the ARC many times before but I am always struck by the smell. It's like nothing on earth. It assaults the back of your throat as you enter and is a mixture of strong disinfectant, acrid urine and dead parrots – which they get a lot of, apparently.

My mate Don, who runs the place, is always telling me how lucrative the rare-bird-smuggling business is. Apparently they come through in suitcases, crammed down cardboard tubes or plastic drainpipes. I remember a big case a couple of years back in which a whole load of birds of prey from the Far East were found, all shoved inside plastic piping. Most of them were dead on arrival; it was the rotting smell that had alerted a Customs officer. The smugglers apparently don't care if the animals live or die. They make £5,000–6,000 on the one or two that get through, the rest they can sell on for taxidermy.

Despite the odd smell, the Welfare office is something of a sanctuary. Bathed in natural light, it is a totally different world from the rest of the airport. The walls are lined with detailed charts and diagrams of bees, wasps, British beetles and butterflies. There are six white clocks in a row on the wall, showing the times in LA, Toronto, London, Cyprus, Bangkok and Sydney. The shelves are stuffed with big leather-bound volumes, everything from the *Dog Law Handbook* to the *Bird Wings and Butterflies of Papua New Guinea*. There are chains hanging up on the walls and weird-looking equipment used to restrain dangerous dogs, plus the odd cleft stick for picking up poisonous snakes. There are plants all over the place, a giant wooden tortoise on top of a cupboard, bottles of sherry and port on the shelves, model airplanes on every surface, and two stuffed penguins on the desk.

Standing in here, surrounded by so many curious things, I

always think this must be one of the most interesting jobs at the airport. If I hadn't hankered after being a pilot so much perhaps I might have ended up working here. Although I know most of the guys here are incredibly qualified with zoology degrees. Don spent twenty years at Longleat. There are also three vets contracted to the unit; some are local, while others work for the International Zoo Veterinary Group. Still, if it weren't for the snakes, I'd quite fancy it here.

I pick up a jar from the row of jars on the desk. I hold it up in front of me, letting the sunlight shine through the glass.

'I always think this is such a great place— Jesus Christ!' I shout, nearly dropping the jar on the desk in front of me. 'What the fuck . . . ?'

Mr Narkpreecha starts to laugh.

'It's snake whisky,' says Jeremy rather nonchalantly as he leafs through a book on his desk. 'All the jars are full of snakes. They're dead, mind you . . .'

'That hardly makes much difference,' I say, my toes curling up inside my shoes.

'Sorry,' he says. 'You really don't like them much, do you?'

'No shit, Sherlock.'

'They can't do you any harm.'

'That's not the point. Anyway, what are they doing on the desk? They're not normally here.'

'Yeah, I know, they shouldn't be there really. Don brought them in. They're from the Far East. Some of the snakes are in whisky and the others are in rice wine.'

'Oh, right, I know the stuff.' I nod, slowly bending over to take a closer but safe look.

Mr Narkpreecha laughs some more and makes a drinking gesture.

'They're supposed to be an aphrodisiac or some such thing,' Jeremy explains.

'Oh.'

'Anyway, it gets confiscated at Customs and we have to check to see if the snakes are actually dead or if they are rare species. The passengers can hang around and wait for us to do our bit and then get the stuff back, but most of them are tourists and can't be bothered.'

'So you get to keep it?'

'That's right.' He looks up. 'D'you want one?'

'No thanks,' I say quickly.

'They make great Christmas presents.'

'Who for?'

'My mum's got loads.'

'Lucky her.'

'Oh, hang on,' he says, running his finger over the page of the reptile book he is studying. 'I think we've found our man. An Albino Reticulated Python.'

'Are you sure?'

'Well, I have had some practice, but I might just get Don to check it out as well.'

Jeremy goes off to have another look at the stowaway snake that he has thankfully caged up next door.

I don't know why I'm questioning his judgement. He knows what he's doing, they all do – they get enough practice. Something like half a million reptiles pass through the centre every year. They deal with some ten thousand dogs or cats, thirty-five million fish, over three hundred thousand birds, and up to six hundred racehorses. They even get more than the occasional lion, tiger or elephant stopping over for a rabies check before they are sent on to a zoo or safari park. Elephants are normally only transported as small calves, but a while back a seven-year-old came through which went on to father two calves at Whipsnade Zoo. Apparently, he was a bit of a handful. Although not as tricky as the boxes of crocodiles Don had to deal with the other day. The smaller ones weren't too bad, he said: they were about seven inches long and packed fifty-to-a-hundred in polystyrene boxes. The large ones, however, were a different story. Packed in wooden cases, they weighed a ton and kept flipping around as soon as anyone tried to move them. It took eight blokes to shift each one of them.

Don walks into the office. His face is red, his nose is even redder and his white hair looks as if it has been blow-dried by a passing 747. He is wearing a thick coat, boots and fingerless gloves.

'Hello there,' he says to me as he walks in. His small blue eyes shine brightly. 'What a pleasure! I haven't seen you for a while.'

'No,' I say, getting out of my seat and shaking his hard, weathered hand. He slaps me hard on the back. 'Not for a month at least.'

'Not since . . .' He tries to click his fingers but they are too cold. 'Not since we had to get that racehorse on a flight for one of those Maktoum brothers. Do you remember?'

'God, yes. The Dubai flight. How much was it insured for?'

'Something like fifty million.' He smiles.

'God knows why it wasn't flying cargo like any other normal horse.'

'No idea.' He shrugs. 'Do you remember trying to get it into its aluminium stable?'

'I remember watching you doing that, surrounded by a whole mass of flunkies and vets and stuff.'

'That would be right. Anyway, how are you?'

'Great,' I say, somewhat overenthusiastically.

Although I have known Don for five years he is not the sort of person one shares one's feelings with. Over the years we have witnessed quite a few incidents together, and we sort of bonded when a macaque monkey escaped from its box on one of our flights – about three years ago now. God knows how it got out of its box. They're devious things. But it did, and when the cargo door was opened it made a bid for freedom. There were about twenty of us running around the plane, trying to catch the thing. It was all co-ordinated by Don, shouting above the noise of departing aircraft. Eventually we got the bastard after it made the fatal mistake of letting itself get cornered in the toilet on the plane. Don and I were always mates after that. Although, if I were being honest, I'd say that we were canteen mates. We've never actually met outside work but we are always pleased to see each other around the terminal.

'You?' I add.

'Fine,' he says, shaking his head.

'Where have you been?'

'Well, I've picked up another one of these guys in Baggage this morning,' he says, taking a Tupperware pot out of his jacket pocket.

'What's that?'

'A scorpion.' He holds the box up to the light. 'Can you see?'

'Yeah,' I say, watching it sprint furiously around its new plastic prison. 'It looks a bit cross.'

'It's bloody livid,' Don says with a laugh. 'It fell out of someone's suitcase on a flight in from the Ivory Coast. It's had about ten pairs of boots trying to kill it for the last half hour. No wonder it's so bloody furious.'

'I'd be a bit pissed off I suppose,' I say.

'It's the third one in the last two weeks.'

'Really?'

'Have you seen the Black Widow behind you?' he asks.

'No,' I say, turning around to inspect another transparent Tupperware pot sitting on the shelf. Strangely, I'm not that scared of spiders, no matter how big, hairy or mate-eating they get.

'That crawled out of some rucksack that came in from the US last week.'

'Oh,' I say, leaning in. 'It's big.'

'Oh yes. Big and black and female.'

'What are you going to do with it?'

'Not sure at the moment,' he mumbles, taking off his coat. 'What have you brought us today?'

'A snake.'

'Oh yes?'

'Came in concealed in an overhead locker.'

'Does it belong to this guy?' Don nods at Mr Narkpreecha who is now sitting down, staring at the bugs on the wall.

'That's right. Jeremy's next door identifying it.'

'Is he? He's great with snakes.'

'Good.'

'D'you fancy a cup of tea?' Don asks. 'Or do you have to get back?'

'I'm here until the snake gets identified and Mr Narkpreecha here can tell us about his animal.'

'Milk and one sugar?'

'Please.'

'What do you think our guest wants?'

'I don't know.'

'I'll get him the same,' says Don as he walks off down the corridor.

I sit down in a red plastic chair, opposite Mr Narkpreecha. I smile at him. He smiles back. It feels great to be sitting down. I have been running around all morning and my shift's only really just started. I've got check-in to deal with and Andy's birthday flight. I'm now really regretting having said yes to the trip. It serves me right, I suppose, for feeling so flattered to be asked.

Jeremy walks back through the door with his book under his arm.

'It's as I expected,' he says. 'It's non-poisonous, it's rare, but it's fine to bring into the UK. All we've got to do now is check to see if the paperwork is in order.'

'Great,' I say. 'Good,' I add, turning to Mr Narkpreecha.

'Good.' He nods back.

'Do you think the snake is hungry?' asks Jeremy.

'I have no idea.'

'It's been on a long flight.'

'That much is true.'

'I could give it some mice.'

'Sounds delicious.'

'Or a rat, a rabbit or a quail?' he continues.

'Whatever's on the menu,' I smile.

The Animal Reception Centre is well stocked when it comes to food. There is a wholesale company on the other side of the airport that supplies the frozen mice, rats, quails and rabbits for the snakes; locusts, millworms, crickets and other insects get delivered twice a week for the lizards and birds. The exotic fruits for the non-carnivorous birds and bats come from the local Tesco, and perhaps rather too grandly, the whitebait needed to feed a whole box of kittiwakes that arrived starving off a plane just the other day came from Harrods. So no-one can accuse the ARC of not bending over backwards to accommodate its guests.

Jeremy catches Mr Narkpreecha's eye. 'Would he like something to eat?' he asks slowly, making a munching gesture with his mouth and rubbing his stomach with the palm of his hand. Mr Narkpreecha seems to understand that food of some sort is being offered and gets out of his seat. But if he thinks it's his hunger that's about to be sated he is surely going to be disappointed.

Jeremy and Mr Narkpreecha meet Don in the corridor, and Don hands over a cup of tea to Mr Narkpreecha.

'They seem to be getting on,' he says, handing me my tea before sitting down in the recently vacated chair opposite.

'It's a mutual love for snakes,' I observe.

'Well, someone's got to love them.' He blows on his tea. 'Not my favourite member of the animal kingdom. I much prefer birds.'

As Don blows on his tea, I can see his face slowly defrosting. His cheeks glow less pink, the bright tip of his nose becomes less ruddy, and he begins to sniff. I know Baggage can be freezing, particularly when a plane lands or takes off. It sends blasts of freezing air right through the open building.

'Did it take a long time to catch the scorpion?' I ask.

'Why?' he sniffs.

'Because you look bloody frozen.'

'Oh,' he says, 'no. There was a muntjac deer on the runway early this morning, strayed in from somewhere. There must be a hole in the perimeter fence.'

'Oh God,' I say. 'They're a nightmare, aren't they? You've told me about them before.'

'Yeah.' He nods and sniffs again. 'So dangerous. I thought they'd fixed the fence, but apparently not. All you need is one of those meeting a 747 and it's curtains for everyone.'

'I suppose so,' I say, taking a sip of my tea.

'We were called out at about eight this morning near runway two.'

'Shit.'

'Yeah. It took us forty minutes to catch the thing and then I went straight to Baggage to sort out the scorpion, which is why I'm so cold.'

'Nice cup of tea should warm you up.'

'Mmm,' he says, blowing into his mug. 'Oh, they had the bird frighteners out this morning as well.' A broad smile cracks across his face. 'The most gorgeous pair of Harris hawks I have seen in a while. Scared the shit out of the pigeons.' He laughs. 'I think they were supposed to see off the swans but I haven't seen any of those for a while.'

Wildlife is one of the major problems for any airport. Situated as they normally are out of town and surrounded by barren scrubland with stretches of water, they attract all sorts of animals and birds. Normally animals such as foxes, deer and badgers are kept out of harm's way by the perimeter fence. But with birds it is a different story. Some airports release crackers or bangers at various intervals to scare them off; others, mainly the smaller ones, employ hawks or falcons to put the frighteners on; the rest just grin and bear it. We only have the hawks or falcons out when some airline has requested them – if they have had a major bird collision with a swan or something and the airport authority wants to look like it's doing something about it. A swan or any large bird can easily ground a plane. It flies into the engine, totally destroying itself and the machinery. Smaller birds are less of a problem. Given the right angle and the right engine they can do a fair amount of damage, but more often than not they are just toasted. The roast bird smell they give off often makes passengers on the plane think that chicken is being cooked in the galley, and they're often surprised when they are given a choice of fish or beef at dinner.

'They're probably all clogging up an engine somewhere.' I laugh.

'Don't say that,' says Don. 'It's not their fault someone built an airport here.'

'Suppose not,' I say, slightly embarrassed. I should really

pick my audience if I'm going to come out with dead swan jokes. 'Um, seen any more of those cheeky parakeets recently?'

The green ring-necked parakeets that live around Don's house in Shepperton are one of his favourite subjects. There is a rather aggressive flock of them, and they've been on the rampage since the seventies. On a summer evening, just as the sun is setting, you can hear and see them squawk past in a green flash anywhere in an area as wide as Esher, Reigate and the North Downs. With no natural predators, these natives to India are doing very nicely thank you, helping themselves to crops from the local fruit farms. No-one knows exactly where they came from. Some say they escaped during the filming of some buccaneering blockbuster at Shepperton Studios; others say – and Don's in agreement with this – that they escaped from Heathrow. They were said to be stowaways on a jet. Don's seen so many animals make a break for it as soon as they land here, he thinks the Heathrow theory is the most viable.

'Unbelievable,' he says. 'I saw a flock of about fifty of them fly past just the other day.'

'Really?'

'They're a right load of vandals. Stripped next door's apple tree of all its fruit. Well, what little there was left at this time of year.'

Don and I sit and drink our teas while I wait for the Thai translator to turn up. Don tells me that earlier last week he was flown up to Glasgow where he was met by a Customs officer and together they boarded a Russian ship. There he found, identified and confiscated seventeen cockatoos that were being smuggled into the country. He looks rather proud of himself as he tells the story, and I can't help but think how great it must be to get that much job satisfaction.

He seems to have had quite a busy ten days. He's had an escaped seal that was so aggressive both he and Jeremy, plus another bloke at the centre called Chris, had to go after it with broom handles and dustbin lids. After a good two hours' running around, they eventually managed to corral the thing back into its cage. Today, it is entertaining the troops at either London Zoo or Longleat, he can't remember which. They also had a tapir escape from its box. Somehow it got out of its crate and made its way to the staff kitchens. Don spent the whole afternoon trying to tempt it out of the cold store with a handful of ants. But the most complicated saga involved an eighteen-and-a-half-foot-long anaconda that came in from the States.

'It was going to be a pet for a member of some Middle Eastern royal family,' Don explains, 'but the thing had no paperwork so we had to impound it.'

'Really?'

'Yeah. There was a helluva lot of fuss about it. Apparently the member of the royal family was pissed off we'd impounded it. The Americans had wanted to get rid of it, and had given it retrospective papers. Tony Blair then got involved. He was having a meeting with the king of the country in question, and he didn't want anything to get in the way of their "amicable agreement".' Don does the quotes-in-the-air thing with his red hands. 'So some Middle Eastern bigwig flew over in a private jet, paid the pathetic three-hundred-pound fine and collected the snake so that there was no hitch in diplomatic relations!'

He starts to laugh. 'Stick around here, mate, we're right at the sharp end of it, I tell you!'

'Sounds like it.'

'Oh,' he adds, 'and we had a couple of stuffed armadillos. They were stuffed post-1980, so they were confiscated.'

'How can you tell?'

'It's all in the stitching,' Don replies tapping the side of his nose.

'Sounds like you've had a busy time of it,' I say, finishing my tea.

'Well, if you're open twenty-four hours a day three hundred and sixty-five days a year, something's got to happen eventually.' He grins, and gets out of his seat. 'Looks like your interpreter has turned up,' he says, nodding towards the door. 'I'd better get on. Will you be at the canteen at lunch?'

'I am aiming to be,' I say, 'but you can never tell.'

'See you there. If not, see you soon.'

'Absolutely. And thanks for the tea.'

It takes me another ten minutes to sort out Mr Narkpreecha with the help of Kelvin, a half English, half Thai student in his twenties who is studying mathematics at the LSE and translates in his spare time. Together we explain to Mr Narkpreecha that although his snake does have the correct papers, as confirmed by Jeremy, it should not have been travelling in the aircraft. We take his name and address in Bangkok and details of where he is staying in the UK, and explain that the airline will be levying a fine, as they themselves might well be fined. As Kelvin escorts him off towards the terminal and transport into town, I can't help but hope the bloke takes a cab. The idea that

Mr Narkpreecha might mislay his albino friend halfway to Piccadilly would stop me from using the Tube for months.

I thank Jeremy for all his help and turn around to leave. Surely things are going to get a little quieter? I've landed my two flights so I've only departures to go. Things should really start looking up from now on.

10-11 AM

I catch a lift back to the terminal on the BA livestock vehicle, which has been commandeered by Qantas to collect a couple of show poodles off its Melbourne flight. BA is the only airline that actually owns a livestock vehicle to ferry animals back and forth from the centre, but it makes sure that the vehicle more than pays for itself in rental. Jeremy and another young bloke from the centre, Paul, are laughing away as we drive along.

'If the owners only knew what sort of conditions their prize pooches were flying in,' says Jeremy, 'they'd never let them out of their sight.'

'They're all the same,' says Paul. 'The heated hold is just a hot pipe from the engine running through the plane. I've seen so many dogs arrive with ice on their bowls I'm amazed they survived.'

'Do you remember that consignment of birds we had the other day that arrived dead as dodos?'

'What happens then?' I ask, staring out of a grey, drizzly window. It has started to rain again.

'Well, someone like Don or me checks them to see if they've been packed properly or look diseased. If not, we shove a thermometer up their backsides, and if they're stone cold we advise prosecution of the airline.'

'Wasn't Qantas sued a few years back for killing a whole load of Rusa deer?' asks Paul.

'Yeah,' Jeremy confirms. 'On a Brisbane to Bangkok flight. A hundred and fourteen of them were flown out for some breeding programme, and sixty-eight died.'

'Here's hoping the poodles are show-ground perfect,' says Paul, blowing on his hands.

'This you here?' asks Jeremy, as the van pulls up outside the terminal.

'Yeah, thanks,' I say, getting out. 'And thanks again for all your help today.'

'Pleasure.' He smiles. 'I really enjoyed it.'

'Good. Next time I get another big snake I'll be sure to call on you.'

'Do. Don's birds, and I'm snakes!'

'What am I?' asks Paul.

'Small rodents,' says Jeremy.

'See you.' I smile and shut the door.

I check my watch. It's just gone ten. There's time for me to have a quick fag and possibly even a cup of coffee. I stand outside the door to the terminal, light up, take a drag and inhale deeply. I know I shouldn't, but it's a habit born of trying to get maximum pleasure in as few drags as possible. It hits the spot. As I exhale, even the drizzle can't dampen my enjoyment.

I can't believe I bumped into Susan today. Of all the days for it to happen it would have to be when I was hot, sweaty and stressed. I couldn't even think of anything amusing or witty to say to her. She must think I am some boring moron. And I could have done without Rachel. I take another drag on my cigarette. She is always bad for my confidence, and now she is going to go around telling everyone that I'm frightened of snakes. Although she was hardly Wonder Woman herself, slowly backing into the toilet. But no-one minds if women don't like snakes; it's not a good look for a bloke, is it? I bet she tells Sue. Like Sue's ever going to look at me anyway. Flight attendants don't go out with ground staff. We're hardly why they joined up, are we? No-one dreams of having an affair with a duty airport manager, do they? It's pilots in their dashing uniforms that girls dream of.

I stub out my cigarette. I've only smoked half of it but old habits die hard. I make my way back inside the terminal.

I walk back through duty free, and the place is packed. There are signs and offers everywhere, and in order to encourage spending they seem to have hung out last year's faded Christmas decorations, despite the fact that it's only the beginning of October. To the looped tune of 'Jingle Bells' and various other festive hits, holidaymakers, travellers and businessmen are parting with their hard-earned cash. And they've got plenty of outlets to choose from: Paul Smith, Harrods, Thomas Pink, Pringle, Bulgari, Gucci, Burberry, and Smythsons. The place looks like Bond Street, and it has rents to match. In fact, the ground rent in this place is one of the highest in the UK, with enclaves closer to the first-class lounges commanding the highest prices. In 2002, BAA earned £479 million from retail alone. It's a wonder some of the shops here actually make any money. Actually, quite a few of them don't. Some of the stores are loss leaders. For some reason, there is a certain amount of kudos attached to having your brand in the airport. With 170,000 passengers coming through a day, I suppose it's partly to do with the advertising potential, but it's also a lot to do with being part of UK plc. It's like being part of some glamorous club. Somehow, showing your face in the airport means that you are a big player in the high street. But boy, do they pay for this pleasure.

The BAA, or Build Another Aisle as it is more commonly known around here, not only charges the shops for the pleasure of being inside the terminal but also coins a percentage of turnover. So they have a vested interest in what you are doing. A mate of mine who runs a WHSmith in another airport says it's a nightmare. 'If the BAA see empty shelves, they want to know why. They are always encouraging competition between shops and challenging our performance. It's exhausting. We have to work hard for our money; we have to rely on thousands and thousands of transactions to make anything.' If we make 10p on a newspaper, he says, we have to pay the BAA 8p. That's part of the reason why no-one at the airport operates the National Lottery. The retailer makes 5 per cent on the lottery and would have to pay the BAA 4½ per cent. 'Last year,' my mate concluded, 'the BAA made a hell of a lot more money from the shop than we did.'

But the retailers are not the only ones to dislike their landlords. The ground staff hate them as well. Not only is the airport so packed with shops it's like Bluewater with a couple of planes parked outside, but BAA have also started to ask passengers to check in two, sometimes three hours before their flights. An unexpected bonus of these longer check-ins for increased security is that we all have to spend more time and money in the shops. The few clocks in the terminals mean that passengers lose track of time, buy more, miss their flights and delay the plane as we have to take their luggage off. It has been estimated that delays cost airlines £1,000 a minute, but they are impossible to quantify. But so long as the profits are up in Gucci, who cares? Another result of the three-hour check-in is that we have to rent our desks for longer as we have to open up earlier. And when one check-in desk costs around £50,000 a year to rent, you can see why we would want to hot-desk it with a little bit more speed. The last airline I worked for is now paying £10m a year for check-in desks alone. The BAA also have ultimate power, so when you have delayed passengers who are going nowhere, a child who has lost its mother and a man who has left his coat on the flight, they still walk up and say, 'Your check-in queue's a bit long – can you sort it out, please.'

The BAA's greatest detractors are the airlines. They pay so much money for landing rights that they tend to begrudge the 40 per cent annual price hikes they have to pay to finance Heathrow's new Terminal 5, or an extra runway at Stansted. The company's monopoly on all the airports in south-east England also gets up the airlines' noses. The relationship between Ryanair and BAA reached rock bottom at Stansted last year when, after disputes about fuel prices and wheelchair charges, BAA opened a mobile sandwich shop at one of their gates, thereby affecting Ryanair's onboard profits. So Ryanair banned all sandwiches from being brought onto the plane, saying that anything bought in the airport had to be put in the hold. These things sound petty, but when the BAA are making something like £286m a year in profit and plenty of airlines are close to the wall, any way to get back at them is to be applauded.

I walk past the Bally shoe shop and notice one of the girls changing the shoes in the window. I've heard they are supposed to do this four times a day depending on who is travelling through in order to maximize their sales potential. They put high golden sandals out for the Arabs in the afternoon and keep the sensible blue shoes for the Europeans in the morning. Well, I suppose that is one way of keeping the BAA off your back.

I carry on towards the baggage check. There's a couple having a fight outside Boots. He's shouting and she's crying. It looks like a good beginning to a relaxing holiday. There's a family being equally fractious in the entrance to WHSmith.

'I want another cartoon book!' the child is shouting as he throws his red and yellow rucksack on the floor.

'They've run out,' says the mother, sounding exasperated.

On towards the X-ray machines, and there's a huge queue. But then there's always a huge queue. These guys are supposed to be at the frontline of airport security, and they spend most of their time confiscating nail scissors and tweezers, or telling people to take their mobile phones or keys out of their pockets.

Although they do now also sponge your bags for nitrates, just to see if you've been handling explosives. Unfortunately, these are also the same nitrates that are found in plant fertilizers that as a nation of Monty Dons and Alan Titchmarshes we put on our gardens every weekend. So come Monday morning the queue can be terrible, as anyone who has so much as communed with nature over the weekend gets pulled over as a potential al-Qaeda operative. Today, it's just a lot of slow-moving tourists who are taking an age to get their coats off and walk through the metal detector.

I finally make it back to our check-in area and the small office at the back. I find Andy in there standing by the kettle, waiting for it to boil.

'Hello there,' he says. 'You all right?'

'Fine,' I say. 'Why don't you forget that and I'll buy you a proper coffee?'

'Cheers, mate.'

'It is your birthday after all.'

'You really know how to spoil a man, don't you?' He smiles, raising his possibly plucked eyebrows.

We both instinctively take off our yellow vests and airside passes, leaving them in the backroom. Wear anything official in an airport and you become a magnet for moronic questions. The number of times people have asked me where the toilets are when I am standing right next to them is enough to turn a saint to sinning. There's a saying at the airport that passengers pack their brains in their suitcases before they arrive; they are always disorientated, distracted and seemingly incapable of looking after themselves. 'Airport brain' is an official phenomenon. It is the only way to explain why perfectly normal people suddenly become useless as soon as they set foot inside a terminal. They seem to renege on any commitment to personal responsibility. They can lose their passport, their ticket, their luggage, their husband and their mind, all between check-in and the gate. Since we are sneaking off for a cheeky coffee when we should be doing something a whole lot more constructive, the last thing we want, or need, is to be disturbed.

We choose a table that is not too conspicuous from the main drag. I don't want any of my staff to see me sneaking off. I get Andy's skinny cappuccino with extra chocolate and my double espresso and sit down.

'Did you sort the snake?' he asks, blowing his foam.

'Yeah,' I nod. 'Thanks for organizing the translator, by the way.'

'That's OK.'

'God, I hate snakes.'

'I know.' He smiles. 'Rachel came through and said you were bricking it.'

'I thought she might.'

'Yeah, well, Sue stuck up for you.'

'She did?' I try not to sound too interested. But Andy's relationship radar is razor sharp.

'Oooh,' he says, giving my shoulder a little push. 'She did indeed.'

'That's nice of her.'

' "That's nice of her." "That's nice of her." What sort of response is that? You want her. You lurve her. I know you do.' He laughs. 'It's pretty bloody obvious.'

'Shut up.'

'It's just as well that she's coming to Dubai tonight, then, isn't it?' he smirks.

'What?' I say, looking up from my coffee.

'That got your attention,' Andy says triumphantly. 'She's coming with Rachel. Slightly unfortunate for you, but we'll work around that.'

'You've invited Rachel and Susan to Dubai?'

'Yes!' Andy can hardly contain himself, such is the joy at his match-making genius.

'I'm not coming,' I say.

'Yes you bloody are,' he says. 'And so is she, and that's the bloody end of it.'

'You're an evil little shit.'

'I know.' He grins. 'Don't you just love it?'

Andy and I sit in silence for a minute. I contemplate the hell that I am about to go through. The idea of spending an entire flight with a woman I think I'm in love with and a woman I really don't like at all is a terrifying prospect. The palms of my hands are beginning to sweat. Or is that the effect of the coffee? Why has Andy put me in this position? He thinks that one day I will thank him for this. That couldn't be further from the truth. Meanwhile he is blissfully pleased with himself, just sitting there, surveying the concourse, looking for talent.

'Those two look rather tasty,' he announces, watching two stewards walk past in their navy uniforms, trailing their suit-cases behind them.

'What about that blond bloke behind?' I suggest, trying to join in.

'Him?' says Andy, shaking his head. 'No, he's not gay.'

'How can you tell?'

'He's carrying his suitcase.'

'Oh.'

'Gay stewards wheel their suitcases like trolley dollies, straight stewards don't.'

'Right,' I say.

'D'you know, my mate who has just started at Stansted has had two stewards in a week,' says Andy. 'Mind you, he is gorgeous.'

'Where?' I ask, taking another sip of my coffee.

'Disabled toilets,' he says.

I am not at all surprised. For a supposedly transitory space, an awful lot of sex goes on in the toilets – a passenger with another passenger, or ground staff with another member of ground staff, or ground staff and a passenger, or ground staff with crew. A month ago we had some seventies band who did an impromptu performance at check-in for all the girls. After they were handed their boarding passes, one of my girls (who shall remain nameless) grabbed the guitarist, took him to the disabled toilets for ten minutes and wished him bon voyage. Andy's track record is hardly scrupulously clean. I know for a fact that he's had sex with a Middle Eastern prince in the toilets of the first-class lounge. Apparently, the young chap was moaning about having to go back home for the summer holidays from his university in the States. He kept on saying how boring it was going to be. Andy saw his way to cheering him up before he got on the flight.

Sometimes these relationships can get out of hand. There

were two lesbians who were working for the BAA and one of them found out that the other was having an affair with another lesbian and they ended up having a huge fight outside Harrods. It was one of the funniest things I had seen in a while.

'He says that Stansted's much friendlier than here,' continues Andy.

'I've heard that,' I say.

'The BAA's the biggest employer in the area so everyone who works there knows one another from school.' He smiles. 'Imagine the stories and the gossip. The girls from Accessorize have all snogged the boys at Prêt à Manger behind the bike sheds. It's hilarious.'

'I can imagine.'

'And apparently Bishops Stortford is packed with cabin crew. They are mainly Spanish and Italian because the airlines can pay them Spanish wages and say they're employed from Spain. Walk down the high street and there are loads of foreign-registered cars. Oh,' he adds, grinning, 'and put Bishops Stortford into Gaydar and it's packed with cruising cabin crew.'

'What the hell is Gaydar?' I ask.

'It's a gay website,' says Andy. 'I can highly recommend it.'

'I'll be sure to give it a whirl.'

A family dressed in matching shorts and Burberry checked hats march past, trailing their suitcases behind them. The youngest child is in tears, the mother looks as if she is about cry and the father is red-faced. In fact, he looks on the verge of a coronary.

'Have you heard they're looking for volunteer hostages again?' says Andy.

'Is it that time of year already?' I say.

'Yeah,' he replies, draining his cup. 'Do you fancy it?'

'I did it last year. It wasn't the most comforting of experiences.'

In fact, it was terrifying. It wasn't so much the exercise itself that was worrying but our seemingly inept response. It was enough to stop me sleeping at night. We do these exercises once a year where we simulate a hijack in the airport. The airport is closed and the police know that it's about to happen, and still they take twenty bloody minutes to find the plane. They may carry guns but they're fucking useless. They sure as hell don't know how to get to a plane quickly, even when they have advance warning and no passengers to deal with. Anyway, last year it went from bad to worse. I was taken hostage in the cockpit with the 'terrorists', and we watched the police approach the plane. The whole thing was risible. They sneaked along an illuminated corridor, rolling against the walls, walking past the windows in such a way that had my 'terrorist' actually been armed he could have picked them off one by one, like ducks at the fair.

But that's one of the things about working at an airport: it makes you realize how untrained we all are and how easy everything is. My mate Garry, who works in Baggage, always delights in telling me how easy it is to get a Semtex bomb through. Semtex apparently doesn't show up on an X-ray machine, unless it has specifically been programmed to test for explosives. It smells of marzipan, so either you make a wedding cake out of the stuff or, so Garry says, you line a suit-case with it in a nice thin layer so that it looks like lining. The detonator and battery are easy. You can get a small detonator that looks like coins and an even smaller Polaroid battery. Together they're tiny, the size of a sachet of tomato ketchup. He says it's simple to do. I always rather hope that it's a bit trickier than he pretends. But, he always adds, if someone is determined to hold up or blow up a plane, they're determined, and there's not much you can do about it. And on that front, I'm afraid, I have to agree.

'I think I might just volunteer,' says Andy. 'It might be a laugh.'

'It's not,' I warn him. 'Trust me. I wouldn't bother.'

'Oh, OK, if you say so.' He shrugs, obviously not that interested. 'Do you think we should get back?'

'Yeah, OK. I've got a whole load of admin to do before check-in hell begins.'

Andy and I get up to go, only to bump into Terry and Derek jogging past as fast as their doughnut-powered legs can carry them.

'Where are you two going with such . . . um, speed?' I ask.

'A shagging cart crash,' says Terry.

'Ouch!' says Andy.

'I know,' says Derek. 'Some fucker has only gone and run over some old bird on her way to Tenerife.'

'Apparently she's a bit deaf, didn't hear the loud bleeping thing on the cart and stepped right out in front of the guy, when he was transporting a whole load of fizzy drinks up to gate forty or something.'

'Nightmare,' says Andy.

'You can fucking say that again,' says Terry. 'As if we haven't had enough grief to deal with this morning.'

'And we're not even halfway through our shift,' adds Derek, heading off towards gate 40.

Neither am I, I think, as I wave them on their way. We've still got the check-ins to come.

11 AM–12 PM

Buoyed up by our double espresso and skinny cappuccino with extra chocolate, Andy and I make our way back through the terminal towards the small back office. I've got a few rotas to check over and I think Andy wants to go through his emails. As a man who regularly makes use of his discount flying perks, he is sure to have a stack of birthday greetings from all over the world.

We walk past the smart Cathay Pacific desks where they are checking in for Singapore, and I notice that two of their staff have been taken to one side and are being breathalysed. This is a new thing brought in by the BAA: they can randomly test anyone with an airside pass, and threaten them with the sack if they fail.

'See that?' I say, digging Andy in the ribs and pointing to my left. 'They're out random testing again today.'

'Shit,' says Andy, turning pale under his orange tan. 'They'd better not come near me. I'm sure I'd fail.'

'Why, when did you last have a drink?'

93

'God, I don't know,' he says, clearly remembering with slight delight the last vodka he slipped down before coming to work. 'But I know it was certainly less than eight hours ago.'

'I could really do without them coming anywhere near my check-in desks today,' I say. 'I know at least three of the girls went to the Flying Club in Luton last night.'

'Jesus Christ,' says Andy, stopping in his tracks. 'Do you have any idea what goes on there?'

'Drinking, dancing, drinking, stripping, drinking. Last time Cathy went she told me someone poured chocolate all over her tits and someone else licked it off.'

'She the one who used to work for EasyJet?'

'That's right. Apparently the Flying Club is big with EasyJet hostesses and baggage handlers.'

'What a combination,' says Andy, shaking his head.

'What, hosties and baggage handlers or chocolate tits?'

'Both.'

'I know.' I nod, my imagination working overtime.

'How many of them went last night?'

'At least three,' I say.

'And you're expecting them in for work?'

'Well, it's not an early start, is it? It's not like any of them are doing the five a.m. shift.'

'That's true, but I am prepared to take a bet that we'll be at least two down.'

'Twenty quid says they all make it in.'

'All of them?'

'Why not?' I smile, my hand out. 'Think of it as an early birthday present if I lose.'

'You're on.' Andy grins and shakes my hand. 'I bet at least two of them call in with "plumbing problems",' he adds, doing the quotes thing, still shaking my hand. His grip suddenly gets tighter. 'Shit,' he mutters under his breath. 'Shit, shit, shit . . .'

'What?' I say, turning round.

'Don't turn around,' he hisses.

'What?' I whisper, turning back, still shaking his hand.

'The breath fuckers are coming this way,' he says, his eyes round with fear. I can feel the palm of his hand start to sweat. He stops shaking my hand and stands there simply holding it. The colour is draining from his face as eight years in the business seem slowly to trickle down the pan.

'I'll get them to do just me,' I say as they approach out of the corner of my eye. 'I'll send you off to do something. Don't worry, I'll look after you, I promise.'

'Sh-ii-it,' says Andy, closing his eyes, awaiting impact. He squeezes my hand tightly. 'Here we go . . .'

I turn around to face the two BAA testers. I place myself in front of Andy so they pick on me first. I get my service-industry smile in place and they look straight through me. It's as if we don't exist. They stand right in front of us, check either side of us for more people to breathalyse, and then walk off left, in the direction of Boots.

'What happened there?' asks Andy, letting go of my hand.

'Don't know,' I say. And then it dawns on me. 'Oh my God!' I start to laugh.

'What?'

'We don't have our passes on!'

'Shit!' he says. 'You're right!' He pats his chest.

95

'No yellow jackets, no passes – we're members of the public!'

'And can be as pissed as we like!'

'Although not too pissed to fly,' I say, pretending to sound authoritative.

'Of course,' agrees Andy. 'But how pissed is that exactly?'

'How long is a piece of string?'

'Thank you, God,' says Andy, looking towards the heavens, his hands clasped together in prayer. 'Thank you for that close shave.'

'I think that was His birthday present.'

'It was the best I have ever had. Now, let's get the fuck out of here.'

On the way back to the office Andy is as high as a kite after his close shave and he can't stop chatting. 'They were there . . . I was holding my breath . . . and then they . . .' He tells me the whole story of what just happened to us as if I had not been standing right next to him at all. I smile. He always does that. I look forward to hearing the whole scenario again in a couple of hours' time, after he has embellished it and given it more topspin. I wonder if my presence will even make the final cut.

We get back to the office and don our airside passes, and there's a middle-aged bloke off the Sydney–Bangkok flight waiting to talk about lost luggage. It appears that he picked up someone else's bag and only noticed his mistake when he went to put the bag into the boot of his car.

'I've been to the long-term car park and back,' he says, sounding exhausted. 'Do you have any idea where my bag might be?'

This really is the sort of thing that Andy should handle, but seeing as he is in hiding from the breath testers and it's his birthday I take pity on him and take over.

'Well, it's very kind of you to bring the bag back, sir,' I say. 'Most people take them home and then call up the airline to come and collect them, demanding that we find theirs and deliver it to their door.'

'Oh,' says the man as he slumps forward, sounding as if he really regrets his generosity. 'I didn't think of that.'

'Next time,' I say.

'Yeah.'

'Anyway,' I say, picking up the suitcase, 'if you'd like to follow me to Left Luggage, let's see if we can sort this mess out.'

The man says nothing and trips along after me, dazed and confused like a small child. The long flight, the constipating food and the jet lag have clearly taken it out of him; what he really wants to do is curl up underneath his duvet at home. That makes two of us, I think, as I weave my way through the crowds. Thank God it's not the school holidays or half term. Otherwise this place would be so packed we could hardly move. I mean, I've often seen the check-in queue snake right out into the drop-off area outside. It's unbearable then. Tempers fray, fights start, children scream, and the bad language starts to fly about.

We pause for a minute as we go back through Customs. They check my pass, check the middle-aged man's passport, ask to see his boarding card stub and eventually we are let through to Left Luggage. Standing behind the desk, looking grumpy and hassled, is Bill. In his late fifties, completely bald, with a red-raw face and skin like a crocodile handbag, Bill spent the best part of twenty years in Baggage but moved to Left Luggage two years ago after he did his back in.

'All right, Bill?' I ask, leaning on his counter.

'No,' he says, pointing to a load of bags piled up next to the office. 'These came in Rush off some Virgin flight and now I've got to deal with them.'

'Oh,' I say. 'That's unfortunate.'

'Telling me,' he says, wiping his scarlet nose on the back of his red hand. 'It's the last thing I need.'

Airlines are notorious for sending Rush bags. It usually means that they are in danger of losing their take-off slot and have decided that it is better to fly the passengers without their bags than miss their take-off time by loading the plane up properly. The bags are only supposed to hang around for twenty-four hours before they are loaded onto a plane, other-wise they have to be checked again by security before they are allowed to fly.

Some airports are infamous for losing bags or having bags tampered with. Heathrow used to have a right reputation. Thiefrow, they called it. The airport was practically porous. They have supposedly cleaned up their act quite a lot, after they employed private detectives to weed out some of the real chancers. But only the other day my mate Garry told me how a bag full of seventy mobile phones split open. 'They presumed they must be moody,' he said, 'so everyone helped themselves.'

Heathrow also has a pretty poor reputation when it comes

to losing bags. Most airports lose about two in every thousand bags, but Heathrow loses eighty per thousand, which means that for every five hundred people who check in to a jumbo, forty won't get their bags at the other end. But that is mainly because the transport times between the terminals are so tight. When the place is busy, which it always is, there is so much luggage being transported between the terminals and so little time to do it in that a lot of the transferred luggage gets left behind. Most of the problems come from arrivals in Terminal 4. There is a tunnel that goes under the airport from the central terminal (i.e. 1, 2 and 3) to Terminal 4. It runs under a runway and the luggage travels along on a belt. All it takes is the belt to break down for the chaos to begin.

Left Luggage wasn't squeaky clean either. A bag used to hang around for three months in a large holding area under the ramp, during which time every effort was supposedly made to track down its owner. If all else failed the bag was opened and its contents auctioned off. However, there always seemed to me to be a slight conflict here as their first priority had to be to find the owners of the bag. Was any effort really made to trace the owners when the luggage could be sold anyway? Needless to say the system is a bit different now . . .

'So, Bill,' I say, rubbing my hands together, trying to engender some sort of enthusiasm in the man. 'We are rather hoping that you can help us.'

'Oh yeah?'

'This man here . . . sorry, what's your name?'

'Mr Hartley.'

'Mr Hartley here has lost his bag.'

'Well, I rather presumed that to be the case,' says Bill. 'Otherwise you wouldn't be here.'

'Yes, thanks for that,' I mutter. 'Anyway, Mr Hartley collected a bag that wasn't his and has brought it back in the hope that either his has been left behind and brought down here, or that we might be able to register him so that when the other person realizes their mistake and brings the bag back, we know how to track him down.'

'Sometimes they don't bring them back,' offers Bill helpfully.

'What?' says Mr Hartley. What little colour he had in his face has now totally drained away. 'But I've got . . .' He gives up.

'Sometimes,' continues Bill, oblivious to Mr Hartley's sensitivities, 'if they like what they see they keep it.'

'Great,' says Mr Hartley as golden cufflinks and expensive Savile Row shirts disappear before his very eyes.

'Yeah, well.' Bill shrugs – like he can control human behaviour. 'What flight were you on?'

Mr Hartley hands over what remains of his ticket and baggage tag, and Bill punches the flight number into the computer. He is using a programme called World Tracer, a global system for lost bags. You type in your name, address, flight number and a coded bag description and the system will supposedly tell you exactly where your bag is anywhere in the world.

'So, we're looking for a . . .' Bill leans over the counter and checks out the large black holdall at my feet. 'A black nine,' he says. 'A black nine . . . black nine,' he mutters. 'Oh,' he says. 'It looks like it might be here. In that pile over there. Do you want to take a look?'

Mr Hartley can hardly contain himself. He rushes over to the bags and starts searching through them as if he is looking for his long-lost daughter. His mind is focused, a black holdall the only thing computing in his brain. It takes him a good five minutes but he finds it, right at the back and covered in what looks like a burst bottle of shampoo. But he doesn't seem to care. He hauls it out to the front, checks the labels and immediately undoes the thing to check that the contents haven't been tampered with.

'Thank you,' he says. 'Thanks, mate,' he adds to Bill. Bill half-heartedly acknowledges him. He's not that interested in the man's find; he is more pleased that there is one less bag in the pile for him to deal with. 'Thanks,' Mr Hartley says to me again. 'Thanks very much for your help.'

'Pleasure,' I say. 'Another satisfied customer,' I add, with a certain amount of irony. 'Do you want a trolley? To take it back through Customs?'

'No thanks,' he says. 'It's not actually that heavy.'

We walk back through Customs together and the mirrored hall appears to be empty, although I am pretty sure there are a couple of blokes keeping an eye on us through the glass. We reach Arrivals and there are the usual mini-cab drivers hanging around with poorly written names scrawled on small pieces of cardboard. There are about thirty to forty hopeful friends, or relatives, leaning against the metal barrier – wives, husbands, children, lovers – their faces trained in our direction, their expectant expressions falling slightly as we walk through. I stop to say goodbye to Mr Hartley, who seems very impressed that he got his bag back so speedily.

101

Poor man, he probably expected his nightmare to continue for another couple of hours. He shakes my hand and walks off in the direction of the complimentary long-term car park buses.

I am about to return to the office when someone taps me on the shoulder.

'Excuse me?'

'Yes?' I turn around.

'Where can I get a taxi from here?' asks a rather short fat man standing underneath a taxi sign.

'You are standing right underneath the sign.' I point it out.

He looks up. His mouth hangs open. 'Oh,' he says. 'Which way?'

'If you follow the arrow . . .'

'What arrow?'

'The arrow on the sign. It's pointing outside.'

'Oh, right,' he says, his face still skywards, his mouth still open. 'It's quite hard to see from here.'

'Evidently,' I say, and start to walk away.

'Excuse me?' the fat man says again.

'Yes?' I turn around again.

'Will they take me to Leeds?'

'Leeds?'

'Yeah, Leeds.'

'That will cost you a lot of money,' I say slowly.

'Oh.'

'I think perhaps you should take the train,' I suggest.

'Oh, right!' he says, as if it's the most novel idea he has ever heard.

'How did you get here?' I ask, wishing I hadn't got involved in this conversation. My stomach is rumbling. It's almost time for my lunch break.

'I took the train,' says the man.

'Right,' I say. 'Then perhaps you should go back the same way you came.'

'OK then,' he says. He picks up his bags and heads off in the direction of the taxi rank.

By the time I get back to the office all I can think of is lunch.

'I'm starving, who's for lunch?' I say as I walk in, only to be confronted by two policemen in uniform with guns and flak jackets, and Andy sucking on a mouthful of mints. 'Oh,' I say, stopping in my tracks. 'Morning, gentlemen. What can I do for you?'

'You the airport duty manager?' one of them asks.

'That's right.'

'We're making the rounds of the airport just to make you aware that there are a few things going on today,' he continues.

'Right.'

'And we'd like you to brief your staff when they come in later.'

'OK.'

'Firstly,' he begins, 'we've been tipped off that there's a gang of Brazilian bag snatchers coming in who are planning to rip the place off and then fly out again.'

'Right.'

'I know it's not really your area, but if you could keep an eye out. They'll normally clean out duty free, move on to handbags and then get the next plane out, thinking we can't catch them. So if you see anything . . .'

103

'We'll call you,' says Andy, putting his little finger to his mouth and his thumb in his ear.

The officer ignores him and carries on addressing me. 'And we've got wind of a gang who might well try to board your Thailand flight this afternoon.'

'OK,' I say.

'We've heard that they might be taking money back to Thailand or that they might be bringing drugs back. Either way, we'd like you to look out for anyone buying an expensive ticket at the last minute. Someone who doesn't look like they should be travelling first or club. Anyone who is at all suspicious.'

'OK.'

'Customs are putting plenty of foxes [plainclothes officers] in the area,' he adds, 'so as soon as you see anything . . .'

'Right,' I say. 'I know the drill.'

I've actually done it before. A few years back when we had flights to South America, I cracked a cocaine cartel through exactly the same means. This gang of young chaps were buying first-class tickets at the last minute to Bogotá, which I thought was a little odd, as eighteen-year-olds don't normally carry three grand around in cash. Anyway, at the last minute they got a telephone call through and asked for another ticket. I told them, untruthfully, that only club was available and they didn't bat an eyelid. I had to let them go because there was no reason to hold them. But then, a couple of hours later, they were all back again. They said that they'd missed their flight and could they fly the next day. They didn't look like the usual duty-free scammers who buy an expensive refundable ticket, say a £600 ticket to New York, stock up on duty free or a half-price Cartier watch, miss the flight, catch the bus to Terminal 2 and then land themselves in the country, claiming their ticket refund as they go. So they must have been up to something else.

I therefore contacted Customs, told them about my suspicions and what time they were coming back, and they said they'd keep an eye out. But when the gang came back the next day there was no-one from Customs to be seen. I was scared and furious. I delayed the gang as much as possible, checking out their passports, that sort of thing. Eventually I telephoned Customs and said something along the lines of 'Where the fuck are you?' They turned around and said, 'We're everywhere. See the old woman at Costa's café? That's us. See the two backpackers in Waterstone's? That's us. See the man with the newspaper? That's us.' They had staked out the whole place with foxes. In the end they let the gang fly and followed them to South America, catching them on the way back with £3m of coke in a suitcase. Six months later I got an award.

'Good,' says the officer. 'Just so long as you are aware.'

'Fine,' I say, taking a step to one side to let the policemen pass. Neither of them looks as if he is moving. 'Anything else?'

'Yes,' says the other officer. 'The government is flying out a terrorist on your Thailand flight.'

'Oh,' I say, not really knowing how else to react.

This is a first for me. I've heard that this happens, but I didn't think I would ever have to deal with it. Governments and security services fly terrorists all the time. Either they are allowing them to fly because the government wants to see exactly what they are up to, or we are repatriating them with as little fuss and nonsense as possible. The airline doesn't have the right to refuse these passengers, but they do have the right to be informed.

'He is being repatriated to Indonesia, via Thailand,' says the officer. 'And there will be two tigers flying with him, even though he is not dangerous.'

'So un-dangerous that he needs only two guards,' says Andy. I shoot him a look.

'You will be given his name later on a need-to-know basis only,' continues the officer, looking down his short nose at Andy.

'OK,' I say. 'That all sounds fine to me.'

'Good. Do we have an understanding?'

'Yes, absolutely,' I say. For some reason I put out my hand to shake his. He rather stiffly reciprocates.

'We'll be in touch,' he says.

'Look forward to it,' I enthuse, like they've invited me to some party.

Fortunately, neither of the officers reacts. I step to one side and they leave the room.

'Fuck!' says Andy, after they've left. 'That sounds heavy. Let's go and have some lunch.'

12-1 PM

All the way to the staff canteen, Snackz, the flying terrorist is Andy's only topic of conversation.

'I wonder if he's killed someone?' he says. 'Or blown anyone up? A plane or anything like that?'

'I shouldn't have thought so for a second,' I reply. 'They'd hardly be flying him club class on our airline if that were the case.'

'If he's going to Indonesia then he's bound to be a Muslim,' he continues. 'D'you think he had anything to do with Bali? Or the World Trade Center? D'you think he was trained in Iraq?' I don't bother to reply. 'I wonder if he has really killed someone? With his bare hands. Or with a gun? I wonder if he's good-looking?'

'Jesus Christ!' I say, stopping in my tracks. 'Does it always boil down to sex with you?'

'Not always,' Andy replies, grinning.

'Anyway, will you shut up about the terrorist. It's supposed to be on a need-to-know basis.'

'What, like everything else around here?' he says. 'I bet half the airport knows already.'

Andy's right about that if nothing else. It is almost impossible to keep a secret around here. I mean, everyone knew about Darren the BAA sex-change supervisor who became Karen after a long and painful operation way before someone sold the story to the *Daily Mail*. People love to gossip about the smallest thing here. And it's worse in the air. They have a false intimacy problem born of hours and hours in a plane together, followed by excessive drinking and most probably sex. But it's quite bad on the ground as well. We spend all day, every day, in small cliques performing monotonous jobs, living like vicarious voyeurs. The smallest thing takes on enormous significance. Just the other day Paul Newman came through and every single detail of his short trip into the airport to meet up with his daughter was passed around the place like gold dust. The fact that he sat in our airport office rather than the first-class lounge; the fact that he ate airline crisps and peanuts while sitting in the office; the fact that he chatted to blushing members of staff – all were noted, commented upon and probably embellished.

I do have to say that I have met so many celebrities passing through this place that I've slightly had my fill of them. There was a time when someone like Anthea Turner or Vanessa Feltz would have sent a frisson through the ranks, but now they have to be quite far up the list for anyone to take much notice. But it is interesting to see how they behave. There are pleasant celebs, like George Michael, who talk to the staff and hand out autographs, and unpleasant ones, like Shirley Maclaine, who was a demanding cow and wouldn't stop attracting attention. Some of them go through incognito, like Gwyneth Paltrow, who pops on a baseball cap and travels economy, ensuring that she is not recognized at all. There are the cheapskates who insist on using the first-class lounge when they have economy tickets and are quite dogmatic about their upgrades. Then there are the glamorous stars, like Tom Cruise, travelling with his children, who get put into the inner sanctum in first class – the lounge within a lounge.

And then, of course, there's the Chelsea Suite. The Chelsea, sited at the centre of the airport, is for royalty and the super famous. Unlike the other lounges, it guarantees you a private bus to your flight so that you don't have to mix with the hoi polloi at any stage of your tricky journey. Built in the fifties with the sort of decor that reminds you of Burton and Taylor in their heyday, it is not the most brash or swish of places but it has everything a VIP traveller could possibly wish for on their short trip through. It takes passengers from any airline just so long as they are important enough. Bill Clinton, Nelson Mandela, anyone on a state visit to the UK tends to go through the Chelsea. Tom and Nicole certainly parked their backsides in there on occasion. Jude Law and Sienna Miller might make it in there at the moment. But your star does have to shine rather brightly to sit in the Chelsea. Then again, I think standards may be slipping a bit these days. I saw Claudia Schiffer in there last week and I couldn't help thinking, surely first class is good enough for her?

Andy and I walk up the short flight of stairs leading to Snackz and through the swing cowboy-saloon doors, picking up a copy of the *Villager* newspaper on the way. Inside the canteen it is as crowded, noisy, smoky and depressing as ever, frequented as it is by any odd or passing sod who shift-works in the airport. An expansive room with lime-green walls, it has steamed-up plate-glass windows with views of the Royal Mail sorting office and seats up to 150 at any one time. It was decorated during some seventies nightmare where purple waves and orange squares were de rigueur, and all the brown plastic tables are nailed to the floor, as are the smokers' chairs. The wicker chairs, reserved for non-smokers, are, bizarrely, allowed to roam free and socialize.

The room is quite cold and the air hangs heavy with grease, cooked meat and stale cigarettes. The food is served at stalls rather like in a motorway service station, each sporting a large, yellow-stained sign declaring its wares. From the Hot Wok to the International Exchange, the dishes are all heavily subsidized and taste more or less the same, whatever world-wide delight you plump for. It is not the sort of place you would choose to spend your lunch hour, but there really are only so many 10 per cent discounted burgers and fries a sane man can eat in a week. At least here you can make a stab at a lamb curry for £3.20, or spare ribs with potato and veg for £2.80, followed by a chocolate pudding with custard for 77p. When you've been on the go since five a.m., having woken up at 3.30, you tend to eat quite a lot, especially when you're not quite sure when your next meal is coming. Fortunately, we get given £25 a month towards our food on an airline card. I'd hate to think I was shelling out too much of my hard-earned cash on this stuff. That would just be too depressing.

I pick up my tray and walk along the stalls trying to work out what is the least offensive option. I plump for a bread roll, an apple juice and the Lancashire hot pot on the Home-style stall where you get a 60 per cent discount if you have a staff card. Andy always goes for the same chicken salad from the same salad bar and complains about the same things each and every time he comes.

'Look at these tomatoes,' he says, sitting down at a nailed-down table. 'They look like they are made of bloody cotton wool.'

'I don't know why you always go for the same shit and complain about it every time,' I say, trying and failing to pull my chair closer to the table.

'I'm a creature of habit – what can I say?' He takes a small box out of his top pocket and lays out a vast selection of vitamin pills. Andy has a pill for every occasion and every ailment. 'I think I might be getting flu.' He shivers. Picking one pill up at a time, he pops each one individually into his mouth and makes a great show of swallowing them, chasing them down his throat with half-pint glugs of water. 'I can feel it coming on. Do I look ill?'

'You look hungover,' I say.

'Do I?' He shivers again.

'And thirty,' I add, for good measure.

'You bitch,' he says, flicking his salad with his white plastic fork. 'I feel terrible.'

'There are a couple of blokes feeling pretty shitty in Baggage today,' announces Garry as he sits down at the table.

'Oh, all right there, Garry?' I say, my mouth full of potato and unidentifiable meat.

'I'm all right,' he says with a sniff. 'It's just a couple of my blokes have come down with runway malaria.'

'Really?' asks Andy.

'Yep,' says Garry. 'It's the third batch we've had this year.'

The blokes who work in Cargo or Baggage are always picking up the strangest things. Exposed as they are to anything that seeps, crawls or flies out of any suitcase, bag or crate arriving from anywhere in the world, it is quite surprising there aren't more cases of dengue fever, sleeping sickness and the like. But of all the illnesses, runway malaria is the favourite. All it takes is one mosquito to make the journey from a malaria-infested region like Gabon in some crappy holdall with a half-undone zip. The beast escapes in the baggage hold, bites a couple of handlers, and they come down with something a few days later. And there is nothing anyone can do.

'How badly have they got it?' asks Andy. He loves a good sickness story.

'I'm not sure really,' says Garry. 'They're both in the hospital for tropical diseases.'

'Oh,' says Andy, a forkful of sweetcorn poised beneath his mouth. 'That sounds quite bad to me. When I got malaria, I never bothered with hospital.'

'Oh?' says Garry.

'Picked it up in Kenya,' he continues. 'I was on a two-week tanning holiday in Mombasa and it really knocked me for six.'

'When was that?' I ask.

'A couple of years ago. You remember?'

'Um, yes,' I reply, not remembering at all.

'I had a week off work at least.'

'Right. It does ring a bell.'

'Hope these guys aren't off that long,' says Garry. 'We're quite short-staffed as it is. Yesterday we had a few blokes busted for smoking marijuana while operating the X-ray machines. You can hardly blame them, it is the most piss boring job in the world. But they were so unsubtle about it. They were bound to get caught sooner or later.'

I have known Garry for a couple of years now and he is not your typical baggage handler. I met him during the *Neighbours* debacle, when they started to slash my tyres and threaten me when I asked for their TV privileges to be taken away. He was the only bloke who understood what I was trying to do, and didn't take offence. Then again, he's not really one of them. A former computer engineer, he lost his job during the recession of the early nineties and ended up working here because he couldn't find anything else. A quiet, conscientious bloke who is more interested in designing computer programmes at home and watching birds of a weekend, he found that the odd hours of five a.m. to one p.m. suited him, as did the triple overtime. So he stayed. Unlike his high-pressured life before, Garry likes earning without responsibility and spends more time thinking about what he is going to do in his spare time than worrying about the job. He is quite stoical about things, and I like that in a bloke.

'How obvious were they?' I ask.

'Quite pathetic really,' he says. 'They were giggling at the vibrators that kept coming up on the X-rays and the whole place stank of skunk.'

'Fairly unsubtle,' I say with a nod.

'Extremely,' he says, returning to what looks like a chicken curry. 'Oh,' he adds. 'You'll never guess what we had through today that sent everyone a little crazy.'

'What?' asks Andy, leaning in.

'Two suitcases of absinthe.' He grins. 'There were twelve bottles in all, six in each of the cases. God knows what had happened to them, but they were smashed to pieces in the suitcases and the alcohol was leaking everywhere. It took us a while to realize what it was. At first we thought it was some sort of perfume, but then we all started to get headaches and some of the guys started to act a bit weird, getting all dizzy. It's strong stuff. A hundred and forty per cent proof. Anything stronger than that has to be signed for by the captain and shipped as dangerous goods.'

'I've drunk it before,' says Andy. 'It's fucking lethal. It sends you crazy. That's why Van Gogh cut his ear off.'

'Yeah, well, no-one quite went that mad, but it hung around in the area for ages,' says Garry, shoving a forkful of rice into his mouth. 'Some of the blokes felt quite sick.'

I smile at Garry and look at the nicotine-yellow clock over his shoulder. It is showing 12.30. A large group of builders walk into the canteen. There are always builders at the airport, extending shopping aisles and cutting back on check-in desks. They are loud and laughing as they load up their trays with sandwiches and biscuits. They sit themselves next to a middle-aged woman in a dark blue World Duty Free uniform who is reading the *Daily Mail*. She shifts in her seat and flicks her newspaper in irritation. On the next-door table there are a couple of Community Police Support officers dressed in plain clothes. Extra eyes and ears for the police force, they are powerless to do anything other than detain you. Neither of them is talking; they are simply gazing into space, their mouths slightly open, chewing on their food like a couple of cows.

I flick through the *Village*. Established twenty-one years ago and run by two journalists out of a small office in Staines, it is one of the organs for the airport and carries all the important stories. On the front page today is a photograph of the Countess of Wessex handing over a 'top airport' award to BAA's managing director. Inside, there are stories about the marvellousness of British Airways, how we are one step closer to a third runway, and something about a lost grey pony. It takes me two minutes to read.

'We had a whole load of khat through this morning,' says Garry, by way of reopening conversation.

'Oh yeah?' says Andy. 'Never quite understood the appeal of chewing a stick to get high myself.'

'Three suitcases of the stuff bound for the US,' he continues. 'You know it's illegal over there?'

'Isn't it here?' asks Andy.

'Nope,' says Garry. 'And that's half the problem. They get couriers out of here to ship it to the US and there is almost nothing we can do. You can always tell it's khat in the suitcases because it stinks of damp wood and they show up really well on the X-rays. Like a whole load of branches.'

'Really?' says Andy.

'All we can do is pull them at the gate, accuse them of

carrying khat, and take them off the flight, and that's it. We can't arrest them. Then d'you know what they do?'

'What?' I say.

'They only go up to Manchester and book themselves on the next America-bound flight out. So we just inform US Customs and they get arrested on arrival.'

'Well, it's not like you didn't give them a chance,' observes Andy, crunching a carrot.

'I know. We've had a whole lot of M16s through today as well.'

'What? Rifles?' I ask.

'Yup,' he says, taking another mouthful of curry. 'And some kitbags full of pistols and stuff from Iraq. We had a couple of Kalashnikovs through last week.'

Ever since the war on terror moved to Iraq we have had much more firearms traffic coming through the airport. Soldiers on their way out to combat, or on their way back, are allowed to travel with their weapons, just so long as they are not loaded and have the correct paperwork. There's a £10,000 fine for the airline if you don't inform Customs that you are shipping weapons or you are travelling with incorrect paperwork. The guns and pistols go in the hold and the ammunition has to travel in a locked box, although Garry says he's always seeing it slung into the bottom of kitbags and no-one seems to care that much. Having said that, it's not allowed to hang around the airport long and it travels back and forth to the plane in caged vans.

Just as Garry is about to launch into the ins and outs of what weaponry he has been handling today, we are joined by two of Andy's acquaintances who work in the airside shops.

'Hiya,' says a young man as he sits down. 'D'you mind? I'm Jay.'

'No, hello,' I say. 'Do sit down.'

'And this is Marie,' he continues.

'Hi,' she says, sitting down next to me. 'Jesus!' she huffs. 'I'm knackered.'

'That's what comes of doing two jobs,' says Jay, wagging his fork at her.

'I know,' says Marie, rolling her bright blue, heavily made-up eyes.

'Two jobs?' asks Andy.

'I work at Burberry and in a bar in town,' she says. 'Five a.m. to two p.m. here and then six p.m. to eleven p.m. at the bar.'

'No wonder you're tired,' says Andy.

'I'm not the only one,' says Marie. 'We're all at it.'

'And you've got a shit hangover,' points out Jay.

'And I've got a shit hangover,' she echoes, cracking open a bag of crisps.

'How's your day been so far?' Jay asks Marie.

'Well, James from Swatch has just pulled the new Asian girl who's working there and it's only taken him a week. Gay Hugo, who's just moved from Thomas Pink to the seafood bar, has found a new flirt with the new bloke who's just arrived in Harrods, and Trisha got given a telephone number by some bloke who was on his way to Helsinki because he fancied her and wants to take her out for a drink. And that's not the first man who's done that to her this week.' She pauses and draws breath. 'Dave from Tiffany stuck a pound coin on the floor this morning to see how many people would stop and try to pick it up, and we

117

had six at the last count, and I had some man say to me this morning as I was wrapping a handbag for his wife, or mistress, that he was "in a hurry and had a plane to catch", so I said, "No shit, sir, you're in an airport," which probably wasn't very clever because he got pissed off. But, you know, what's a girl to do?'

'It sounds like you've had an exhausting morning,' I say, still wrestling with my meat and potatoes.

'Not really,' she says. 'It was quite boring actually.'

'Oh,' I say.

'Oh! And I saw that Jenny Powell off *Wheel of Fortune* having a coffee,' she announces to Jay.

'Really?' he says, leaning in. 'What did she look like?'

'Exactly like she does on the telly.'

'Oh.'

'I know, bor-ing,' says Marie with a wave of her crisp. 'I only like it when they look shit or are really short. I saw that Cher the other day. Made me feel a whole lot better about myself, I tell you. She looked, to me at least, like a right old fright as she came off the plane. It's amazing what they can do with hair and make-up these days.'

'Did you hear about the fight outside Bally?' asks Jay.

'No,' says Marie.

'Some German hit his wife and she fell to the floor.'

'Germans are always doing that,' declares Marie.

'Are they?' I say.

'Oh yeah,' she says, finally putting the prawn cocktail crisp into her mouth. 'All the time.'

'Did you hear they had some Russian sniffing around the ten-grand bottle of whisky at World of Whisky?' asks Jay.

'No,' says Marie. 'And did you hear about the Russian who pissed himself?'

'What?' says Andy.

'Oh yeah,' says Marie. 'Apparently he'd been held at gunpoint before he got onto the plane and had wet himself on the plane. He turned up at Austin Reed damp and shaking and asking for new trousers.'

'That sounds terrible,' says Jay.

'I know,' agrees Marie, 'but I suppose that comes with the mafia territory, doesn't it? The Russians are all like that . . .'

Marie and Jay then launch into a conversation about which nationality does what when it comes to duty free. The best shoppers, apparently, used to be the Americans, but now it's the Spanish and the Italians. The Arabs buy most of the whisky, particularly the Johnny Walker Blue at £99 a bottle, and particularly the Dubai flight. The Japanese love their fish, their foie gras and their caviar (luxury items have a tax on them, but caviar is not considered a luxury item and is therefore not taxed). The Nigerians on the Lagos flight are real big spenders and walk around with wads of cash, as do the Russians. The best-selling drink is vodka. And if you want to buy more alcohol than is allowed you can, because who are they to enforce the rules?

'I agree,' says Jay. 'I mean, if I wanted to work in Customs, I would.'

'I know,' says Marie. 'Anything for an easy life.'

'Yeah. So, how are you, Andy?'

'Fine,' says Andy. 'It's my birthday today.'

'Oh my God!' says Marie. 'I wish I'd known. I would have got you something.'

While Andy, Jay and Marie chat about Andy's birthday and commiserate with him for turning thirty, I make my excuses and move on to the Café Plaza just around the corner for a cup of strong black coffee and a cigarette. Garry follows me to do the same. The Café Plaza is supposed to be the slightly more upmarket food section. It's a dark red area only dimly lit, with armchairs and filter coffees. It's a favourite with the flight attendants. There are a group of three of them laughing away in their pillbox hats, their small suitcases at their feet, when Garry and I arrive. They look a little intimidating, so we pick up our coffees and sit next to a grey, slightly sweaty-looking bloke I recognize from Ops, or Operations.

'Tricky morning?' I say as I sit down.

'You could say that,' he says, taking a long drag on his cigarette. 'BA had a plane go tech in Miami and it's put all the others out of whack. I've got a whole load of service crew who have gone out of hours in Johannesburg and there's no way of getting them back. There's also snow predicted in New York and fog here later.'

'Right,' I say. 'That sounds exhausting.'

'I thought there were a few things going on,' says Garry. 'We've had an odd morning for luggage.'

'Well, you would,' says the grey man.

Ops is one of the jobs I would least like to do in the airport. The realm of clever men and organized women, it is almost as stressful as air traffic control. Stuck in an airless room in front of a large screen that shows exactly where every plane is at any one time, it is their job to juggle crews and planes, making sure that they get planes in to land in time for them to be re-equipped, refuelled and re-staffed ready to take off again on schedule. It is a finely tuned operation with little margin for error. All it takes is snow, a punctured tyre or a pilot off sick for you to have thousands of passengers diverted to the wrong place, and the whole thing collapses like a house of cards. The plane arrives late from LA, which means that it can't take off on time to go to Cairo, and the crew who were waiting to man the Cairo flight go out of hours, i.e. they have been on duty too long – over 12–15 hours – and another crew has to be scrambled to the airport; meanwhile, the cost to the airline in delays, compensation and staff wages is spiralling skywards. The worst-case scenario would be for Swanwick itself to go down. The newly privatized and computerized £623 million air traffic control system has been known to collapse and then the whole of UK airspace becomes a nightmare. There are delays, and planes get backed up; it's the same as having snow and fog in all the airports and the guys in Ops end up tearing their hair out. It's no wonder, then, that the grey bloke looks so low and so knackered. It's also no wonder that the guys in Ops and Air Traffic Control have the best parties. You can see why they might need a stiff drink at the end of the day.

Talking of which, I really fancy a vodka shot or a drop of whisky. The most stressful part of my day is about to kick off and I could do with a little lift. I knock back the rest of the coffee in one, inhale as much nicotine as I can, stand up and stub out my cigarette. Time to face the public, get that service-industry smile in place.

1-2 PM

By the time Andy and I make it back from Snackz, a couple of the check-ins already seem to be branded and raring to go. As a small airline we don't have permanent check-in desks: it would cost us far too much money, and there's nothing we hate more than giving money to the BAA. So we hot-desk our check-ins, opening as close to take-off as we can. We'd like to open two hours before the flights go, of course, but ever since the BAA have started advising passengers to turn up three hours before their flights we sometimes open one or two a little earlier.

Just as our desks aren't exclusive, neither are our check-in girls. Some of them work for us full time, but the majority work for a ground-handling agent and are sub-contracted to a few airlines at the same time. They could start their shift working for us, go via Olympic Airways and end up with Air Portugal. Sometimes they change their uniforms, sometimes they re-accessorize with a hat, a scarf or a red jacket, but a lot of the time they just turn up in something non-specific like a neutral blue suit, shove on a motif name badge and they're done. The logic behind sub-contracting staff is simple: they get none of the perks that keep the full-time staff sweet, we don't pay them their benefits, and they don't get subsidized plane tickets. And we, in theory, get to keep the ticket price down, perhaps even to increase our profit margins.

Today, if I remember correctly from checking the rosters earlier on, we've got Cathy fresh from having her chocolate breasts licked at the Flying Club; Debbie, who also went to the Flying Club; Chanel and Trisha, who may or may not have gone; and a bloke I haven't worked with before called Dave. Cathy works for us full time, but the others are sub-contracted. I know the girls are at the beginning of their shifts but I'm not sure about Dave. He could easily have done four hours with Air France before coming here.

'D'you know how far Dave is into his shift?' I ask Andy.

'Who's Dave?'

'The bloke we have on check-in today.'

'No idea.' Andy shrugs.

'Right.'

'Are you prepared to start losing money?'

'What?'

'Our little bet from earlier.' He smiles. 'I can see Cathy and Debbie are here, but not the others.'

'They might be in the office,' I say.

'Yeah, right. Like anyone is going to go to the Flying Club

and survive. Looks like twenty quid is coming my way. That's the easiest cash I've earned in a long time.'

'There's no need to be so smug,' I say. 'Anyway, we've still got ten minutes before they are officially late.'

'Seven.'

'A lot can happen in seven minutes.'

'That's why I love you,' says Andy, patting me on the back. 'You're ever the optimist.'

I walk into the back office and look around hopefully. Neither Chanel nor Trisha is in there.

'All right there, Cathy?' I say.

'Ouch,' she says, rolling her eyes. 'I've felt better.'

'Right,' I say, my smile slightly stiff.

'I never knew Bacardi Breezers could make you feel so shit. Mint?'

'What?'

'Want one?' She proffers a tube of extra strong mints. 'Stop me breathing alcohol all over the punters.'

'Good idea. And no thanks. Any idea where the others are?'

'Debbie's here,' she says, pointing to her friend, who looks sheet white, as if she is about to throw up.

'Afternoon, Debbie,' I say.

She can only nod, and even that motion seems to cause her pain. There is hungover and toxic, and this girl is clearly toxic. If I had more staff I would send her home without any pay as she is clearly not fit to work.

'What about the other two?' I ask.

'Oh,' says Cathy. 'Last time I saw them both they were

getting up close and personal with some blokes who work in Baggage at Luton.'

'OK.'

'We left them there,' she adds.

'Any idea if they are planning on coming in?' My patience is beginning to reach its limits.

'Oh, they'll be here.'

'How do you know?'

'I've got Chanel's flat keys.'

'How?'

'It's a long story.'

'Good night?' asks Andy, who is standing behind a check-in desk putting up a branding board.

'Great,' says Cathy, flicking her long, ironed-straight, burgundy-coloured hair. 'It was a mate of mine's leaving thing from Luton and all her male colleagues did the Full Monty striptease in her honour. They were ever so good.' She smiles. 'They did it right down to these gold pouches and a couple of them went totally naked. Wasn't that funny, Debbie, when those two blokes went totally starkers?'

'Mmm,' says Debbie as she turns her computer on.

'Sounds like a top night,' says Andy.

'You'd have loved it,' says Cathy. 'You must come down with us next time.'

'Possibly.' Andy sounds uncharacteristically unforthcoming.

'No, you should,' I say, sensing it is not his thing at all.

'Absolutely,' says Andy, flicking me the Vs behind Cathy's back. 'And you should go too.'

'Yeah, go on,' says Cathy, her eyes brightening. 'You'd love it.'

'Oh look,' I say quickly, changing the subject. 'What visions of loveliness do I see before me?'

'Oh shit,' says Andy.

'Twenty quid.'

'All right. Keep your bloody toupee on.'

Chanel and Trisha are weaving through the crowds towards our check-in desks. Bearing in mind that neither of them has probably been home, they look amazingly showered and shiny and ready for work. Chanel's very yellow hair is scraped back into a tight pony tail, while Trisha's brown and blonde striped hair swings as if she has just stepped out of a salon. I have to admit I am impressed. They are both dressed in their navy blue ground-handling uniforms but have remembered to accessorize with our red and white scarves.

'You two are dirty stop-outs,' says Cathy, wagging a white square-tipped fingernail in their general direction. 'What did you get up to last night?'

'Never you mind,' says Chanel, raising an eyebrow that has been plucked completely away and then drawn back on again. 'Sorry we're late,' she says to me, with an insincere smile.

'You're not.'

'Did you cop off with that big bloke?' Cathy persists.

'My lips are sealed,' says Chanel, zipping up a pair of pink glossed lips. 'A lady never tells.'

'How about you, Trish?' asks Cathy, bored by Chanel's refusal to play gossip.

'Ditto,' says Trisha.

'You two are no bloody fun,' moans Cathy. 'I'm not taking you again.'

'We don't need you to go next time,' says Chanel.

'Ooh, hark at her!' says Cathy. 'Well, you can get someone else to look after your keys next time you want to shag some baggage handler.' She throws over the set of keys.

'Customs and Excise, actually,' corrects Chanel, catching her keys.

'Whatever,' says Cathy, making a W shape with her thumbs and fingers and pointing it in Chanel's direction.

'Can you two stop bickering?' I say as I look at all four of them standing in a row behind their desks. 'We've got a full plane to check in and we're a bloke down.'

'It's always a full plane,' mutters Cathy.

She's not wrong. Our planes are normally overbooked by about 20 per cent. We do it as a matter of course, mainly because there are about 20 per cent no-shows on any one flight and the airline doesn't want to be out of pocket. These days there are so many ways to book tickets and so many people who don't pay until the last minute that it's hard for the industry to keep up. The days of everyone booking months in advance and paying their fare in full to their travel agent are long gone. People's plans are always changing. Most of the time, because this is a long-haul flight to Sydney via Bangkok, we can successfully juggle passenger numbers. It's the short-haul flights, where passengers' plans are more likely to change and the flights are overbooked by as much as 35 per cent, where the real problems are.

But there are some passengers who make money out of not flying. It happens more in the States, but it does go on over here as well. Known as 'compensation flyers', they book the cheapest non-refundable tickets on very over-subscribed flights then turn up late in the hope that there is no room on the aircraft, and we have to compensate them. Denied Boarding Compensation can be quite substantial, between £300 and £600 a flight, so you can see the appeal. There are some people who spend whole days booking themselves onto flights out of JFK and never going anywhere at all. It is quite a lucrative way of earning a living, just so long as you time your arrival correctly and are always the first people in the queue to accept the invitation not to fly.

Unfortunately, some people also think this is the best way to get an upgrade. If you arrive late enough for the plane, there will be no economy seating left and we will have no choice but to upgrade you. In the days of yore, before frequent flyer cards and loyalty schemes, this may well have worked. But now these card-holders are marked 'Vol Up' (suitable for voluntary upgrade) before the puffed-out passenger who arrives late for the flight. In fact, being late and stressed will only mark you out for special treatment. Check-in staff often take sadistic pleasure in handing you the worst seat on the plane, in the middle of the back row, right by the toilets, if you arrive late and give them any sort of grief. The more you huff and puff and complain about how difficult your journey has been, the worse your seat. Well, they get paid £11,000 a year for an eight-hour shift on the service frontline; you can understand they have to keep themselves amused somehow.

And it's not as if we haven't heard the upgrade excuses before. 'My wife's pregnant.' 'My wife's got her period.' 'My wife had flu.' 'We're honeymooners.' 'I have a headache.'

'My back is bad.' 'I've got unfeasibly long legs.' 'But I always fly first/business – my secretary must have made a mistake.' It's enough to make you put them next to the fattest, most flatulent person on the flight.

And it's always bollocks. In the years that I have been doing this, never has anyone produced a medical certificate if they've been asked. And as soon as we call Derek and Terry over, if they're really pleading and insistent they normally undergo a miraculous recovery worthy of Lazarus.

Then, of course, there are the bribes. Usually the preserve of the Nigerians and the guys from the Gulf, the slickest way of securing an upgrade is to slip a couple of fifty-pound notes into your passport as you check in. We used to have a terrible problem with cash for upgrades. Last year I found seven passengers on our Sydney flight who had paid at the check-in for the privilege. I got the purser on the flight to explain that they could sit in their seats, but the cabin staff wouldn't be able to serve them on the flight. They all sat still and ate nothing all the way to Sydney.

But there are plenty of other ways to be on the take. We used to get a lot of Premiership football business on our short-haul flights and one of our check-in staff was only too keen to upgrade them in return for tickets and season passes. But it was one of our check-in staff in South Africa who proved to be truly problematic. He was in the pay of people smugglers and was getting illegal immigrants onto our flights despite them all having forged passports. It was a nightmare for us at this end because we were being charged £2,000 per repatriation. It took UK immigration a while to work out what was going on, but eventually our check-in bloke was arrested. It caused no end of problems for our duty manager over there. The smuggling gang didn't like the fact that their business had been compromised and they started to threaten the duty manager's family. He was quickly moved out of South Africa and sent to New York. But it all got quite hairy. So you can understand why it's a good idea for me to keep an eye on proceedings.

'Right,' I say. 'Dave is obviously not showing up, so Andy and I will take it in turns to do first and club, and the rest of you are on economy.'

'OK,' says Cathy. The others nod in agreement.

'Do you all know how this system works?' I ask. 'Business is rows eleven to twenty-seven.'

'Yeah,' says Chanel, glancing over at a pale, grey-looking Debbie. 'Not sixty to seventy like in BA.'

'Can you chat on these computers?' asks Trisha with a small grin on her face.

'Oh yes,' replies Andy. 'We've still got the old system here.'

'Not too much,' I warn them, trying to keep control. 'We've got a lot of people to check in in a very small amount of time.'

'Spoilsport,' mutters Andy.

'I know what you're like,' I say, tapping the side of my nose.

Depending on what computer system the airline uses, check-in staff can talk to one another via simultaneous email. So when check-in staff seem to be taking an age to type your rather short name into the computer, they are probably sending one of their mates a message – usually about you or occasionally about someone else in the queue behind you. These messages range from the basic – 'Have you seen the nose/tits/arse/gut on her?' – to the more malicious – 'I've got a right old cunt here; can anyone suggest a screaming child for him to sit next to?' They can also add comments or messages to your ticket that flash up as you arrive at the gate. So the cabin crew are warned in advance that a 'twat' is approaching or a 'difficult bastard' is on his way and that you should be treated accordingly – i.e. given your dinner/drinks last, asked to move at the last minute to a seat next to an enormously fat man. You see, it really does pay to be pleasant at check-in.

There are a few passengers already forming queues by the time we are ready to open. Fortunately, we don't have a uni-queue policy (or one queue for all flights) as favoured by some airlines. I don't know why they bother to do them. They're a bloody nightmare. Every time anyone finally gets to the front of the queue, they are always pissed off at having to wait that long and feeling panicked about missing their flights. It's not that democratic either: most of the time staff are trawling up and down the queue pulling people to the front who are late for their flights; meanwhile, the ones who turned up with plenty of time to spare get penalized.

I walk up and down behind the desks. The check-in seems to be going fine. There is no sign of the gang the police are looking for. However, I do notice that every time Debbie bends over to slip a luggage tag on a bag she retches. I swear, if I don't let her go and get a glass of water she is going to puke any second.

'Debbie?' I say.

'Mmm?' she says, her dry lips held tightly together.

'Why don't you have a quick break and get yourself a glass of water?'

'Oh,' she says, looking a bit surprised. 'Um, thanks.'

Debbie walks into the back office for a sit down and I take over her desk.

'Good afternoon, madam,' I say to a rather efficient-looking woman with hard blonde hair, accompanied by three young boys whose ages, I'm guessing, range from about six to twelve.

'Is it?' she says as she heaves her luggage onto the scales and slaps down four passports.

'All the way to Sydney?' I ask.

'That's right,' she replies, not bothering to look me in the eye. I start to type in her name. 'Could you upgrade my children to business?' she asks in a manner that implies we hand out almost £21K worth of tickets for free every day of the week.

'Oh,' I say. Here we go. 'I'm afraid we don't usually upgrade children into the cabin. If you would like to fly with your children I suggest that you downgrade to economy. I could sit you all together next to an emergency exit for extra leg room if you'd like?'

'Right,' she says, having clearly ignored everything I've said about her downgrading. 'Are you sure you can't put them in business? You see, I've done it before.'

'Not with this airline you haven't, madam,' I say, sort of trying to laugh.

'I have,' she insists. 'Every time I've flown, in fact.'

'Well, it isn't our policy to upgrade children. We have customers who have paid a lot of money for some peace in the cabin and I'm afraid they don't really expect children to be there.'

'I don't care what the other customers do or do not expect,' she continues. 'I fly your airline all the time and my children always get upgraded.'

'Do you have a frequent flyer card?' I ask.

'Of course not!' she barks. 'I don't have a Sainsbury's Nectar card either. Dreadful things.'

'They aren't quite the same,' I point out.

'You've got a right old slag there.' A message from Andy pops up onto my screen.

'Do some work,' I type back.

'Look at her hair. She looks like a right old harridan.' I ignore him.

'I want to speak to the man in charge,' she says.

'I am the man in charge,' I reply.

'You!' she says.

'Yes, me.' I smile.

'Oh.' She looks only marginally wrong-footed.

'It's the children I feel sorry for,' Andy types. 'Look at their miserable little faces.'

'Um,' she says, 'I'll be back in a minute.'

'Madam!' I say as she walks away. 'You can't leave your children, luggage and passports here.'

She ignores me, and flounces off down the long queue to make a phone call. The three small boys sit on their suitcases like little lost souls and wait for their mother to return. I move her bags off the scales and carry on checking in.

'What?' comes a shriek from the next-door queue. 'It can't be.'

'I'm afraid it is,' says Chanel, her face impassive. 'By two months.'

'Can't you make an exception?' asks the harassed-looking woman.

'No,' says Chanel. 'Your passport is out of date, you are not allowed to fly.'

'But it's only just,' tries the woman.

'Two months is two months,' says Chanel.

'I can't believe you won't make an exception. I'm English, and Australia is an English colony.'

'It's a country in its own right,' explains Chanel. 'And I'm afraid we can't let you leave the UK with an out-of-date passport.'

'Well, fuck you!' says the woman, suddenly giving up and giving Chanel the finger. 'Fuck all of you!' She marches off into the terminal in tears.

'You all right?' I ask, leaning over to Chanel.

'What?' she asks, looking at me as if I'm insane. 'Course I am.'

'Good. It's just that some people get a bit upset being sworn at.'

'Nah,' she says. 'Water off a duck's back.'

'Right!' says the hard-haired woman, who has returned to the front of my desk and slapped the passports down again. 'I've come to a solution.'

'OK,' I say.

'The children will fly tomorrow as unaccompanied minors and I shall travel today in business.' She smiles. 'I don't know why I didn't think of it earlier. So much easier for everyone all round.'

'Right,' I say. Much easier for you, I think. 'You'll have to go to the ticket desk to change the children's tickets. And if you give me yours, I'll check you in all the way through to Sydney.'

'Isn't that a good idea?' She smiles again, looking down at her children. 'Nanny Stewart is on her way to collect you. And I shall see you in a couple of days.'

With hard-hair checked in to Sydney and her children waiting for the lift back to London, Debbie makes a return appearance.

'Better?' I ask.

'Yes, thanks,' she replies, looking only marginally less grey.

I vacate her desk and walk up towards Andy and the club/first class check-in. As I walk past Cathy she turns round and takes hold of my arm.

'Can I have a quick word?' she asks.

'Course,' I say.

'See the man behind me?' she whispers, pointing over her shoulder towards a small weasel of a man in a thin grey suit.

'Yes.'

'Well, he's got such bad BO. I don't think he should fly.'

'Really?'

'Yeah. Can't you smell it?'

I lean forward and inhale slightly. Jesus Christ! The smell is overpowering. It's so acrid it makes my eyes water. 'You're right,' I say. 'He stinks.'

In the airline regulations manual there is a passenger acceptance list which gives a whole load of reasons for refusing admission to a plane. Drunk passengers, rowdy passengers, barefoot passengers, infants less than a week old (unless its parents have a doctor's note allowing it to fly), passengers with communicable diseases such as chickenpox, passengers who look like they might be on drugs – and passengers with body odour. And this man really does have body odour. Offensive body odour. Revolting enough to make anyone sitting close to or around him on a long flight to Sydney want to complain.

'Um, I think you should take him to one side, explain the rule and tactfully suggest that he goes to Boots to buy some deodorant. Otherwise he can't fly.'

'Oh, good idea. Excuse me, sir,' Cathy says, turning around, 'can I have a word?'

I leave Cathy to deal with her smelly passenger and arrive behind Andy just as what I can only conclude is our terrorist turns up. It's not the most subtle of arrivals. Firstly he is so closely flanked by two tigers he can hardly move without treading on either of their toes. Secondly, the terminal suddenly appears to be crawling with foxes, all of whom seem to be sitting and staring at our check-in. It would be hilarious if the man weren't presumably so dangerous. For a bloke who just over an hour ago was so gabby and interested in our friend's dodgy past, Andy is remarkably taciturn as he checks them all in. In fact, he is so tense he forgets to ask any of them if they packed their bags themselves, or if they have any sharp objects to declare.

'The last row of club all right for you gentlemen?' he asks, his hand shaking slightly as he types. One of the tigers nods. The terrorist says nothing. He is staring at the floor, stroking his long black beard. 'Great,' says Andy, his voice suddenly slightly high-pitched. 'Enjoy your flight!'

'Thank you,' replies one of the guards.

'Oh my God! Did you see that?' asks Andy as they turn the corner. 'Jesus Christ, he's definitely a bomber and he's definitely killed people. I could feel it. Just feel it on him. Couldn't you?'

'He looked like an old school teacher to me,' I say.

'You're such a bad judge of character,' declares Andy, running his hands through his highlights. 'You've got no idea.'

I leave Andy to wallow in his close encounter with terrorism and go into the back office to put a call through to Chris, the purser in charge of the Bangkok–Sydney flight. He needs to be informed that he has a terrorist and a couple of tigers on his flight, in order to brief his cabin crew. When I get through, it turns out that Chris and the captain already know who they are carrying to Bangkok. I tell them they are all sitting in the last row of club and Chris suggests that, as I have already met the man, I should come to the crew briefing just to make his staff feel a bit more at ease with the whole situation.

'The last thing I want is anyone being at all hysterical,' he explains. 'You know how they can be. And seeing as you have already met the man . . .'

It seems like a good idea. Just as I walk over to Andy to tell him where I'm going, the weasel with BO returns. I can tell by the look on Cathy's face that the trip to Boots has made no difference at all.

'Don't worry, Cathy,' I whisper in her ear. 'I'll take this from here. Excuse me, sir?'

'Yes?' says the man. His voice is quite nasal and he is beginning to sound a little pissed off.

'Could I have a word?'

'What about?'

The queue of passengers is growing behind him and they do not seem to be at all amused by the delay.

'If we could just move to one side?'

'Look,' he says, 'I've already lost my place in the queue once. What do you want?'

'Um, the whole personal hygiene thing . . .' I start.

'I've already been to the chemist and bought some deodorant.'

'I realize that, sir.' I smile. 'But it just isn't working.'

'Well, there's nothing I can do about it.'

'You could go and buy a new shirt,' I suggest as gently as I can.

'What?' The man looks stunned. 'A new shirt? No way.'

'Well, in that case I can't let you fly.'

'You can't do that!'

'I'm afraid I can. For the sake of other passengers.'

'Jesus bloody Christ, what sort of bloody outfit is this? I can't bloody fly unless I buy a new shirt?' His cheeks are growing red with fury, and possibly with embarrassment.

'That's about the sum of it,' I say. 'I am terribly sorry, sir, but I am only following regulations.'

'Don't talk to me about fucking regulations,' he says, his teeth gritted.

'I'm sorry, sir. I just can't let you fly.'

'Fuck you!' he says.

'Quite possibly, sir,' I say.

'And fuck your airline!' he says, walking away from me.

'That too.'

'Fuck the lot of you!'

I nod and smile again.

'Where's the nearest fucking shirt shop?'

'Round the corner to the left, sir,' I say. 'Thomas Pink, you can't miss it.'

2–3 PM

It's a long walk to the crew briefing room. It's almost at the other end of the terminal from where we are. But I can't say I mind. It's a great excuse for me to get outside the building, spark up a cigarette and see some daylight. Although I have to say now that I'm outside the light is grey and the weather is awful. Apart from that brief outburst of sunshine when I was at Animal Welfare, it must have been drizzling gently all morning. What is it about the weather in this country that means it can go off half-cock like this for days at a time? I wish it would just piss it down and be done with it. Suddenly, I think as I take a drag on my cigarette, the jaunt to Dubai doesn't seem so bad after all. Anything to get away from here, no matter how short the trip.

I walk along the pavement outside the terminal and watch a loving couple kissing each other goodbye. I wonder what Susan is doing. She should be showered and tucked up in bed by now. Lucky girl . . . lucky bed. I can't believe Andy invited her to Dubai. He can be a right old shit sometimes. Messing around with other people's lives and relationships. It's not amusing at all.

I spot what looks like a plainclothes security fox standing at the end of the pavement, watching people arrive. He is wearing shades and leaning against the wall. He's holding a newspaper that I'm sure has eyeholes cut out of it for easy viewing. He looks about as subtle as a Secret Squirrel cartoon. All he needs is a flasher's mac to complete the ensemble. I wonder if he was one of the guys who was watching our check-in just now.

Andy suddenly calls through on my radio.

'Hi there,' he says.

'Hi.'

'I just wanted to tell you that Dave has turned up for work.'

'Oh, right,' I say, leaning against a pillar. 'Well, he's over an hour late for his shift.'

'I know,' says Andy. 'But you know we have another flight to do today and you are over there and the queue is backed up to the BA check-in.'

'Shit,' I say. 'Really?'

'I know,' he says.

'How did that happen?'

'Oh, we've had one too many difficult passengers, heavy bags, excess baggage – you know the score.'

'Tell him yes, then,' I say. 'But we won't pay him his full shift.'

'Fine,' says Andy. 'Send my love to the flight crew!'

'Yeah, right.' I smile.

'Roger,' he says. 'See you later.'

I put my radio back in my pocket, turn the corner, go through a side door and walk to the end of a white, strip-lit corridor where I find the crew room. It's a small, unattractive office full of chairs, desks, computers, plane-charts, a map of the world with all our routes drawn on it, plus some telephones and tea- and coffee-making facilities. The place smells of a new carpet, instant coffee and the sweet floral scent of cheap perfume. Chris is leaning, buttocks first, on a desk, asking his gathered crew of nine various security questions.

'So, Diane. If there is a fire in the cabin, what do you do?'

'You get the extinguisher and put it out,' she replies, her red glossy lips cracking into a self-satisfied smile.

'That's correct,' says Chris. 'And what don't you use?'

'Oxygen,' the whole group reply.

'Excellent,' says Chris. 'Diane, can you show me how to do a Heimlich manoeuvre on Sally here.'

Diane gets out of her seat, smooths down her tight navy skirt, grabs the dark-haired Sally from behind and starts thumping her on the back.

'Um, no, Diane,' says Chris.

'Oh God, sorry,' says Diane, collapsing in a fit of embarrassment. 'Sorry, sorry, I forgot. Can I do that again?'

'Be my guest,' says Chris.

Diane takes Sally from behind again, places both her hands in a clasped fist below Sally's rib cage and gives her an almighty tug. Sally pretends to cough up whatever was obstructing her throat and everyone seems pleased.

143

'Excellent,' says Chris. 'I knew you'd get it in the end. So' – he claps his hands – 'those are all the safety questions dealt with.'

It's not often that I get to sit in on a crew briefing. An hour and a half before any flight takes off the crew always gather to go through various quick safety checks, the passenger list and any other idiosyncrasies of the flight. Normally they'd be expected to answer the safety questions straight off; these days they sort of seem to pride themselves on being safety officers. The whole trolley dolly, waitress in the sky idea is supposedly long gone. Attendants are on the terrorist frontline, in charge of the key to the flight deck, the only thing between the captain and a shoe bomber. Some of the super-keen even go on unarmed combat courses so that they know how to deal with drunk or dangerous passengers. However, judging by Diane's performance, this safety movement seems to have passed our lot by.

'OK,' says Chris, his eighties wedge fringe flopping forward across his face. 'Before we all CPA, does anyone know where Tom is? Alex?' A skinny bloke shakes his head. 'Daniel?' The other steward looks equally blank. 'Well, this is terrible,' says Chris, shaking his head. 'I've called his mobile and there is no reply. I'll give him a bit longer before I ring one of the stand-bys, but quite frankly . . .' He looks at his watch and sucks his back teeth. 'OK.' He looks up. 'Can we all CPA?'

All the flight crew stand up, get out their handbags, rattle around in them for a moment, and pull out their compacts to 'check personal appearance'. The two stewards retrieve hand mirrors out of their top pockets.

'Sally?'

'Yes?' she says.

'Have you waxed your arms?'

'Chris!' she moans. 'Course I have.'

'Well, after last time,' he tuts.

'I know, but I've learned my lesson,' she says, walking towards him, extending both her arms for inspection.

Chris takes hold of her hands and turns her forearms up towards the light. 'You know it's because you're dark,' he says.

'I know,' she agrees. 'It's the half Greek in me.'

'Only half?' comments Daniel. 'Doesn't sound much good.'

'Shut it, Daniel,' says Chris, wagging his finger. 'They're snooker-ball smooth,' he opines, running his hands along Sally's arms.

'Told you,' says Sally.

'Your nails,' Chris continues, squinting slightly as he moves in closer. 'Are they the regulation red?'

'Yes.' Sally rolls her eyes. 'Rimmel Titian,' she confirms, 'just like everyone else.'

I'd forgotten quite how strict they are when it comes to uniforms and make-up. They make quite a song and dance about it all. It's worse than school. Each flight attendant is issued with a booklet when they are first handed over their uniform, which details the dos and don'ts of cabin dress – no facial hair, no tattoos, no visible piercings, no far-out make-up deviations like blue nail varnish. There are approved hairstyles, like bobs, French pleats or pony tails or whatever women do to make their hair look neat. They can't do that just-got-up, pole-danced-their-way-through-a-Britney-Spears-video sort of look. And no obvious dyeing. It's all about looking neat, sweet and efficient. Some airlines have a choice of five or so make-up colours; we, like Emirates, only allow red. And only one type of red at that. Jewellery is minimal – gold earring studs, small diamonds, plus the old-school pearls.

Physically, hosties have to be strong enough to open the plane door and tall enough (over 165cm) to reach an overhead locker. I know it doesn't sound much, but you'd be surprised how many wannabes fail the height/strength test. And they're not allowed to be fat or to get fat. No-one says that, of course, because that would leave the airline stranded in some large legal minefield. But there is some weird rule that height and weight have to be in proportion. Some airlines have a free Weight Watchers programme for all flying staff and they are quite strict on the uniforms themselves: they won't issue a larger size for any attendant who has put on weight. As a result the flight attendants who do chub up end up letting out their uniforms themselves.

And the cardinal sin for a flight attendant? A VPL. For reasons of elegance and decency, they are checked for visible panty lines before each and every flight. And with those regulation tight skirts, it's hard not to have one. So much so that many attendants actually fly pantyless. Some wear girdles, some have thongs, but the majority don't bother with knickers at all. I remember Susan telling me some story about when she was working for another airline, the Cabin Service Director made her bend over and pick something off the floor to check if they could see either her buttocks or the gusset of her pants through the split in her skirt. Sounds like my kind of job.

'Ah.' Chris smiles, having finally spotted me at the back of the room. 'All right mate?' he nods. 'Thanks for coming over to talk to us.'

'That's fine,' I say.

'Do you mind sitting there for a sec? We've just a few more bits and pieces to get through. And, I think' – he mouths this like it's a bit of a secret – 'the captain's on his way.'

'No, that's OK,' I say.

I have no idea what the hell I am going to say to this lot. It's not as if I ever actually engaged the terrorist in any conversation. Perhaps I should just leave. It's hardly going to be the most enlightening of chats.

'Would you like a coffee?' asks a blonde hostess who I know is called Denise.

'That would be great,' I say. 'Black no sugar.'

'Strong and black – just like my men.' She laughs.

'Yes, quite,' I say. A couple of the other flight attendants giggle.

'OK,' says Chris, clapping his hands, pushing his wedged hair away from his eyes. 'Concentrate, everyone. I'd just like to go through the passenger information list. Just to make sure everyone is OK about what is going on this flight.'

Everyone sits back down to listen to Chris go through the PIL [Passenger Information List].

'As you know, we have a terrorist on board,' he begins. 'Our duty airport manager will be able to tell you a bit about that later.' He nods towards me. 'But before he does I'd just like to tell you about a few of our special-needs passengers. There is a Mr Parsons on board in, um . . .' He looks down his list.

147

'Thirty-four B. Mr Parsons has one leg shorter than the other. He's had a leg amputation so he needs extra room for his prosthetic. Sally?'

'Yes, Chris?'

'We might have to move Mr Parsons. Can you check how mobile he is when he boards and make sure that in the event of an evacuation he is not going to block anyone in? You know we don't allow the disabled to sit on the end of a row, do we? We don't want them to put other people in danger. The immobile are put in a window seat, remember?' Sally nods. 'For the safety of the other passengers?' Sally nods again. 'So make sure Mr Parsons is mobile. If not, you'll have to move him. I can't risk that on my watch.'

'Yes, Chris.'

'Lorraine,' Chris continues.

'Yes?' smiles a young pretty redhead I haven't seen before.

'You're in first?'

'That's right.' She smiles.

'Well, there's a Mr Andrews in first who is ovolacto sensitive.'

Chris looks at Lorraine. Lorraine stares back, waiting for some sort of clue.

'Ovolacto,' she repeats, rather slowly.

'Intolerant to eggs and milk,' he explains.

'Right.'

'Thing is, I'm not sure if it's a dietary affectation or if he's actually life-threatening allergic. OK? So pay attention to that. He has got a special meal somewhere, so be sure not to give it to someone else. I'm not sure where he's sitting as he hasn't pre-booked his seat. Just watch out,' he concludes, pointing to each of his own eyes with his index finger.

'Other than that,' he continues, 'we've only got one overly large person, a Mrs . . .' he runs his finger down the list. 'Mrs Price, who is obese and very embarrassed about her condition. She has booked two seats and we have also ordered up a seat-belt extension so she can fly. But remember not to serve her any meals because she won't be able to get the tray down, now will she? She is bringing her own onboard food, but remember to be as tactful as possible.' The crew nod. 'She's in economy. She's over twenty-five stone so you can't miss her.'

'Afternoon, everyone.' The captain walks in behind Chris. He has four stripes on his jacket and scrambled eggs (a brocade) on his cap. 'Sorry to interrupt.'

'Absolutely, Captain,' says Chris, stepping quickly to one side. 'You go right ahead.'

'Afternoon, everyone,' he says again. His voice is soft, smooth and terribly reassuring.

'Afternoon, Captain,' the crew reply in unison.

Quite a lot of the time captains are not much to write home about. They are technical-minded control freaks who spend most of their lives sitting on their backsides and moaning about mortgages as they fly across the Atlantic. They only get laid so much because they've got great uniforms and are in positions of power. This bloke, however, is in a different league. Tanned, toned and in his late thirties, he's got a jaw like Action Man and a twinkle in his eye. All the hosties sit up straight. A couple of them cross and uncross their legs. Another flicks her hair.

'My name is Captain Nick Jones,' he says with a smile, 'and I shall be taking you all the way down to Sydney.'

And a few of you in Sydney, I think, judging by the reaction he's getting. I notice he's wearing a rather shiny new wedding ring. Not that that makes much difference downroute. There's honour among thieves once the chocks are off. I remember one of our older pilots had one family in London and another in Sydney, and neither knew about the other. Until he came to retire, that is. Then the poor bloke really was up shit creek. I think he opted for the UK lot in the end. Perhaps the Aussie maintenance was cheaper.

'The flight is full today,' continues Captain Jones. 'The weather seems to be fine, if a little damp.' A couple of the girls laugh. God, life must be easy if you're a captain and you're tanned and good-looking. 'But I am expecting a bit of turbulence as we go over the Alps, so maybe we should get the drinks out early and wait until we are over the Med before we do the main meal.'

'Absolutely, Captain,' says Chris.

'Thanks, Chris. We've got a bit of a tail wind down over the Middle East so we might well be a bit early into Bangkok. The flight time is eleven hours give or take half an hour. We'll restock in Bangkok and then continue on down to Sydney. I'm not sure what the weather is like Down Under at the moment but I shall be checking in to see if it's Bondi or straight to the bar when we land. Um, any questions?'

'No, Captain,' says Chris.

'Oh, one other thing,' adds Captain Jones. 'I understand we have a terrorist on board. I'm not entirely sure what he is supposed to have done or who he is supposed to work for, but let's just see if we can get him to Bangkok with the minimum of fuss, shall we? Then we can get on our way to Sydney as soon as possible.'

'Yes, Captain,' reply the crew.

'On no account should any of the other passengers find out who he is or what he's supposed to have done. I gather there are two guards with him?'

'A couple of tigers, yes,' says Chris.

'I gather there is someone coming over from ground staff to tell you a bit more about him?'

'That's correct,' says Chris, pointing me out at the back of the room. 'He's here already, actually.'

'Good,' says the captain, not bothering to acknowledge me. Captains are famous for never remembering the names or faces of any of the ground staff. Because we don't fly, it's almost as if we don't exist. He turns to exit the room and pauses. 'Oh, I almost forgot,' he says, smiling and tapping his square forehead. 'The password to get on to the flight deck today is, um . . .' He looks around the room. 'Beaver.'

The whole room bursts out laughing.

'Beaver?' queries Sally.

'That's right.' He winks. 'And do try to get it into a natural-sounding sentence.'

Captain Jones leaves the room and everyone suddenly starts chatting. 'Isn't he great?' 'This is going to be a good trip.' 'I wish I was working in first, so I'd get to talk to him.' 'How long d'you think he's been married?' He's clearly charmed the pants off all these women. It's just sad that half of them aren't wearing any.

151

'Settle down now, everyone,' says Chris. 'I'm just going to hand out per diems to those of you who are having them. Denise?' he says.

'Yes?' she replies.

'I've got you back on per diems now. Is that right?'

'That's right,' she confirms. 'I've done up my kitchen. New washer, the works.'

Per diems are the daily allowance the airline gives the flight crew to spend while they are out of the country. The amount of money is worked out according to the cost of living in each country the crew are staying in, and can differ quite widely. In an expensive country like Japan, the per diems are quite impressive and much higher than for a country like Egypt. In some countries, like India, the cost of living is so low that they become known on the circuit as charity flights as you get almost nothing from the airline to live off. This extra money used to be a bit of a perk, but now the government taxes it at source which has slightly taken away the joy of having the airline give you money.

Sometimes handed out as cash in envelopes or as travellers' cheques, per diems can (for a 2½ per cent handling fee) also be dished out by the hotel where the flight crew are staying. You check in for your five-day, seven-day or two-week turnaround and collect the wad of cash at reception. Sometimes, though, in order to save money towards a car or a kitchen or something substantial, flight attendants choose to forgo their per diems, adding them to their basic £16,000-a-year wages instead. It's a way of stopping them irresponsibly splashing out as soon as they touch down. However, if everyone else is irresponsibly splashing out and you're the one in your room eating an apple or an in-flight meal you have squirrelled away in your bag before leaving the plane, this can lead to downroute tension. Those who are not saving invariably end up forking out for those who are building a nest egg. I remember Rachel telling me, when we were actually speaking to each other, about the huge rows they used to have in restaurants whenever the savers said something annoying along the lines of 'I only had a salad' and those with per diems always ended up paying.

Chris hands out the per diems in small brown envelopes like school dinner money. All the attendants gather round, excitedly pocketing their cash. I have always thought that working as a flight attendant is not that dissimilar to a life of endless school trips. The way they are looked after, collected from the airport in buses, ferried to the hotels, given their daily spending money, the drinking, the partying, the bad behaviour – it's all rather similar to releasing a group of teenagers for the first time in Paris. You would think they'd all know one another and get along well, but that's not the case.

It's truer of the smaller charter companies, although this intimacy does have its consequences. Andy's flatmate Craig had to leave Britannia after one particular flight when he arrived and realized that he'd fucked every hostess on his plane. Fortunately, none of them knew that he had bedded any of the others, but he decided to leave before they all found out. But in the larger airlines many of the flight attendants don't actually know the people they are flying with at all. They meet for the first time in the crew room and have to start relationships from scratch every time. This can lead to a different kind of problem, mainly isolation and loneliness. If you're not one of those people who can bond on the bus on the way to the plane, you can end up on your own for the entire three- or four-day turnaround. I have a friend who was asked to look into flight attendants' concerns for a large national carrier and she came back with such terrible stories of temazepan, vicodin and valium addictions prompted by the odd hours and the isolation that they had to set up an internal helpline open twenty-four hours a day.

Ours is a medium-size carrier, so we span the divide. You can drop your pants with a certain amount of impunity, though sooner or later your past will catch up with you. Andy and I both have a bet with Craig that it is going to take him three years before he has a planeload of ex-shags to deal with. So far, it's looking like we might get paid a little sooner.

'OK,' says Chris, with another clap. 'I have given him the benefit of the doubt and Tom is clearly not turning up. I'm going to have to call in a standby.'

As well as flying days, part of the shift system also includes periods spent on standby. All flight crew on shift have to live within ninety minutes of the airport crew room in full make-up so that they can be called in at short notice. In any one week an attendant can have three flying days and two spent on standby for which they also get paid. In the smaller airlines such as ours they get called in to fly at short notice about 70 per cent of the time. This can happen at any time during standby. If you have been on standby all day, unable to drink or stray further than ninety minutes away from the airport, you can be called in at 5.50 p.m., in the last ten minutes of your shift, and asked to do a seven-hour night flight. I have lost count of the number of times flight attendants have been caught out, glass of wine in hand, as they clock off an hour or so early.

'Which Tom are you talking about?' I ask, thinking I might be able to help.

'Tom Raven,' replies Chris.

'Oh.' I smile. 'I might give Andy a call. He goes out with Tom quite often.'

'Would you? That'd be great.'

I radio through to Andy and mention that Tom is missing from work. He doesn't seem at all surprised. He says he'll look into it and call me back as soon as he can. Two minutes later, he's as good as his word.

'So?'

'Well,' says Andy. 'Slightly delicate . . .'

'OK.'

'He's handcuffed to a bed on the sixth floor of the Kensington Intercontinental and can't get out.'

'Right,' I say, slowly taking in the information. 'How do you know this?'

'Because he was out with me last night and I know the bloke he went back to the hotel with, so I gave him a call.'

'Oh.'

'It's one of those pranks that went a bit wrong.'

'No shit.'

'Yeah, well.'

'Is there any way he can be released?'

'Not in time for the Bangkok–Sydney flight, no.'

'Right.'

'Whoops.'

'Double bloody whoops.'

'We can probably get him here in time for Singapore–Sydney,' suggests Andy optimistically.

'Sadly, not the flight he's scheduled for.'

'No,' says Andy.

'No,' I reply.

'Any luck?' asks Chris from across the room.

'Well,' I smile. 'I think it's probably better if you can get a standby. Tom seems to be incapacitated. Some family problem . . .'

'Oh.' Chris nods. 'He could have phoned in.'

'Yes. Unfortunately he can't get to a phone.'

'Oh,' says Chris again. 'Sounds bad.'

'Yes. Most unfortunate.'

'I'd better sort out a replacement,' declares Chris. 'I hope they can get here at such short notice.'

'Good idea,' I agree. 'You'd better get your mate to release Tom,' I whisper to Andy.

'Roger that,' says Andy, starting to laugh.

'See you back at check-in.'

'OK, mate.'

Chris rattles through his list of standbys and manages to find someone who lives unfashionably close to the airport and can make it in half an hour. It seems that Tom is off the hook. I look at my watch. It's 2.55. I really have got to get back to the check-in. I had no idea I had been sitting here for so long.

'Um, Chris?' I say.

'Yes, mate.'

'I've got to head back across . . .'

'Oh, right. Any quick words of wisdom on the terrorist?'

'Oh, um, of course,' I say. A whole room of expectant faces turns towards me. 'Well, let's see. He looks like an old school teacher.' They all nod. 'And wasn't that frightening at all.' They nod again. 'He is the brains behind things, not the brawn. Um, not dangerous in the slightest.'

'Why does he need two guards?' asks Chris.

'Oh, well, you know – regulations.' I smile.

'Of course,' says Chris.

'Anyway, better go. I'm sure I've got a load of late passengers to deal with.'

'See you on the ramp,' says Chris.

'Absolutely,' I reply.

'And thanks for the talk. It was really very useful indeed.'

3-4 PM

By the time I get back to check-in via a small cigarette break just next to the put-down area outside, the crowds have disappeared, Andy's nowhere to be seen and there is a shouting match going on, involving the very hungover Debbie and a rather small woman in a leather jacket with a fur-trimmed collar. It seems to be just about to hit its stride.

'Look,' says the short woman, sounding exasperated. 'When I came to check in and didn't have my passport, you told me I had enough time to call my flatmate and get him to bring it to the airport, and now . . . and now . . .' Her voice is getting louder. Her face is increasingly puce. 'And now you are refusing to check me in!'

'You're too late, madam,' says Debbie, not looking her in the eye. 'I know that you've gone to a lot of trouble for nothing. But you are just too late. We've closed the check-in.'

'But you knew I was coming!' replies the short woman,

looking astounded. 'I'm hardly unfamiliar. It's not like I have come out of the blue, like some big fat surprise. I've been standing next to you for over an hour.'

'That's as may be, madam,' says Debbie, her face looking slightly less grey than when I left. 'But we closed the check-in ten minutes ago and you are too late.'

'The plane is still here, you are still here, what's the problem?' she says, raising her voice another decibel.

'The check-in is closed,' Debbie insists. 'There is nothing I can do.'

'Yes there is!' shouts the short woman. 'You can check me in for my flight to bloody Australia and be done with it!'

'There's no need to swear,' says Debbie.

Oh dear, here we go, I think, as I walk towards the situation.

'You call "bloody" swearing?' exclaims the woman, making little quotation marks in the air in front of her.

'I'm afraid I do.' Debbie is not handling this well.

'Bloody isn't swearing,' the short woman bellows. 'Fuck! Cunt! Arsehole! Now that's swearing. If you want to hear swearing I can carry on.' But her voice is growing a little weaker; she seems to be on the verge of tears. 'Fucking cunting cockhead. There! Now that's really something to complain about.' She sounds triumphant. I have to admit, as swearing goes it's a pretty good combination, possibly some of the worst we've had in a while.

The passport-dash passengers are always the most difficult, mainly because they can't believe they've been so stupid as to leave their passports behind. And it usually happens to the most cool, well-travelled people. Granted, there are a few dickhead novice passengers who forget their passports, but more often than not it's the ones who are quite relaxed about travelling who don't bother to check for their tickets and passport three times before leaving the house. They turn up, feel like twats, and then go into a total tailspin panic. They clockwatch while someone races to the airport with their documents, tension mounting all the time, and then they collapse completely when they are too late for the plane.

But I have to admit that I think Debbie is being a bit harsh here. Perhaps she's had a shit shift and is being bloody-minded just for the sake of it. Or more likely Little Miss Shouty got up her nose the first time she tried to check in.

'Can I help?' I ask.

Debbie looks relieved. The short woman spins around.

'Yes!' she says. 'I'd like to speak to someone in charge.'

'I'm in charge.' I smile.

'Oh good. This woman here' – she points at Debbie but can't seem to bear to look at her – 'is refusing to check me in, even though I have been standing here for over an hour.'

'OK.'

'You didn't have the correct documents and now the check-in is closed,' mumbles Debbie from the other side of the desk.

'Do you have much luggage?' I ask.

'Just this bag.' She indicates a suitcase that, at a push, is small enough for hand luggage.

'Well, let's see what we can do.'

Her face breaks into an enormous smile. 'Really?'

'We'll see,' I say, reaching for my walkie-talkie.

Truth is that just so long as the plane is still here I can get anyone onto it I like. VIPs are always delaying flights and arriving at the last minute. But our flight is still very much on the ground. It doesn't take off for another twenty-five minutes and they've only just started boarding. All I have to do when calling through is to use the correct code to elicit the correct response. If I start the sentence 'We have . . .' it means I want them to reply that it is too late to accept the passenger. However, if I say 'Any chance . . .', the woman will get on the plane.

I page through to the gate and get Andy.

'There you are,' I say.

'Well, someone's got to start the boarding,' he says. 'And seeing as you weren't back yet . . .'

'OK, point taken. There's an LRP. A late reporting passenger.'

'I know what an LRP is,' he says, sarcastically.

'I was just checking that you were awake.' I laugh. 'Anyway, any chance of getting her onto the flight?'

'You know it's fine,' says Andy. 'Just get her along quickly. We are actually boarding.'

'Good,' I say.

'What?' asks the short woman.

'It's fine.'

'Oh my God!' She yelps and leaps into the air with joy. She runs up to me and puts her arms around me. 'I love you, I love you,' she says, kissing my right bicep, nuzzling her face into my armpit. 'Thank you so much. Thank you so very much. You've saved my life. You really have.'

'That's perfectly all right, madam,' I say, trying to extricate

162

myself from her embarrassing embrace. 'Follow me as quickly as you can. You have a plane to catch.'

'Right, of course,' she says, picking up her bag. She stops and turns towards Debbie. 'Um, sorry about all the shouting and swearing. I was a bit overwrought. I just have to leave for Sydney today. My sister's getting married.'

'Oh, right,' says Debbie. 'Don't forget your passport again.'

'No,' agrees the woman. 'Never again.'

As we jog through the airport towards the plane, the short woman won't stop talking about how grateful she is and how marvellous I am for sorting her out. To start off with it's enough to make a guy's head swell. I feel quite chuffed with myself and pleasantly pleased. If only it were possible to elicit this sort of response from everyone we help. But by the end it is rather like being followed by a yapping, rather over-excited poodle. She really won't shut up, no matter how many times I pretend to be self-effacing. When we finally reach the gate I freely admit I'm pleased to be rid of her.

'This your HAG?' asks Andy, rather absentmindedly as he takes the short woman's boarding pass.

'Um,' I say. Shit, I think.

'What?' she says, stopping in her tracks and pulling herself up to her full diminutive height.

'Sorry?' says Andy, looking down his tanned nose.

'What did you just say?'

'What?' says Andy, unaware that he has actually said anything.

'You just called me a hag,' she blusters.

'Did I? Oh I'm sorry. I'm not sure I did.'

'You did,' she replies. 'I heard you. Did you hear him?'

She looks at me, her newfound friend, for confirmation. I shrug and think about starting Andy's defence. But he launches in himself.

'Oh God, I shouldn't worry, madam,' he says, shoving her boarding card through the computer. 'It's a technical term, you know, that we use in the industry.'

'Is it now?'

'It means "have a go" passenger,' explains Andy, not lying for once. He looks up and smiles. His white teeth shine. 'We use it all the time to mean people who are late but who give you some sort of story as to why they are late.'

He is being so disconcertingly honest that the short woman's chest deflates. 'Oh,' she says.

'Yeah, I know.' He nods. 'I can see the confusion. Anyway, have a good journey.' He points her in the direction of the plane, then looks at me and rolls his eyes. 'That woman needs a fucking Valium,' he mutters with a cheeky grin.

'I heard that,' she says, turning around and marching back along the corridor towards us. 'You're a supercilious old queen!' she yells.

'Oh, don't use words you can't spell,' says Andy, his voice sounding deeply jaded.

'Madam, why don't you just board the plane?' I suggest. 'I really think it would be better for all concerned.'

'I shall be complaining about you,' she says.

'Who, me?' I ask.

'No, him,' she says, pointing at Andy.

'Go right ahead,' Andy says with a smile.

'I will,' she insists, stamping her foot.

No sooner has she turned the corner than Andy is on the radio to Chris inside the plane.

'Chris, mate,' he whispers. I can hear some vaguely garbled reply. 'Listen, you've got a right old bitch coming through. Seat number . . .' He taps away at the computer. 'Forty-four C. Anyway, just to warn you guys that she is coming and if someone wants to spit in her coffee, be our guest.' Chris says something that makes Andy giggle. 'That sounds great. Mmm . . . yes . . . short . . . fur-trimmed leather thing . . . got her?' Chris says something else. 'I know. You're right, it's always the short ones. Thanks, mate. Over and out.' Andy turns to me and smiles. 'That's sorted. Her dinner is going on the floor of the toilet before it goes on her plate.'

You may think he is joking, but he's not. Piss off the ground staff enough that they radio through to their colleagues on the plane and you really are in for a bad flight and probably a couple of bad tummy days when you arrive at your destination. Flight staff can spit on your food, piss in your coffee and wipe your steak around the rim of the toilet before it gets anywhere near you. And you would be none the wiser. Some of the more badly behaved cabin crew carry laxative powder that they use to spike the drinks and food of those who get on their tits. It's a simple form of revenge that is not readily traceable. So the best way to get the best service is to be pleasant and affable from the off.

Andy looks very pleased with himself as he puts on his service-industry smile again and carries on processing boarding passes. Ordinarily I should be giving him a gentle bollocking for his Valium comment, and perhaps for the HAG thing, but the woman was a nightmare and she'd already shouted her head off at Debbie and bored the backside off me, so quite frankly I'm glad to see the back of her.

And anyway, there is something much more interesting going on in the far corner of departures. A large woman has been pulled over, and someone from Baggage along with a Customs official is going through her bags. Alerted by swiping her boarding card through the computer at the gate, these two officials would have been waiting for her to turn up for a while. Her bags must have failed any one of the various security tests that luggage is subjected to after check-in. Most irregularities such as weird electrical goods are discovered right from the outset during X-ray, almost as soon as they are put on the conveyor belt, provided that the scanners aren't too stoned, lazy or tired to keep their eye on the screen. But if there's something the scanner can't quite discern, the computer alerts the operator and the bag is moved and taken to the next level. Level two is a 3D scanner, which looks at the bag from every angle and dimension. If the operator is still not satisfied the bag is searched by hand. There are apparently some substances, such as marzipan, that the scanners actually can't see through at all. Garry is always saying that it's the affianced couples and newly-weds we should watch out for, as wedding cakes are potentially lethal. If a bomb is suspected, then the Bomb Squad are called in and the suitcase, through a system of volunteers, is removed from the baggage area.

But this situation, as I approach it, looks like none of the above to me. There was a time when women with big tits were pulled over all the time for the amusement of the Customs and Baggage guys. Bra underwiring shows up on the scans, and when things were slow and they were bored they'd pull over the woman with the most underwiring and therefore the biggest tits just for a gawp. But those days are long gone, and the only reason why this admittedly large-breasted woman would be pulled at this late stage is if something battery-operated had switched itself on in her suitcase and was making a noise.

Sure enough, just as I arrive ready to ask the woman if she needs any help, the Customs official pulls out a pink buzzing cock. The woman doesn't bat an eyelid. Either she is playing it cool, like people pull bright pink cocks out of her suitcase all the time, or she is so embarrassed that she can't move. I turn and try to catch her eye, only to notice that she has two puce patches on her cheeks. She is mortified.

'Everything OK here?' I ask.

'Mmm,' she says, not able to speak.

'Not quite,' says the Customs official, holding the cock in one hand and riffling through her baggage with the other. 'We still have a noise going on in here. Are there any more?'

'Mmm.' The woman appears to nod in the affirmative.

'Aha!' he says, pulling out a small, veined, flesh-coloured vibrator that is not switched on. 'Oh,' he adds, sounding disappointed. 'No, that's not it.' Both he and the Baggage guy stand still, their heads on one side. 'Can you hear anything?' the Customs bloke asks the Baggage bloke. 'Or is it just this one?' He waves the pink cock. 'There's definitely something else. I can hear it.'

This scene is beginning to remind me of the occasion when we pulled over an elderly family entertainer only to find that he had a suitcase full of big buzzing vibrators. Even though my back is turned, I can sense Andy beginning to take an interest. He loves this sort of thing.

The Customs official digs a little deeper and finally brings out an enormous shiny black vibrator that is not only buzzing but, like some rampant snake, also appears to be bending and stirring the air at the same time.

'Jesus Christ,' declares Andy from across the other side of the room, boarding pass hanging limply in his hand. 'That's huge!' He has a habit of voicing what everyone else is thinking.

'Right,' says the Customs official as he puts the two cocks on the table. 'That seems to have, um, cleared the matter up. Would you mind taking the batteries out of these please, madam, so they don't start up again.'

The woman mumbles something and, picking up each of the vibrators in turn, tries to remove the batteries. She sweatily fumbles the batteries out of the pink and the flesh-coloured vibrators, but when it comes to the big black cock her grip slips and it is launched across the floor of the lounge in a frenzy of buzzing and writhing. Everyone – the Customs official, the Baggage bloke and the last remaining passengers – just stand there, mouths ajar, staring. None of us knows what to do. We all stand stock still, watching it crawl and weave its way over the carpet tiles.

Andy is the only one to move. He speeds across the room, whips up the dildo, removes the batteries, and hands the whole lot back to the woman, with immense deftness and grace.

'Have a nice flight,' he says with a smile, then turns back towards his post. 'Right,' he says loudly. 'Now, who's next? Let's get you all on board this plane before we're delayed.'

Soon we are closing the door on the last passenger, and Andy and I are quite relieved to get the flight away. It's only a couple of minutes late on its stand and hasn't missed its departure slot. It's been quite exhausting getting all the tigers, terrorists and loud-mouthed aggressives on the flight, and I feel in need of a large cup of strong coffee and a sneaky cigarette to celebrate. We have an hour and a bit before the next check-in, so neither Andy nor I is in a particular hurry to get back to the office and catch up on the paperwork that I know awaits us both.

'Shall we have a go on the computer games?' suggests Andy as we walk past one of the many amusement arcades that are in the airport and only ever seem to be used by staff. 'Do you want to do the dancing one?'

'What?' I say, stopping on the concourse. 'There's a machine that makes you dance?'

'Oh yeah,' says Andy. 'I come and use it quite often when I'm on a break.'

'When are you ever on a break?'

'You know those times when you can't find me . . .'

'You're dancing?'

Andy looks sheepish. 'Well,' he says. His mobile rings in his top pocket. 'Saved by the bell.' He smiles. 'Hello?'

While Andy 'noo-os!' and 'reallys?' with extreme enthusiasm, I stand and watch the endless stream of passengers pour past on their way to their gates, or madly dropping silly money on unnecessary must-haves in duty free. We are near the cigar room, a Mecca for the larger man and the vacantly curious teenager. One big bloke seems to be stocking up on boxes of Monte Cristos while his bored wife looks on. Further up, the seafood bar is going great guns with a gaggle of blondes tucking into smoked salmon sandwiches for their afternoon tea.

'Excuse me,' asks a youngish bloke with a rather pale face, tapping me on the shoulder. 'D'you know where the toilets are?'

'Oh, hello.' I'm half asleep. I'm obviously developing airport brain myself. 'Right behind me,' I say, pointing to the toilet sign. 'You can't miss them.'

'Thanks,' he says, weakly wandering off.

'Fucking hell!' says Andy, his eyes shining, high off the back of his chat. 'That was Tom.'

'Oh yeah?'

'He's finally been released from the hotel room. He was strapped to the bed, stark bollock naked.' He grins. 'Hotel security had to let the other bloke in.' He laughs. 'Fucking funny. Can you imagine? Being laid out like a starfish? So embarrassing! And to have hotel security let the boyfriend, or whatever he was, in. Hilarious. It could only happen to Tom.'

'Sounds like it,' I say, not really listening.

'Anyway, the great thing is that Tom can now come to Dubai with us tonight!'

'Great.'

'I know, isn't it?' Andy's bouncing around all keen and excited. 'After he missed Bangkok–Sydney, he's got to work the Dubai flight tonight. He's due for a stopover in Dubai anyway before going on to Sydney or Melbourne or wherever, so he's taken it. He'll work our flight and join us in the hotel.'

'That's great news.'

'This is going to be the best birthday,' says Andy, rubbing his hands. 'I can't fucking wait. Tom, you, me, Craig, Rachel . . .'

His voice goes down an octave. 'Oh, and,' he smiles again. 'Sue, Sue, Sue!'

'Before you take the piss any more, I need one,' I say. 'Wait here, will you?'

'Sure,' he replies. 'Don't be long now,' he adds, wagging his finger. 'We've got dancing do.'

I walk into the toilets just as one of the cleaners is finishing up. Wearing industrial-strength maroon rubber gloves, he is wiping down the last of the urinals and then turns the same cloth onto the basin and taps. I stop slightly in my tracks. My mouth hangs open. How am I meant to wash my hands now I know where his cloth has been? He doesn't seem to notice the look on my face. In fact, he doesn't seem to notice or engage with much at all.

'Afternoon,' I say as he walks past me, his head down, his back hunched. He doesn't bother to reply. I shrug and unzip my flies.

There appears to be no-one else here in the toilet; all I can hear is the dripping of a tap. I am alone. What a relief. Sometimes it's nice to have a bit of time out, away from shouting passengers and chatting cabin crew. One of the things that is so difficult about this job is that you always have to be 'on'. You've got to have the right smile on your face, the correct, helpful cadence in your voice, ever ready to assist. It always amazes me that the customers expect this sort of service. It's not as if anyone looks after you and your children like this if you get on a bloody train. Who cares if you left your jacket at Clapham Junction? Or that you're allergic to nuts? What's it to me that your legs are a bit too long for the seat? It's all some hangover from the days when it was glamorous to fly, when airports were destinations and people would dress up to go on a flight. Today, I may as well be running a bus station.

Just as I zip up my trousers, I hear what sounds like crying coming from a cubicle behind me.

'Hello?' I say, my voice echoing. I turn around and notice the locked door. 'Anyone in there?' The crying gets a little louder. 'Anyone there?'

'Go away,' comes the reply. It sounds like the voice of a young man.

'You OK in there?'

'Leave me alone.'

'Are you all right?'

'No,' he says. 'My girlfriend's left me. I hate myself. Leave me alone.'

'What are you doing in there?'

'None of your business. Leave me alone.'

'Do you want to talk? I can help you, if you want.' I am beginning to sense something is not at all right and it scares me. I've been in this situation before and it's not good.

'Leave me alone,' he says, sounding increasingly agitated. 'Let me die on my own.'

'What do you mean, let you die?' I say, my face right up against the toilet door. Here we go, I think.

'Go away!' His voice is growing louder. 'Go away! Go away! Go away!' There are now proper heavy sobs coming from inside the cubicle.

'Maybe if you talked to me I could help,' I suggest, as calmly as I can.

'I don't want to,' he says, struggling for breath between sobs.

'I want to be on my own.'

'Well, I'm afraid I'm not leaving.' I try to make it sound like it's a joke.

'It's too late anyway,' he says, his voice now growing weak, his crying more resigned.

'What do you mean?' I ask, looking under the door. His white trainers are pointing towards me. He must be sitting on the loo.

'I've already taken the pills.'

'What pills? How many pills?'

'I don't know.' He sounds confused. 'Pills. Pills. White pills. And a few of them.'

'Wait there, I'll be back in a sec.' I run out of the toilets and grab hold of Andy. 'Listen, mate,' I say, taking both his shoulders, 'there's some bloke in the bogs who's taken some pills, trying to kill himself.'

'Shit,' says Andy, paying attention.

'Go and get Barry the chaplain and Terry and Derek. And be quick about it.'

'Fuck,' says Andy. 'Sounds serious.'

'I think so.'

'Is it that young bloke you directed in there while I was on the phone?'

'What?'

'He hasn't come out yet.'

'Could be,' I say.

'It'll be another one of those teenager, jilted-lover cries for help.'

'I don't know. I think this one might mean it.'

173

4–5 PM

Andy and I have a toilet each and are trying to engage the teenager when Barry arrives all red-faced and out of breath. Tall and overweight, with a rolling, fat voice designed to resonate all the way up the nave, Barry is the sort of gentle, ebullient fellow you want to confess all to.

'Sorry, sorry, sorry,' he says as he stands outside my cubicle, his black shirt sticking to his chest, his black trousers all creased. 'I got caught up in Customs. Terrible business.' He shakes his head. 'Now,' he smiles, concentrating on the matter in hand. 'What do we have here?'

I get off the throne and beckon him outside, thinking it better to explain the situation out of earshot of the suicidal teenager.

'He's young,' I say to Barry, who is nodding away, his arms crossed over his girth. 'I think he has taken some pills.'

'Pills, you say,' says Barry. 'What sort?'

'No idea. I don't even know if they are life-threatening, but I suspect they are.'

'Oh dear. I do hope they're not paracetamol. I hate it when they take paracetamol. You think you've sorted them out, got their stomach pumped, and then they die of liver failure three days later. Evil stuff.'

'Well, I'm not sure what it is, but he does seem quite keen on killing himself.'

'Right. Girlfriend?'

'Girlfriend,' I confirm.

'Has he just said goodbye to her?'

'I think so.'

'And is due to board the plane?'

'Looks like it.'

'OK. Police and ambulance?'

'On their way.'

'So I'm not late.'

'No, you're the first.'

'Good.' He smiles. 'Let's get on with it, then.'

Barry and I walk back into the toilets together. We are immediately followed by two Italians.

'I'm sorry,' says Barry, turning around to stop both of them in their tracks. 'We have a problem in here.' Maybe it's the dog collar, or the powerful tone of his voice; either way they leave immediately and with no fuss. 'Andy?' he asks. 'Could you stand outside and stop people coming in?'

Andy gets up and vacates his cubicle.

'Any progress?' Barry asks Andy as he walks past.

'None,' he replies. 'I still can't get him to give me his name.'

Barry knocks on the teenager's locked door.

'Hello there,' he says. 'My name's Barry and I've come to help you.'

'Go away,' comes the reply.

'Nothing would give me greater pleasure,' laughs Barry. 'I hate spending time in toilets. Filthy, stinking places. What are you doing here?'

'Leave me alone.'

'I'm afraid I can't do that. Why don't you tell me what you are doing here?'

'I don't want to.'

'I'm not going anywhere until you do.'

'Like I care.'

'Well, you should,' says Barry. 'Because I haven't had any lunch yet and I'm starving. If you could see what a big bloke I am, you'd know how important food is to me. Are you hungry?'

'A bit.'

'When did you last eat anything?'

'Breakfast.'

'You must be starving. What did you have?'

'Frosties.'

'Oh, I love Frosties,' says Barry. 'Only thing is, I'm such a big fat bloke I'm not allowed them any more. My wife's banned them from the house.'

'No way.'

'I know,' says Barry. 'You should hear the other stuff I'm not allowed to eat. As if it makes any difference. I've always been a fat bloke and it's not going to change just because she's banned bread from the house.'

'What else?'

Within three minutes Barry manages to do what Andy and I have spent the last fifteen trying to do: he seems to have engaged the teenager and won some sort of trust. But then I suppose this is his job and he's had plenty of practice. We get quite a few people threatening to kill themselves in the airport. Most of them are young and have just said goodbye to their lover, or loved one, and they think it's the end of their world. They all think they are Romeo and Juliet and retire to the toilets for one last *grande geste*. Others are deportees not wanting to go home, or they are businessmen who have stuffed up, or who can't cope any more. Either way Barry, or one of his team, is the first port of call.

The chaplaincy team are quite an extraordinary bunch. There's a Catholic priest, Benedictine brothers, two sheikh advisers, a rabbi, an Islamic adviser, two guys from the free churches (Methodist and Presbyterian) and a couple of members of the Salvation Army. It's rather like a mini United Nations, which I suppose is the only way to cater for the huge cross-section of people who come through the airport. They run the chapel and the multi-faith prayer rooms but are also asked to attend to some of the more day-to-day aspects of airport business. They meet coffins, counsel the bereaved and deal with the homeless; they attend births in toilets, perform quickie marriages in the chapel (which they will only do for parish members) and take confession all over the airport. They are hard pushed at Christmas, but their busiest time of year comes around January/February during the haj, when some sixty thousand British Muslims descend on Mecca. Most of them come through the airport to connect up with specially chartered flights. The place is packed with people in white robes randomly putting down mats in the lounges and shops to say their prayers. It's an extraordinary sight. Sometimes, even to someone like me who last went to a church in a christening robe, it can be quite inspiring.

And a lot of the team's time is taken up with those too frightened to fly. You'd be surprised how many people come to an airport and still can't get on a plane. Paralysed with fear, they normally make it as far as the departure lounge but can't bear to go any further. The airline staff usually try to take care of the situation, but if all else fails they call in the God squad. Barry tells great stories of actually having to escort people to their seats, all the while explaining that flying takes them closer to God. Although, given that what people fear most is crashing and death, I can never understand quite how proximity to their maker can be a reassuring thing.

I hear Terry and Derek outside the toilets and rush out to head them off at the pass. Barry seems to be doing such a good job with the teenage boy that the last thing we need is for these two to come in and ruin it all with their banter and cynicism.

'Barry's in there at the moment,' I say.

'Right,' says Terry. 'Any idea of the situation?'

'Teenager's said goodbye to his girlfriend and says he has taken some pills.'

'One of those.' Derek yawns, stretching his arms above his head. 'How long has he been in there?'

'About half an hour.'

'Probably crying wolf,' says Derek. Terry nods in agreement. 'How long shall we give Barry?'

'Five minutes,' says Terry.

'He should get him out by then,' I say.

'You sound very confident,' says Andy.

'You didn't hear him in there. Anyway, you two took your time. Where have you been?'

'A couple of wheelies,' says Terry. 'And this piss artist.' He shakes his head.

'Oh my God,' says Derek laughing, 'you wouldn't believe this one even if you were bloody there.'

'This bloke gets off the plane, right,' says Terry. Andy and I nod. 'He leans on the finger gangway arm thing, right, and someone's not secured it properly so he falls straight through onto the tarmac below. All hell breaks loose. We're called. We've got a dead man on the ramp! Everyone's screaming and shouting. No-one can believe it. We get there. He's lying flat out on the tarmac. He looks dead. But I can feel a pulse. I put an airway into him. A tube. The lot. He doesn't flinch. Derek has the spinal injury unit ready and we're moving him on the count of three when he wakes up.'

'Un-bloody-believable,' says Derek, shaking his head.

'He opens his bloody eyes, mumbles something like "How did I get here?" and stands up. Pulls out the tube thing, brushes himself off and stares at us all. Turns out he was so pissed, his body was so relaxed when it hit the ground, that the bastard bounced.'

'Amazing,' says Andy.

'That's the first time I've seen that,' says Terry.

'I know a couple of blokes who've fallen out of planes before,' offers Derek, 'but none of them has ever made it.'

'He's going to feel it tomorrow,' says Terry.

'That's true,' says Andy. 'That'll be the hangover to end all hangovers.'

We are all laughing when Barry appears at the entrance to the toilets, his arm wrapped around the ashen-faced teenager.

'This is Paddy,' he says. 'And he's had a bit of a rough time of it.'

'All right there, Paddy?' says Terry, immediately springing into action. 'How are you doing, mate?'

'OK,' says Paddy, looking anything but.

'Now, have you taken anything?' Terry continues, taking the boy's face in his hand and shining a small torch in his eyes. 'What have you taken, Paddy?' The boy suddenly seems to go floppy in his hands. He falls to the floor, only to be caught by Terry just before he hits the deck. A huge burp of puke shoots out of his mouth and covers Terry's shoes. 'Oh fuck,' says Terry, not even noticing the vomit. 'What the hell has he taken?' Andy's going through his bags, I'm in his jacket pockets, Derek's calling for back-up, Barry runs back inside the toilets. 'Come on! Come on!' says Terry, putting the boy in the recovery position. 'Someone find out what this fucker has taken.'

'Here it is!' says Barry, coming out of the toilets carrying a small white pot.

'What is it?' asks Terry.

'Paracetamol,' replies Barry, his face falling.

'You stupid bastard,' says Terry gently. 'Let's get him to hospital.'

Within minutes the toilet area is a mass of green jumpsuits, police, drips, tubes and trolleys. Paddy is wrapped in a red blanket and strapped into a stretcher, a mask over his white, impassive face.

'What do you think?' Andy asks Terry as Paddy is wheeled away.

'It doesn't look good,' says Terry, whistling through the back of his teeth. 'Looks like he took all forty-eight of the pills in one go.'

'And that's bad?' asks Andy.

'Put it this way, it's not good. Paracetamol is a slow burner. It takes days to eat up your system. It's painful too.'

Barry is sitting at the end of a row of yellow plastic bucket seating, his head in his hands. He looks very downcast. I go over to him.

'You OK?' I ask, sitting down next to him.

'What?' he says, looking up. 'Oh, sorry, mate.' He smiles. 'It's been a bit of a difficult one so far. That's my second death today.'

'He may not be dead,' I point out optimistically.

'I don't know,' he says, shaking his head. 'He looked pretty much on his last legs to me, and I don't have a medical background.'

'What was the other one?' I ask.

'Oh Lord.' He sighs, getting up out of his seat and brushing down his black trousers. 'Do you fancy a cup of coffee?'

'I would actually,' I say.

I'm not feeling that good myself. It's not every day a situation that we all read so nonchalantly goes so badly wrong. For some reason I'm feeling guilty. I know it's mad, but I can't help wondering if I'd acted sooner, broken down the door even, perhaps the situation could have been a bit different. Maybe if I had noticed his sad face when he'd asked for directions to the toilet in the first place he would not have had the opportunity to take the pills. I know I am not responsible. But somehow I feel I am.

Barry and I walk over to Caffè Nero and order two strong black coffees.

'I shouldn't be drinking one of these,' mutters Barry as he takes a sip from the paper beaker. 'My wife's put me off caffeine.'

'Right.'

'No idea why. Apparently it's not very good for me. But anything that stops me eating so much . . .'

'I can't get through the day without it,' I say. 'There have to be some advantages to having no-one at home.'

'That's true.' Barry smiles.

'So where were you this morning?' I ask, hunching over my coffee.

'Customs,' he says.

'Oh, right.' Perhaps I shouldn't press him.

'They had some Nigerian drug smuggler in there who had swallowed sixty condoms of heroin.'

'Jesus.' Barry looks at me. 'Sorry,' I mutter.

'Anyway, he'd already passed some twenty condoms while sitting on the glass toilet they have in there and was waiting for the other forty when he suddenly got it into his head that one of the condoms might burst. He panicked and started screaming that he didn't want to die, and in fear of death he turned to a police officer and announced that he wanted to be baptized.'

'What?'

'Yeah,' nods Barry. 'I've done it before, but this was much more difficult. Anyway, they called me in and I spoke to the prisoner in order to work out if he was of sound mind and reasonable understanding. Which he was. Under the circumstances. And then I baptized him with a cup of water right there in the cells. I have to say that there are ways, and ways, of coming to God. That wasn't one of the best.' He stares into space and takes another sip of his coffee.

'So is he OK?'

'No. Turns out he was right about the condoms. Some sort of premonition. Or perhaps he'd just worked out the odds. Three of them burst about half an hour after he was baptized. He died about forty minutes later. Apparently, according to the Customs official I spoke to, he had only wrapped the heroin in one condom when he should have used two. The stomach acid rots down one with relative ease. The longer they stay in there, the higher the risk.' He looks at me across the table. 'What a terrible, terrible business.'

'At least you baptized him,' I offer.

'Well, I suppose so,' says Barry. 'Thank heaven for small mercies, eh? Oh look,' he adds, pointing over my shoulder. 'There's Robert, one of our Salvation Army boys. Robert! Over here!'

Robert, a young blond chap in the black and red uniform of the Salvation Army, comes over.

'Afternoon, Reverend,' he says. 'How are you?'

'Not too bad. How about you?'

'Oh, it's the end of my shift and I've just come over from one of the prayer rooms in another terminal.'

'Oh yes?'

'Very disappointing.'

'Oh dear.'

'Lots of Muslims today and no Christians at all.' Robert looks crestfallen.

'Oh well,' says Barry, 'there's always tomorrow.'

'That's true,' nods Robert. 'See you then.'

'Absolutely. See you.' Robert disappears and Barry smiles. 'The enthusiasm of youth,' he says. 'It's just a shame that some of that didn't rub off on that young boy Paddy.'

'That's true,' I say.

'Anyway,' says Barry, knocking back the remainder of his coffee. 'Can't sit around moping all day. I've got a homeless meeting to attend to.'

'Right. The Lord's work is never done.'

'Something like that.' He smiles, getting up from his chair. 'You should look after yourself,' he says to me, putting a hand on my shoulder. 'You're looking tired.'

'The stresses and strains of life,' I say.

'You should get some early nights.'

'Absolutely.'

'I'm always at St George's Chapel or the office if you need me.'

As he walks off in the direction of the terminal, I watch as he is accosted by some old lady loaded down with duty free. She touches his arm, tugging at his shirt. I can't hear what is being said but she doesn't detain him long. Some pleasant words and she is off, on her way again, a smile on her face.

'What were you two gossiping about?' asks Andy as he plonks himself down opposite me.

'Oh, nothing really,' I reply. 'I think perhaps we should get back landside. We've got check-in soon.'

'Don't I just know it.' Andy yawns. 'D'you think that boy will be OK?'

'I don't know. I don't think it looked too hopeful. Why, what did Terry or Derek say?'

'Nothing much,' says Andy. 'Which I always take as a bad sign. I prefer it when they talk.'

'I know what you mean,' I say, getting out of my seat. 'Shall we go?'

As Andy and I make our way back through Customs it starts to pour with rain. In any other airport in the Western world this would not make much of a difference. Here, however, it's a different story.

'Shit!' says Andy.

'Shit!' I echo.

We sprint back to the office to get out the baking trays and buckets. There are other airline staff scattering to their stations in front of us. It's a nightmare. This place leaks like a sieve. They keep saying they are going to do something about it, but they never do. All you need do is look up towards the ceilings next time you come through here to see all the peeling paint, the patches of damp and the drips. Baggage is the worst. It pours through in there. But that's what comes of having an ancient airport that no-one maintains. We've got one terminal so damn ancient that archaeologists come and paw all over it. The upstairs floor is made of the largest piece of granite in Europe, which means that it has a preservation order slapped on it and hundreds of fossil hunters crawling about. It also sadly means that downstairs the terminal can't be raised or refurbished and will always remain poky and low.

Andy and I make it back in time to get out the buckets and trays without too much rainwater making it through into the back office. I've lost count of the number of times all our paperwork's been rendered a useless pulp by a sudden downpour. We are also back in time to witness something else. As we turn the corner, he starts to shout.

'Step away from the fucking microphone! Will someone get some fucker who can use this fucking technology! No-one can understand you! No-one! No-one ever has been able to understand you!'

It's my old mate Jim, who works for another airline and has had the misfortune to have spent the last ten years standing underneath a Tannoy that has sent him slightly deaf.

'What the hell's got into Jim?' I ask Andy as we both stand outside the office and stare.

'Fuck knows,' says Andy. 'But I like what he's saying. He's really laying into that Tannoy.'

He is too. He's standing underneath it, hands cupped around his mouth, using the sort of language last heard from someone with vicious Tourette's.

'Will someone learn to use the fucking microphone properly!' he shouts. 'It's not that fucking hard! Step back and enunciate properly, you ignorant cunt!'

Someone has obviously called security, because on the use of the c-word Jim is rugby-tackled to the floor and dragged out of public view.

'What the hell happened there?' asks Andy.

'I've no idea. But I have a feeling it has been brewing for some time.'

'Yeah,' agrees Andy. 'Another casualty at the coalface of the service industry.' He smiles. 'You'll be next.'

'Piss off,' I say. 'Is that a check-in queue I see before me?'

'You slave driver,' he says as he looks over his shoulder at the gathering masses. 'It's only a matter of time before they take you away in a white coat. Mark my words.'

'Work!' I say, an irrational note of fear sounding in my voice.

5-6 PM

There's no time to dwell on deaf Jim's departure or quite why he decided to snap on this particular rainy afternoon; there is also no time for the extra cup of coffee Debbie seems to be brewing for herself in the back office.

'No time for that, I'm afraid, Debbie,' I say, trying to bristle with efficiency. 'We've got two flights to get out back to back, so the quicker you get this one off the less of a nightmare the next one's going to be.'

'Oh,' she says, batting her eyelashes. 'Just a little sip. I need the caffeine to get me through. Go on.' She gives my arm a little tap.

Sometimes I really do wish I was gay. Her desperate display to butter me up and flirt with me is so goddamn poor, it's pathetic she thinks I'd even go for it.

'Come on,' I say, quite sharply. 'All the others are out there. And we've got a Lagos queue next door. We need to be cracking on.'

'Fair enough,' she sighs, putting down her mug. 'Seeing as it's you . . .'

If she'd said 'seeing as it's a Lagos queue' I might be more impressed. The queues for the Lagos flights are notorious. For not only are they long and packed, not only do they seep into surrounding queues – hence my desire to have all hands on deck and all eyes to the front – they are also always the most difficult to board. Mainly due to the huge amounts of luggage everyone always seems to take with them. I know it's a cliché to say that on some flights they take everything including the kitchen sink. Well, on the Lagos flights I have actually seen a great big aluminium kitchen sink, not to mention a sofa, a desk, armchairs, a couple of car tyres, a bicycle, a Breville sandwich maker, and sacks and sacks of rice. All of which we are supposed to be able to let fly under the 30kg weight restriction or indeed the 32kg BAA restriction. The boys downstairs won't carry anything heavier. It's more than their lower backs are worth.

My favourite, however, was a rather large lady who turned up in traditional dress wheeling a huge mahogany coffin. Fortunately it was empty (we checked); still, the thing weighed a ton. We did try to persuade her to leave it behind, or send it as cargo, but she was insistent on bringing it back because it was so beautiful and such a bargain. Eventually we charged her through the nose for it and shoved it at the back of the hold. I never found out who it was for. Had she picked it out for herself, or had she had plans for a certain unsuspecting relative?

Even though the Nigerian flights are a nightmare to board, that's not to say they are unpopular to work. They're not. They can be highly lucrative, particularly if you are not the most scrupulous member of the check-in staff. A lot of the bags are stuffed with wares bound for the markets of Lagos, so in order to make the weight requirement, or cut down on excess charges, bundles of cash regularly cross the counter tucked inside passports or, less subtly, brown envelopes. The temptation to pocket the money and look the other way when it comes to weighing in another tractor tyre is extreme.

Sadly – or is it perhaps fortunately? – we no longer do flights to Lagos. Ever since terrorists pointed surface-to-air missiles at planes coming out of Kenya's Mombasa airport we've dropped all our Africa flights. Except for Nigeria, none of the others was making us much money anyway. There weren't enough business passengers and too many holidaymakers on air miles. We all knew the missile thing was a timely excuse really. It just meant that we cut down on the sort of flights, like South Africa and Tanzania, that I used to enjoy taking at 10 per cent of the cost.

No such problems with this Singapore flight. It is usually so full of businessmen that we regularly overbook by 20 per cent. Again, you'd be amazed at the number of no-shows we get. Meetings change at the last minute, and quite a few of them cut it fine in the late-afternoon traffic after trying to fit in one last telephone call before getting into the cab. Why should the airline be left out of pocket?

I am standing at the end of the row of desks. All the girls seem to be checking in nicely. The break seems to have done their humour some good, and it appears that Chanel and Cathy have got over their brief spat earlier because they keep sharing tight smiles about various handsome-ish or rich-looking business passengers. After one of our check-in girls managed to pull and marry an American millionaire business-man last year, they all live in hope. After all, there are plenty more Adnan Khashoggi types out there to make them think it's still possible.

The queues don't seem to be moving too slowly at the moment. Everyone has apparently packed their own bags and no-one's got nail scissors in their hand luggage. Towards the back of Trisha's queue I notice a guy in a large lobster-shaped hat. I have no idea what he thinks he looks like, but there's something about him, other than the hat, that requires closer inspection. I walk up to the back of the queue.

'Good afternoon, sir,' I say.

'Hello there.' Turns out the man is American, and he looks to be in his fifties – a little old, perhaps, to be wearing such a hat.

'Those your bags there, sir?' I ask.

'Sure are,' he replies.

'Did you pack them yourself?'

'Yes, sir.'

'Good, because sometimes people are given things to carry on board that later turn out to be a bomb. Can you vouch for all the stuff you have with you, sir?'

The bloke's face falls a bit; his cheeks turn a pale shade of pink as he looks directly at the carrier bag he is holding.

'Well, um, I suppose this video camera is new.'

'Right.' I smile. 'New, sir? Where did you get it?'

192

'Rome,' he says. 'It was given to me by my cousin.'

'Oh, so you have family in Rome?'

'No.'

'Oh. But you just said that your cousin gave it to you in Rome.'

'Yes, that's right . . . I bought it.'

'You bought it? But you just said that your cousin gave it to you.'

'Yes I know, but—'

'Do you have a cousin in Rome, sir?'

'No.'

'No. Right. Were you given the video camera in Rome?'

'No.'

'No. Right. Have you been to Rome?'

'Yes.'

'Yes, you have, good.' I smile again. 'Finally we are getting somewhere.'

'Today,' he adds, triumphantly.

'Today indeed. And you were given the video camera today? In Rome?'

'No,' he says. 'I bought it.'

'You bought it,' I repeat. 'OK . . . duty free?'

'No, from a man in the departure lounge.'

'Oh.'

'I think they were stolen,' he admits. 'But he said I could have one for a hundred dollars.'

'OK,' I say, standing back and looking at the carrier. 'I'm afraid I'm going to have to call the police.'

'I'm not in trouble?' asks the man, panic rising in his voice.

'Well, you have lied to me and trafficked in stolen goods, but other than that you're fine.'

'There are two of them in there,' he says finally.

'Two what?'

'Video cameras.' He smiles. 'Well, they were only a hundred each.'

I call the police on my radio and they arrive in no time at all. They confiscate the bag and disappear, leaving two men behind in charge of the American. Although it is highly unlikely that Lobsterman's bag is carrying anything other than video cameras, we can't be too careful. A few minutes later the police return, looking perplexed to say the least.

'We've X-rayed the bag,' one of them tells me, 'and, um, we've found nothing that indicates there is anything electrical in there.'

'Oh,' I say.

Lobsterman looks troubled. 'What does that mean?'

'There are no video cameras in the boxes?' I suggest.

'But I bought two of them,' he declares.

'I know.'

'We're going to get two of our boys to open the bag,' says the police officer.

'OK,' I say.

Having ascertained that there is nothing electrical in the bag, therefore ruling out a bomb, they decide to open it up in front of the American. But they are still careful and a little ginger about it. Sliding the box slowly out of the bag, they gently lift the lid. Everyone stands back. One officer takes out the wrapped contents and peels off the cellophane. He places

194

the object on the floor in front of everyone. I lean over. It's not what anyone was expecting at all. Turns out that Lobsterman's hundred-dollar video cameras are in fact black painted wooden boxes with photocopies of a video camera stuck on the front of them. Inside, to give them the necessary weight, the boxes have been filled with sand. The policeman steps back and raises his eyebrows. It looks like he's biting the inside of his cheek, trying not to laugh. I needed an explanation as to why a fifty-year-old man would be seen dead in a lobster hat, and now I have it.

'Oh dear,' I say as I watch his puzzled expression. 'Often when things are too good to be true, they are too good to be true.'

'But that's not what he showed me,' he replies.

'Better luck in Singapore.' I smile and show him towards the queue. 'You get plenty of bargain electrical goods over there. Just pay a bit more attention next time.'

'Yes, sir,' he says. 'I'm never going to be caught like that again.'

He says that, but there have been plenty who have. Only last week I had some bloke in the queue who had a bag of onions inside a box that he thought was a computer. But I have to say that black boxes of sand are not really my target when going up and down a queue, although supposed gifts are the first things I'm looking for when I'm security-checking a flight. After all, it was a teddy bear full of explosives that Anna-Marie Murphy unwittingly tried to take on to an El Al flight in 1986. But there are certain things you check for and certain things that automatically mean you pull the passenger. A lot of them are quite simple: you check to see if the names and baggage tags match, that they are carrying their own bags; you look for Middle Eastern stamps in passports, or anomalies such as a Lebanese baggage tag coupled with a passenger who is a US passport holder, with an Israeli stamp in their passport, as you are not allowed into the Lebanon with Israeli stamps. But I have to say that, bombs aside, most of our problems centre on entering rather than leaving the UK.

One of the more amusing aspects of the security check is watching the reaction of people further back in the queue. There is always some bloke who suddenly remembers he's got some dope, a wrap of coke, or a couple of Es still on him and who disappears off to the toilets, either to finish off his own supply or to flush it down the loo. The cleaners are always discovering discarded wraps in the landside toilets. And it's not just the toilets. Rubbish bins and fast-food boxes are also favoured places for dumping drugs. Just the other day a large fistful of grass wrapped in clingfilm was discovered underneath a whole pile of Crunchies in WHSmith. Some pothead must have panicked and shoved it there for safekeeping.

The thing that gets me is that they all think they have been so subtle about it when they return to the queue. But there is no greater coke-snorting giveaway than some twitchy bloke with a stinking cold who won't stop trying to chat up the check-in girl, or telling her fascinating facts about himself. If we suspect that you have more on you than what you have put up your nose, we'll stop you, call customs and have you searched. Shoes, hats, underpants, bras, up the backside – they'll take their time and they usually find what they are looking for. Two days ago a girl came through with what seemed like terrible flu. Her bags were X-rayed and her talc bottle was filled with what came up as 'organic material'. She was pulled just before she boarded the plane and was just a bit too jumpy and a bit too quick with her answers for anyone's liking. Turned out in the end that her talc bottle contained ten grams of coke, which she claimed was for personal use. Judging by her unfortunate streaming cold, I was inclined to believe her. Not that it would have made much of a difference. She was in big trouble whichever way you look at it.

It's always a difficult call pulling people you suspect are using or carrying drugs if it's only for their personal use. I remember when a mate of mine who was working for another airline had this problem with the lead singer of a well-known British band. The airline had sent a limo to collect him from his west London home and it was clear that the bloke had been up all night. He kept the limo waiting for over an hour while one girl after another left the flat, and when he finally got into the car he made the driver go via Earls Court where he met a dealer in the street, money changed hands, and he picked up more of what he was taking. The driver then drove him to the express check-in and went and informed my mate. By the time my mate arrived to speak to the popstar in question it was clear that he had taken most of what he had just bought. He was bright-eyed, bushy-tailed and very talkative.

'I mean, what was I to do?' asked my mate. 'Pull him for having a system full of class A drugs? Then we would have to start checking everyone, even the more subtle user. I mean, if he wants to fly to New York ripped to the tits on coke, that's his business. Personally it is my idea of hell, having to sit down while full of fidgety energy. But each to their own.'

So they let him fly. They warned the flight attendants to watch him and make sure he didn't misbehave. Apparently he went and did a few more lines on the plane, but nothing they couldn't handle. In fact, if you are going to abuse drugs, they'd prefer it on board that you took class A rather than B/C, or whatever marijuana is supposed to be these days. Smoking in the loos is against Civil Aviation Authority rules and is punishable by a huge fine or imprisonment, depending on the airline; chopping out a line is not, even though, just as alcohol in the air is different from a drink on the ground (one in the air equals three on the ground), so coke at altitude can make you a little more odd, crazy and violent. We had one wired guy once try to kick the door open mid-flight. He then turned around and fractured the flight attendant's jaw as she tried to wrestle him to the ground. He was arrested as soon as the plane touched down.

It's more often than not a case of trying to work out which is the lesser of two evils. When another flight attendant I know confiscated all the marijuana from a rowdy American heavy metal band after they all lit up a joint in first class, she knew they just went straight to the toilets to take coke. But then, as she put it, 'What am I supposed to do? Famous people don't seem to be able to fly straight.'

The Nigeria flight next door now seems to have some sort of hold-up. There is what looks like a family of eight all wanting to travel first class, and wads of cash are being slapped down on the counter. I smile. Happy days, I think, as I watch the check-in girl break into a sweat. I look back across to my own check-in and at the front of Trisha's queue there seems to be something going on. Trisha is looking insistent and a middle-aged woman is appearing defiant.

'I am sorry, madam,' I can hear Trisha saying, 'but the photograph looks nothing like you.'

'But it *is* me,' the woman insists. 'Look, what else can I show you to prove that it's me? Here' – she empties her wallet – 'look. Credit cards, all with my name on them. Look. Parkes . . . Parkes . . . Camilla Parkes.' She snaps one card after the other down on the counter. 'They are all mine. See? The same name is on the passport. The same name is on the ticket.'

'I'm afraid that credit cards are not considered a form of ID,' says Trisha. Her white, square-tipped nails type some message over to Debbie on the next-door check-in. Debbie promptly bursts out laughing. 'Anyway,' says Trisha, a conspiratorial smirk on her lips, 'you could have stolen them.'

'Oh Jesus Christ!' says Ms Parkes. 'Now you're accusing me of being a thief!'

'Can I help?' I ask.

'I don't know,' replies Ms Parkes. 'Can you?'

'What seems to be the problem?'

'The problem is that this woman here is claiming that I have stolen my own credit cards along with my own passport.'

'And all these are legitimately yours?' I ask.

'Of course they are,' she replies, with heavy sarcasm.

'May I?'

She hands over her passport with a hefty sigh which wafts mildly acrid old champagne breath in my direction. I open up the back page and take a look at her photo. Shit! Trisha is right. The old woman in the shot looks nothing like the forty-something honey standing in front of me. The date of birth of the woman in the passport makes her fifty-six; Ms Parkes must at most be in her mid forties. Yet they do look similar.

'Um,' I say. 'Are you sure you haven't picked up your sister's passport, or your aunt's, by mistake?' I suggest.

'Oh for God's sake,' shouts Ms Parkes. 'I've had a bloody facelift! Look – here, here, and here.' She frantically yanks back her blonde hair and pulls forward her ears to reveal the thinnest of scarlet scars. 'See?' she says, snatching back her passport. Her face is red with fury and the indignity of it all. 'It is *supposed* to be a subtle job,' she mutters, putting her passport back inside her handbag.

'It is,' I reassure her.

'Yeah, right,' she replies. 'I'm unrecognizable.'

'No, it's just a bad photo in the passport,' I try, weakly. 'They always are—'

'No, it's too tight,' she says. 'I told the surgeon it was too tight. Do you think it's too tight?'

I'd like to stand around and discuss the merits of Ms Parkes' extreme make-over – which is, for the record, far too tight – but I notice that Debbie is now having a few problems of her own. I inform Ms Parkes that hers is the best job I have ever seen and make my way over.

'Everything all right here?' I ask.

'Well,' replies Debbie, keeping her tone high and cleverly light (she's no fool), 'I think sir here has had a bit too much to drink.'

'No I haven't,' slurs a middle-aged bloke in a pin-stripe suit. He is looking at me, but it's clear from the way his bloodshot gaze meanders that he can't quite determine which of the two or possibly three of me to look at.

'He's only had a couple,' says his mate, unwisely slapping him on the back, propelling the drunk a few fumbling steps forward.

'Only a couple,' the drunk confirms, nodding. 'Of bottles!' he adds with a huge childish snigger.

'Yeah,' grins his friend. 'He's emigrating!'

'Not today he's not,' I say.

'What?' says the pin-stripe drunk. 'You can't do that!'

'I'm afraid I can. You're under the influence of alcohol, and as it stands you are too drunk to fly.'

'I'm not!' he declares, throwing his loose arms around in indignation. 'Who are you to tell me that I'm too pissed to fly?'

'I'm the duty airport manager and it's one of the many aspects of my job to see that passengers are fit to fly. You, sir, I'm afraid, are not.'

'I'm fit,' he says, winking at his friend. 'I box three times a week.'

'You may well be fit, sir, but sadly not fit to fly.'

'Oh, come off it,' he says. 'Of course I am. I've got to fly. I'm emigrating.'

We always have one or two over-enthusiastic emigrators a week. They arrive at the airport accompanied by a group of pals, sink a few jars in departures, and before they know it they are too pissed to fly. Their mates, instead of witnessing their last glorious send-off, end up having to accompany them

201

on an ignominious journey home. So this bloke is not exactly exceptional.

'Listen, sir,' I say. 'If you can walk in a straight line and prove to me that you aren't as drunk as you appear to be then I shall let you fly.'

Debbie shoots me a look. I smile gently back at her. It's obvious that this bloke is so plastered he can't even piss straight, let alone walk in a straight line.

'You're on!' he says, going to tap the side of this nose but missing.

'From here to the end of the check-in,' I say.

He inhales. He clenches his fists. He chews the side of his mouth with determination. The concentration is pathetic. His friend is willing him on – the last thing he wants to do is take his mate home again. He starts off, one foot slowly in front of the other. He gets halfway and stops, trying to control a wobble.

'Keep going,' I say.

He carries on, suddenly looking quite steady. Shit. I am now worried that the drunk bastard is going to prove me wrong and I'll have to fly him all the way to Singapore. Will and determination drive him on. I look at Debbie. She pulls an 'I-told-you-so' face. This is not looking good. How can someone this drunk be able to walk this straight? He makes it to the end of check-in, spins around to punch the air and immediately stumbles backwards and disappears behind a pile of seven heavy suitcases a large Nigerian woman and her three small children have lined up on the floor. He lies there, legs in the air, applauding himself and laughing, still convinced he has made the flight.

I walk towards the scene and end up standing over him, shaking my head.

'I'm afraid you're not leaving the country today, sir.'

'Fair enough,' he shrugs.

'Back home.'

'I've sold that.'

'A hotel then?' I suggest

'You can come back to mine,' says his friend.

'Thanks, mate,' says the drunk, gathering himself on the floor.

'Remember,' I tell him, 'a little less celebrating and we'll see you on Monday.'

'Yeah, right,' he replies sarcastically. 'Next time I'm not flying Shithole Airways, I'm getting myself a decent airline.'

His friend starts to laugh. 'Come along, Justin. Let's get you home.'

As Justin and his drunken pal stagger off in the direction of the taxi rank, I find myself apologizing to the Nigerian woman in the queue, saying that we don't normally infringe on the Lagos flight, it's usually the other way round. I'm all laughing and engaged; she looks neither entertained nor interested. She has three children to look after and a whole house to move half-way across the world. Justin falling over her luggage is just another inconvenience to be endured.

I walk back to the other end of check-in. Our Singapore queue is beginning to die down a bit, only standing about five to seven deep at the desks now. It's time to converge a couple of queues and open up the Dubai flight.

'Not long to go now,' says Andy, rubbing his hands together

with excitement. 'In just over two hours it'll be you and me with gin and tonic in our hands.'

'Sounds great.' I smile.

'And Susan.' He winks.

My smile tightens. As if I could forget about that.

6-7 PM

I slip into the back office for five minutes to have a quick look through the passenger list for the Dubai flight, just to check if we have any VIPs, problem passengers, or anyone I should be vaguely aware of. The rain seems to have abated a bit. It's only dripping gently through the ceiling and into the three buckets and the baking tray that we've lined up in the office. The whole place smells of damp and that very particular rusty metal aroma that you get from leaks and polluted water that's travelled through the insides of a building. I think about making myself a quick cup of coffee, but all the spoons are dirty and crusted with half-dissolved powder, and the industrial-size tin of Nescafé we have back here looks a little hard on top, as if it's been contaminated with rainwater. So I decide against it.

It looks like we've got a few notables coming today. There's some Arab sheikh who has a star by his name, which denotes that a certain amount of buttering up is required. Secondly, it looks like we've got a boy band flying with us this evening. My heart sinks. Andy will get all giddy, so will the girls, and I will undoubtedly never have heard of them. It says here that their PR has phoned ahead and requested that they go into the Chelsea suite. What a load of old bollocks, I think, running a line through the request. What is the point of having an extra-selective VIP area if any old Tom, Dick or talent-show winner can go in there? It says that they are travelling over to entertain the troops in Iraq as part of a ten-day tour of the region. Well, at least that's something for them to look forward to. After months in the desert, being shot at and avoiding suicide bombers, five nice dancing boys. I bet they're thrilled.

There's also a note in the paperwork that I must have missed earlier, or actually just haven't had the chance to see. It's about updating our EPIC press pack and asking for volunteers. Manned 24/7 by a skeletal staff, EPIC, or the Emergency Procedure Information Centre, is what the world's media would turn to in the event of a plane crash or an onboard terrorist bomb blast. They have press packs on all the world's aircraft, airlines, their history, their turnover, a summary of their company reports, plus photographs and footage of flights in happier times. It is an extraordinary set-up that each airline contributes to. Located deliberately off-site, it has banks of computer and television screens and looks like something out of NASA. I have, fortunately, only ever had one friend who has had the occasion to use it, when he was working for Kenya Airways and their KQ 431 Abidjan flight crashed in January 2000. I remember him telling me not only what hell it was trying to co-ordinate everything, but also that one of the weirdest questions the media asked when he was managing the nightmare was how many white faces they could get in front of camera. He was, I think quite rightly, rather appalled. I make a note to myself to sort out the EPIC packs when we get back from Dubai and to see if I can get some of our lot to join the voluntary BA staff who man the place. I suppose I could even do it myself. It's not as if I have anything else going on in my life.

I walk back out to the check-in. All the girls seem to be coping fine. We still have two cleaning up the Singapore flight and the other two, plus Dave who is on first/club, dealing with the Dubai flight. Andy, while supposedly supervising, is grinning and bouncing around looking very upbeat indeed. It's actually quite sweet to see a grown man that excited about his own birthday.

I smile as I walk past and give him a tap on the back.

'What?' he says, turning round.

'Not long now.'

'I know,' he says. 'And Fun Five are on our flight!' He rubs his hands and raises his eyebrows. 'Dave's checking them in right now. And guess who's going to escort them through to the first-class lounge!'

'They don't have first-class tickets,' I say.

'I know, but who's counting? It won't hurt anyone, now will it?'

I pause for a second. 'I suppose not.' It would seem churlish to turn him down. After all, what really is the difference between the first- and club-class lounges? Colder air con? A fatter sofa?

A better class of sandwich? A more expensive brand of champagne? Speedier internet access? A shower and a massage, maybe, but who has got time for that when they're about to leave the country? Anyway, it's all sitting there so it may as well be used. I have to say, I'm not someone who is terribly precious when it comes to the lounges. There are some duty airport managers working for other airlines who, even if they upgrade someone like a journalist writing about the flight, or someone they've bumped up from economy, won't allow them into the lounge. Personally, I think it's pathetic. Their reasoning is that they haven't paid for the flight so they are not entitled to the perks.

'Anyway,' adds Andy, 'how else are we going to keep them away from their fans?'

'How else indeed,' I agree, looking around for a screaming rabble. 'They look overrun.'

'There's no need to be sarcastic. I'll have you know they are very popular. Their music's excellent.'

'Excuse me,' says Chanel, leaning over her desk.

'Yes?' I say, turning round.

'Would you mind if I went and asked the band for an autograph?'

Andy's face beams triumphantly.

'No, no,' I say. 'Go right ahead. I'll take over from you.'

'Thanks ever so much,' she says, smoothing down her yellow blonde hair as she comes out from behind the check-in. 'It's for my six-year-old niece,' she adds. 'She'll never forgive me if she found out that Fun Five had been through and I didn't try to get their signatures. She's got their posters all over her bedroom.'

'A super fan?' I ask.

'You could say that.'

'Rather like Andy here.'

Chanel looks puzzled; her painted eyebrows curl into a frown. Andy flicks me the Vs and walks off down the other end of check-in towards the band. Chanel follows, and I take her place behind check-in. I look down to find her computer showing a message: 'Does anyone have a baby I can put this rude stressed bastard next to?' I think it's come from Debbie, because Cathy and Trisha are still dealing with the last three passengers before closing the Singapore flight and Dave is handling first/club.

'How rude exactly?' I type.

The message comes back immediately: 'Upgrade request, bulkhead request and now the I've-got-long-legs rude.'

I look across at Debbie. She is smiling away, grinning through her hangover, pretending to be helpful. She is concentrating so hard on keeping her service-industry smile in place that I don't think she has noticed it's me she's dealing with now, not Chanel, who is currently flirting with the boy band at the end of the row. I check out the passenger in front of her. He is slouched on the counter looking bored and surly, like he can't believe he has been kept waiting, and that the service here is so goddamn bad. I suddenly feel a bit sorry for Debbie, sitting there, right at the coalface, having to keep it together all day while drunks, hysterical women, cantankerous bastards and poisonous children all do their worst.

'No can do on the kid front. But see I have one big fat bastard coming up. Put them together?' I type and send.

'Good one,' comes the return.

I look up the seating plan and find a row of four in the middle of the plane. 'Suggest 30D aisle for my fat bloke and 30E middle middle for rude boy?'

'Done,' comes the reply.

As I check in the couple in front of me I can hear her spinning the tale next door.

'The plane is very full today, sir.' She is smiling away. 'What with it being nearly half term.'

'Half term?' he questions. 'Is it?'

'Don't you have children, sir?'

'Do I look old enough to have kids?'

'No, sir.' She laughs. 'Of course not.' And of course Debbie knows this already. Half term. I smile. I wonder how many times she has used that one on some unsuspecting bachelor. 'So I have done my best with your seat, sir,' she says, handing him a boarding card. 'Have a good flight.'

'Cheers,' he says, picking up his holdall. 'See you around.'

Debbie turns to grin conspiratorially at Chanel and finds me. 'Oh,' she says, her eyes and mouth round with surprise. 'It's you. I thought . . .'

'I know what you thought,' I say.

She doesn't know what to say. She stares at me blankly and then turns. 'Good evening, sir,' she says as another passenger slaps down his passport and tickets. 'Dubai?'

'Looks like it,' he replies.

I check in my passenger of exceptional girth, placing him next to the irate rude boy, and hand back over to Chanel. Over at the Singapore check-in, both Cathy and Trisha are shutting up and changing over when a hysterical woman arrives, all hair, bags and paper. She is politely told that the flight closed some ten minutes ago and she promptly bursts into tears. Now, I have been around long enough in the job to learn that there are tears, and then there are tears. And these are clearly of the crocodile variety. There is an awful lot of noise and very little water. In fact, the woman is wailing so loudly you would have thought she was at a funeral of a dearly beloved, recently departed relative, rather than at an airport check-in desk. Trisha is handling it well. She can be quite a tough customer herself, although perhaps not quite tough enough today.

'Is there some problem here?' I ask.

'She won't let me on the plane!' the woman wails, her mouth wide open, revealing a significant amount of dentistry.

'I'm afraid you're too late,' I say.

'But it's still here!' she cries, wiping away a very dry tear for good measure.

'It's actually boarding,' I explain, 'so no matter how fast you run, or how light your bags, there is no way we can clear security in time to get you on board.'

'But I have to be there!' she wails some more.

'Madam,' I suddenly snap, 'no matter how loud you cry, or how long you weep, you will not be allowed on this plane.'

'Well, fuck all of you,' she says through a determined, thin mouth, and picking up her bag she marches across the terminal.

I am just about to launch into an explanation about drama-queen tears to a rather stunned-looking Trisha when I spot the arrival of my Arab sheikh. He is standing at the first-class check-in with what look like a couple of wives. Dave is giving him the benefit of his full white smile, but I can tell the man looks a little pissed off at not being meeted and greeted with the full flunky entourage.

'Sir!' I say, rushing towards him, my arm outstretched before me. 'How lovely to see you again.'

'There you are,' he says in perfect English. 'I was just asking where exactly you were.'

'I was dealing with a slight problem at the other end.' I point behind me. 'But now I am all yours. Why don't you give me your passports and tickets,' I continue without drawing breath, 'and I shall check you in myself. Just the three of you today?'

'Yes,' replies the sheikh, pleased that normal service has been resumed. 'I am travelling light.'

I laugh a little too loudly and a little too long, but he doesn't seem to notice. Well, he is one of the few big spenders we have who regularly uses our airline. I give the sheikh a fixed smile while making sure that Dave puts him in 1A and 1B and gives 2A and 2B to his wives.

Dave looks a little white when I request the seats. 'I've given them away,' he mutters.

'What?' I turn round to smile at the sheikh to reassure him that all is well. I then turn back and whisper to Dave, 'What the fuck did you do that for?'

'Andy,' he says feebly.

'Andy what?' I hiss out of the corner of my ever-smiling mouth.

'He requested them for Fun Five.'

'But they only have club tickets!'

'I know, but Andy said that we don't have many first-class passengers today so to upgrade them.' He's beginning to look flustered, running his hand over his bald patch.

'Think about it,' I hiss again. 'This is a well-established flight that goes to Dubai twice a week, in the Gulf States. How likely is it that we would have problems selling first-class tickets? It's not exactly air miles territory, is it? Like bloody Orlando, bloody Florida?'

'It is increasingly a holiday destination,' tries Dave.

'Don't answer back,' I say wearily. 'Just get the boy band out of first and give me my front-row seats.'

'OK,' he says, still looking flustered.

'Don't worry,' I add, 'I'll sort Andy. Give me the new Fun Five boarding passes and I'll give them to Andy in the lounge.'

'Everything all right?' asks the sheikh, approaching stealthily from behind.

'Absolutely. Of course. I was just making sure that you got your usual seats.'

'Good.' He smiles. 'Very good. Will you be escorting me through today?'

'Absolutely. I know it's normally Andy, but today you have me.'

'Good,' says the sheikh. 'I have a little business to attend to, but my wives would like to go shopping.'

'Great,' I say. My face smiles but my heart sinks. Where's Andy when I need him? 'Shopping . . .' I nod and smile some more. 'Every man's dream.'

Dave hands over the boarding passes for the sheikh and his wives, as well as those for Fun Five. The sheikh wafts off in a puff of white robes, and I am left with his two wives. Dressed head to foot in black chadors, with only their dark eyes visible, they stand and stare at me like a couple of shadows, awaiting my suggestions.

'So,' I say, rubbing my hands together, 'where would you like to start?' Neither of them replies. It is immediately apparent that they don't speak any English. 'Um, Gucci?'

'Gucci.' They both nod.

'Gucci it is then.'

I walk them through passport control and wait the other side while security swab their Prada bags.

'All right, ladies?' I say as they arrive. They say nothing, but one of them hands me a £20 note. 'No, really,' I say, smiling, stepping backwards and holding my hands up in the air. She taps me vigorously on the chest with it, nodding away.

'Take,' orders the other one.

'Oh, OK,' I reply.

We disappear off to Gucci where I watch them drop nearly £8,000 on four handbags, a watch and five pairs of shoes. They hand me the bags and we move on to Harrods, where they buy eight teddy bears, a tin of shortbread and a selection of Wedgwood cups. Again, they hand me the bags. We move on to Burberry where they buy two small checked handbags, a baseball cap and an extra-large checked shirt. In duty free they buy four bottles of Coco Chanel, a couple of YSL lipsticks they have smeared very discreetly on the backs of their hands, and then, after much to-ing and fro-ing, I understand that they want me to buy three bottles of Johnny Walker Blue at £99 each. In the space of about ten to fifteen minutes, on a small spree between check-in and the lounge, they have shelled out what Dave, Cathy or Debbie earns in a year. By the time we arrive at the first-class lounge I have requisitioned a trolley for all their purchases. There is only so much retail one man can carry on his own.

We walk into the lounge and I show their passes and see them settled into a large, accommodating sofa. The taller of the two reaches into her handbag and pulls out a crisp £50 note. I have to admit that this time I make no show of not wanting to take it. My hand is out and it's been trousered before any of the other staff notice me, the manager, pocketing tips. I wish them a good trip, bow obsequiously, then set about trying to find Andy.

I walk the length of the first-class lounge that we, in fact, share with another airline. Full of red carpet, curved walls, comfortable sofas, glass tables and interestingly groovy shelves of untouched books and obscure cigar magazines, it also has a sumptuous stuff-yourself buffet laid with plates of smoked salmon, Parma ham, fresh blinis, stacks of fruit, croissants, Danish pastries, and every conceivable bottle of alcohol that the parched, weary tycoon/businessman/traveller could wish for before he begins his journey. Over in the far corner there are shower facilities, conference rooms, a massage area, a row of computers with free internet access, and banks of television screens all showing CNN. But Andy is nowhere to be seen.

I look around the lounge again. I finally spot what looks like most of the band, up at the far end, surrounded by cans of Red Stripe and packets of cheese and onion crisps. They have clearly yet to get to the macrobiotic stage of celebrity. I walk up to them.

'Evening, lads,' I say. They turn and face me, their facial topiary and gelled fringes smacking of the same stylist. 'Um,' I continue, slightly wrong-footed by the cloning. 'Have any of you seen Andy?'

A slight snigger goes around the group.

'Not for a while,' says the one with black gelled hair.

'Oh,' I say, a bit confused. 'He should be here with you.'

'You could try the toilets,' suggests the one with ginger gelled hair.

Everyone sniggers.

'Right,' I say, turning around.

I'm going to kill him. If I catch him shagging one of the members of the band in the toilet, birthday or no birthday, I am actually going to suspend him. He has done this one too many times. I know he thinks it's all very witty and amusing to pull on the job. I know he thinks it's one of his check-in perks. All part of the service, as it were. But it is not a good look for the airline. And to be frank, it's a sackable offence.

He is also beginning to develop a bit of a reputation. His favourite trick, in an overnight delay situation, is to invite a passenger or two back to his flat. He's done it a few times. He suggests that there might not be enough room at the hotel where we are putting up delayed passengers and indicates that there might be room in his inn, which is handily near the airport. You'd be surprised how many takers there are for a night of tequila and sex round at Andy's.

As I walk into the men's toilets, Andy and the one with blond gelled hair walk out. They both look flush-faced, bright-eyed and slightly dishevelled. They also smell of sex.

'Ah,' says Andy, stopping in his tracks and smiling, 'I was wondering where you were.'

'I was wondering the same thing,' I reply, staring him in the eye.

'I was just helping Chase here,' he says, indicating the one with the blond gelled hair. 'I spilt some beer down his trousers and I was showing him how to dry them before he got on the flight.'

'Yeah, that's right.' Chase slips past me. 'Thanks for that, man.'

'Pleasure,' Andy says with a smile. 'Any time.'

I know that Andy is lying. He knows that I know he is lying. But his story has been corroborated by a passenger and there is very little I can say. I could accuse them both of lying, but what is the point? The truth is I like Andy very much and I would be loath to let him go.

'Now that you're here,' I say, moving on, 'I have a problem with the boarding passes that I need you to sort out.'

'Right away,' he says, running his thumbs along the waist-band of his trousers. 'Anything you say.'

I talk him through the seating changes, explaining that much as I would love to put the boy band at the front, the sheikh kind of takes priority. He does, at least, have the decency to look slightly embarrassed. But we both decide not to down-grade the boys. Well, there is only a finite amount of room in club, and quite frankly Andy, Sue, Rachel and I rather have our eyes on those wider leather seats ourselves. We are all flying standby, with space-available upgrades, so it's rather in our interest to make sure that there is actually space available.

'That's all sorted then,' I say to Andy.

'Yup,' he says. 'So I'll meet you at the gate?'

'Not long to go now.'

'Can't wait,' he says, rubbing his hands together again.

'I'm just going back to make sure that the last passengers check in OK.'

'OK.'

I turn to go. 'Oh, Andy,' I say.

'Yes?'

'Don't do that again.'

'Do what?' he says, coming the innocent.

'You know what.'

He smiles. His earlobes turn red. He knows exactly what I'm talking about.

7-8 PM

Coming out of the first-class lounge, I run slap bang into a group of some of the sickest-looking people I have ever seen. It is a shocking sight, like some sort of weird hospital breakout of the living dead. There's a whole convoy of them shuffling slowly past with zimmer frames, sticks and crutches; some are in wheelchairs, others are sporting portable drips. They all look terrible, with white skin and rheumy red eyes. I stand back, leaning flat against the corridor wall, making room for them as they go by. They are accompanied by a small attachment of concerned nurses and a flurry of benevolent-looking nuns.

'Lourdes?' I ask one of them as she walks past.

'That's right,' she smiles.

'I hope you have a successful trip.'

'Oh, it will be.' Her eyes glow with all the certainty of a believer.

It's been a while since I've seen a Lourdes flight leave the airport and I had forgotten quite what a sobering and depressing sight it can be. A couple of my friends have done the flights themselves, when their plane has been wet-leased by some charter company. They said that the flights were quite hairy; they packed extra oxygen on the plane and crossed their fingers, hoping for the best. Fortunately, France isn't that far away.

As wet-leasing gigs go, Lourdes is not one of the most popular runs to be on. Then again, wet-leasing is a precarious business. A way for airlines to make their planes and crew work for them when they are supposedly on the ground, wet-leasing is when one airline hires out its plane, crew and pilots to another for a short charter. It's the closest a charter company comes to being a virtual airline. So, a company like Thomas Cook can wet-lease a Qantas plane that would otherwise be sitting on the tarmac all day (having arrived early in the morning, it won't be leaving until later that night). Qantas supplies a crew who have been downroute for a couple of days who fancy earning some extra cash doing a day trip to Greece. Thomas Cook stocks the plane with its own catering and duty free, and provides its own tickets. And everyone makes money. There are plenty of travel companies or organizations at it, like P&O, who wet-lease planes to ferry their passengers to and from Mediterranean cruises. There are also some who dry-lease. They supply the crew and the pilots but they effectively rent the plane for the day from another airline. It's one way to keep the accountants happy.

The Lourdes party eventually pass and I wander back through

the inappropriately festive duty free towards check-in. 'Jingle Bells' is on a loop and the purple and silver Christmas tree parked outside Harrods is flashing away at full wattage. It really does depress me that they bring Christmas this early to the airport. We spend so long getting into the spirit of things that by the time the big day arrives I find it quite hard to give a shit.

Ahead of me, struggling with what looks like a heavy suitcase, is a pilot. I can't work out which airline he is from, but his suitcase looks cheap and his uniform is shiny and shoddy. I wonder if he is carrying cash for the BAA. There are some airlines whose credit rating is so bad that they have to pay their BAA landing rghts and fuel bills in cash. This bloke is certainly a likely-looking candidate.

Turning left as I come through the other side of security, I can see that there is something odd going on at our check-in desk. As I get closer, I can see that Cathy's check-in desk seems to be covered in toiletries. She has bottles and bottles of shampoo, conditioner, soap, bubble bath and shower gel, in fact a whole Boots counter, laid out in front of her.

'Good evening,' I say.

'Hi.' She smiles and rolls her eyes as the passenger in front of her hauls out another three bottles of body lotion from her bag.

'Overweight?' I ask the woman who is rattling around in her luggage.

'It seems so,' she puffs, bringing out a giant pot of Marmite and placing it on the counter. 'I'm moving to Dubai for a couple of months, and I just wanted a few of my home comforts with me.'

'I'm sure you can get shampoo out there,' I reassure her with a smile.

'Yes,' she agrees. 'But not lemon fresh Head and Shoulders.'

'Oh, right,' I say.

'My mate who organizes the ex-pat hash runs and stuff warned me that it's ever so difficult to get exactly what you're used to,' she says. 'So, you know, I've been to Marks and stocked up' – she pulls out six pork pies and a packet of scotch eggs – 'on the little things that remind me of home.' She then places a family-size jar of pickled onions on the counter. 'That should do it, don't you think?' she asks Cathy.

'I'm sure it will. Put the bag on again.'

The woman drags her bag back onto the scales. Cathy and I take a look. It's still a good seven kilos over, but I don't really have the heart to ask her to unpack more.

'That looks fine,' I say.

'Oh, really?' says the woman, her fat cheeks bright red with exertion. 'I've still got a Battenberg cake I could take out.'

'No, don't worry,' says Cathy.

'Or the Jaffa cakes?'

'No, no, that's fine,' I say.

'That's a relief. I promised Pauline a proper English tea when I got there.'

'Looks like you'll keep that promise,' says Cathy.

'Um, what would you like us to do with all this?' I ask, gesturing to the small market stall in front of me.

'Oh,' she says, 'you'd better have it.'

You'd be surprised how often the check-in girls go home with bottles of shampoo and conditioner or jars of face cream

as they are usually the first things people take out of their suitcases when they are overweight. Though we have been left
with stranger stuff – whole hams, boxes of toilet paper, tins of
peaches, electric irons, and packets of dried-up meat.

Chanel, Cathy, Debbie and Trisha gather around like
gannets and in a matter of seconds have selected the best pick-
ings. Dave has a little more dignity and doesn't seem that
interested. I pool together the leftovers and take them into the
back office to give to Barry for the Church. Although quite
what he will do with a giant pot of Marmite, two bottles of
Head and Shoulders and some scotch eggs is anyone's guess.

Back out front there are still a few more passengers to check
in. A couple approach and then split up as soon as they reach
the desks, pretending that they don't know each other. I walk
up and down behind the check-in just to make sure they are
who I think they are – a couple of middle-aged adulterers off
on a long dirty weekend. They do this sometimes. They buy
their tickets together and then pretend they don't know each
other when they arrive at the airport. I don't know who they
think they are kidding, because as soon as one of their names
is typed into the computer, the other name automatically
appears alongside it. It's very strange. The only thing that does
happen as a result of this is it makes it more difficult to work
out who is travelling with whom in the event of a crash. And
it's not just men and their mistresses who do this. I can recall
a supposedly very heterosexual pop star arriving with a handsome young man in tow. They booked into separate seats on
the plane and the singer proceeded to ignore his 'special friend'
throughout their time in the first-class lounge. Not even so

much as a glance in each other's direction. The sad thing is, if they had booked in together and sat together on the flight, no-one would have given it a second thought. It was the subterfuge that aroused suspicion.

Mr and Mrs Illicit Weekend check in and make their separate ways towards security just as Susan and Rachel arrive. You can always tell an air hostess a mile off, even when she is off duty, and these two are no exception. Despite the jeans, the shirts and the jackets they are both sporting, there is something about the way they apply their make-up and do their hair, that sort of extra-soignée appearance they have, that non-flyers simply don't possess.

'Recovered from the snake debacle?' asks Rachel, as she puts down her passport.

'Yes, thank you,' I say, stepping behind the desk to check them both in.

I can feel my face getting hot under Susan's gaze. I look down at the screen and feign interest in it. This is pathetic, I think, looking up and trying to smile at her. My cheeks twitch. What the hell do I think I am, some sort of love-struck teenager?

'Looking forward to this?' I ask Susan, desperate for something to say.

'Well,' she says, sounding dubious. 'I hope my liver can cope.'

'Yeah.' I laugh with far too much enthusiasm. 'Mine too!'

'Andy at the gate?' interrupts Rachel.

'Um, yes,' I reply. 'He's escorting some boy band onto the plane.'

'That's his idea of heaven,' she says.

'I know.' I nod, smiling at Susan.

'So, are we all in club?' Rachel asks.

'What?' I say.

'Is there room for us all in club?' she asks again, looking down at the check-in computer.

'Oh, sorry. I'm sure there is. I think Andy blocked off the whole of the front row.'

I look down and start to type. The whole of club-class seating comes up in front of me. It looks remarkably full. Andy has blocked off the front row as promised so we are all OK to fly, but the rest of the compartment is packed.

'That's odd,' I say.

'What?' asks Rachel, always the first to pick up on anything resembling a weakness.

'Club class is full.'

'I knew it! One simple thing like flying a small group to bloody Dubai and you and Andy can't even manage that! Come on, Sue, let's go, because there's no way I'm flying steerage.'

'No, it's not that,' I reply.

'Oh,' says Rachel.

'We're all fine to fly.'

'Oh,' she says again.

'Good,' smiles Susan.

'It's just that club looks very full indeed. I don't remember it being that fully booked. Dave?' I turn towards Dave, who already has his coat on at the end of his shift. 'Do you know anything about this?'

225

'What's that?' he says, sounding excessively nonchalant.

'Do you have any idea why there are so many people in club?'

'No idea, mate,' he replies. 'I just checked them in.'

'Right,' I say. Something is not quite right here. 'Are you hanging around for a while?'

'Me, mate?' he asks, like I might be talking to someone else. 'Yes, you.'

'No, mate. I've got to shoot off.'

'Oh.'

'See you around,' he adds as he walks off, putting his hands in his pockets and pulling his coat collar up around his ears. He disappears off into the crowd, his bald patch shining under the strip lighting.

'What do you think has happened?' asks Susan.

'I'm not sure yet,' I say as I watch him go. 'I'll know more when I get to the gate.'

Susan and Rachel disappear off into the club-class lounge while I pack up the check-in and see off the girls. The hatchets of earlier in the day seem well and truly buried now as they clatter around in the back office, reapplying make-up and spraying themselves in clouds of perfume, discussing going out for a drink locally or perhaps meeting up in town later. Cathy's the only one who is back on duty with us tomorrow; all the others have different shifts starting at different times for various other airlines. Chanel, if I overhear correctly, doesn't appear to be working at all. She's got the day off and is going to spend it having her hair dyed. I can't think why, I muse while looking at her, it looks yellow enough to me. I thank them for their hard work, and they all pocket their free toiletries and disappear off in a whirl of blue uniforms, red and white striped scarves and high heels, and a cloud of strong, sweet-smelling perfume. All except Cathy, that is, who is also boarding the passengers on to the Dubai flight. She makes her way towards the gate and I tell her I'll catch her up in a minute before turning to lock up the back office. The next time I open this door I am going to be feeling very unwell indeed. The idea of my impending hangover and enforced jolly drinking makes me want to run for it. But I can't. I can't let the side down. I can't let Andy down. And more importantly, when am I ever again going to get the opportunity to spend any time alone with Sue?

I pick up my passport, my boarding card and my small rucksack and make my way through security. I am still wearing my airside pass so they wave me through. As I wander through duty free on my way to the lounge, I radio Andy to check that he is not boarding yet.

'We've got a half-hour fog delay,' he replies.

'We have?'

'Yup,' he confirms. 'The plane was late out of Abu Dhabi.'

'OK,' I say, standing at the Clinique counter wondering whether I should buy some scrub and cream for his birthday or wait until I get back and get him something more personal. I buy him a pot of his favourite turnaround cream just so that he has something to open.

'The captain also says there's a landing light problem.'

'Oh?'

'Yeah. He's just trying to work out if we can fly with it.'

'You're not allowed to fly without a landing light,' I point out.

'I know that, you know that, Richard the captain knows that, but is he going to risk delaying three hundred passengers and thousands of quid in profit for the sake of a landing light? I don't think so.'

'Yeah,' I agree. 'Particularly if we have a daylight landing in Dubai.'

Pilots fly with legal faults every day, from small things such as broken toilets and dodgy seats to seemingly rather important pieces of equipment such as a broken 'yaw damper', which stops the plane from oscillating and prevents the passengers from feeling sick, or even a thrust reversal engine brake that's not working. Then there are faults, such as a broken landing light, that you are absolutely not allowed to fly with. There is a minimum equipment list, or Defects Book – a manual to which the captain refers when he has a problem. In it is everything that has to be functioning properly in order to fly legally. If your fault is not on the list then you have no excuse not to fly, indeed the airline will sack you if you don't. It costs them far too much money to have you hanging around on the ground.

But this is a self-policing industry, the Civil Aviation Authority is funded by the airlines themselves, and all fault reporting is down to the staff. Although their safety record is excellent, the pressure some of the CAA inspectors are under to pass planes as fit to fly must be immense. When it comes to maintenance and checks, I've heard extraordinary stories of some aircraft that haven't been serviced for a year or more and are still flying. They have done over a hundred thousand flying miles without so much as someone checking that the cargo door still locks. A couple of years back, one very well-known airline used regularly to lose the logbooks for their parts (each aeroplane part has a birth-to-death logbook in which everything that ever happens to it is written down). When it came to inspections, they would miraculously find them. Either they had somewhat amazingly been found down the back of the filing cabinet, or they had been made up overnight. Either explanation is, of course, not remotely satisfactory.

Along with paperwork problems, there are also stories of engineers who don't know their backsides from their airsides. I know of an airline in another UK airport that used car mechanics to check over their planes instead of properly trained aeroplane engineers. There's also a debate raging at the moment about whether the visual checks planes get while sitting on the ramp are actually enough or should other, more technical tests be used. When an Airbus A310 recently lost its twenty-eight-foot-long rudder over the Caribbean, there were those who said there was no way anyone could have been able to check the viability or deterioration of such an important part of the plane through sight alone. And as the November 2001 disaster, when 265 people died after American Airlines flight 587 crashed shortly after take-off from JFK, proves, sudden rudder loss can be fatal.

All I know is that the smallest thing can bring down a plane – a locked landing gear, a frozen windspeed pipe or, in the case of the Air France Concorde that crashed over Paris in 2000, an exploding tyre. I remember the story of a plane crashing into the Potomac River in the US after the crew did not activate the anti-ice system. The instruments froze and the pilot couldn't read them properly. He thought he had reached maximum engine thrust when he was nowhere near it, and he failed to clear the 14th Street Bridge that crossed the river. The plane went through the ice and all but six people died.

Then again, as they say, shit happens. You buy your ticket and you take your chance. I know Richard will choose to fly tonight, faulty landing light or not. We will therefore be what is known as 'illegal to crash', or, more specifically, uninsured. But if he lands safely in Dubai, who's to know? The airline is more likely to bollock him for not flying tonight than the other way round.

I arrive at the gate and find Andy, who reports that, sure enough, Richard has chosen to fly. He doesn't need the light to land in Dubai so he's not grounding the flight. However, should we need to make an emergency landing just outside the UK due to a heart attack or the rapid onset of childbirth, then he will, indeed, be fucked. But Andy's too excited about his birthday to care about that and I am far too tired to bother much either. I just want to get on this flight and get the whole thing over with.

The fog delay isn't helping matters either. We've got passengers at the gate who are bored and want to board. We've got passengers drinking in the terminal. We've got passengers still in the lounges. The whole thing is chaos. I like a nice neat board, and this is clearly not going to be one of those. And to top it all we have a club class problem. I explain my suspicions to Andy.

'I think Dave's been taking cash for upgrades, or something like that is going on.'

'Are you sure?' asks Andy.

'Well, I know we get a lot of frequent flyer card holders on this flight, but there's something about this that smells a bit dodgy. Club is too full for this time of year. And Dave was far too keen to push off at the end of his shift. Let's just keep an eye on things.'

'I'll have a word with Cathy.'

'Can you check that bloke coming in now?' I say, pointing to a short, slim guy in a well-cut suit.

'OK,' says Andy, and he starts to walk towards the check-in. He stops suddenly in his tracks and turns to look at me, a pleading look on his face.

'What?'

'Do I have to?' he mouths.

'Yes.'

'Excuse me, sir,' I hear him say as I approach from behind.

'Oh, hello,' says the short guy, with a wide smile. 'How are you?'

'Fine,' says Andy. 'I'm sorry to have to do this, sir, but could I check your ticket and your boarding card?'

'Of course,' says the short man, handing them both over. 'But how are you?'

'Fine,' mumbles Andy again, staring at the ticket. The tips of his ears are growing red. I move in closer. 'I'm afraid this upgrade is illegal,' he says.

'Oh?' says the short man.

'Yes, sir, I'm sorry, it's definitely illegal.'

'Will you stop calling me sir,' mutters the man. 'We've had sex.'

'I'm sorry, sir,' continues Andy without missing a beat, 'but we do have a problem.'

'I was offered an upgrade for two hundred in cash at check-in,' he says.

'Do you have a receipt for that, sir?'

'Was the sex that bad?'

'Sorry?'

'Was I that disappointing?'

'No, it's just that you have an illegal upgrade and I can't allow you to fly in club.' Andy gets out his pen and taps into the computer. 'So I am downgrading you to, um, thirty-six B on the bulkhead. You'll have plenty of leg room.'

'Fine,' says the man, snatching back his boarding card. 'Just get me my money back.'

'Give me your name and address and I'll sort something out,' says Andy.

'You know my name,' hisses the man.

'Of course I do,' lies Andy.

'Here's my card,' he says, after rootling around in his top pocket. 'And don't call me.'

'No.' Andy smiles.

'Because quite frankly you weren't much cop yerself,' the man says, marching off to sit down at the other end of the lounge.

'Oh dear,' I whisper into Andy's ear. 'Who was that?'

'Oh God,' says Andy, shaking his head. 'The marketing director of some make-up brand. I met him at a party a couple of weeks ago.'

'Right.'

'I told you I didn't want to deal with him.'

'Now I can see why.' I smile. 'Why don't you check out that married couple over there. No danger of intimate knowledge with them.'

'You never know,' smiles Andy. 'It's always the so-called straight ones who are the most deviant.'

Finally I get to call the flight for boarding and we spend the next fifteen minutes checking all the boarding passes against all the tickets, looking for more of Dave's victims. All in all we find five people who have been illegally upgraded. One of them even has NSUG (Not Suitable for Up Grade) typed by his name, which means he must have been rude to one of the girls before he was even approached by Dave. I have to say that Andy and I are both gobsmacked by Dave's brass neck. I mean, I've heard of people taking bribes for upgrades – that goes on all the time – but I have never heard of someone actually flogging them at check-in. I should go and report him myself right away, but I've got a plane to catch. I put my own boarding card through the ticket machine and walk towards the plane. Part of me actually rather admires Dave. He managed to pocket a grand in an afternoon. That's quite something. He will keep until I get back. Hangover or no hangover, that's the first thing I'll sort out when I touch down.

'Get a move on,' says Andy, pushing me along the finger towards the plane. 'Sue and Rachel are waiting to get the drinks.'

'All right, all right,' I say. 'Anyway, what's the hurry? There's still quite a few people ahead of us.'

8-9 PM

'Fuck you, madam. Fuck you. Thank you, sir . . . this
queue. Fuck you, sir? That's right. Fuck you. Fuck you. Fuck
you? Both of you . . .'

I can hear Craig from the back of the line as I wait to board
the plane. Andy turns around and smirks.

'Can you hear him?' he asks.

'Yes,' I say, rolling my eyes.

This is one of the oldest tricks in the book, telling passengers
to fuck off in the politest and most pleasant of voices while at
the same time pretending to say 'far queue'. Craig does it every
time he boards a plane and still somehow it manages to amuse
him – and now, seemingly, Andy, who is quietly corpsing
in front of me. I've heard it so many times before I'm afraid
that it no longer tickles me. It ranks up there with farting in
passenger's faces, which is another flight attendant favourite.

If you know they're at it, then face-farting is actually quite easy to spot. It's usually directed towards someone who has pissed off a check-in girl, or who has been difficult and unpleasant during food service. The flight attendant will travel down the aisle and pause to talk to someone else, bending right down, forcing their buttocks into the face of the annoying passenger. And then they will break wind. Cabin pressure makes everyone far more flatulent than when on the ground because the stomach bloats, so it's much easier to fart to order in the air. There are some attendants who pride themselves on this extremely useful skill. Craig, needless to say, is one of them.

'Fuck you, Andy,' says Craig, taking a look at his ticket. 'Fuck you, sir,' he says, smiling at me. 'Are you two the last?'

'Yes,' I say. 'As far as I know.'

'Fuck you both,' he says at the top of his voice as he ushers us along. 'This is going to be a great flight.' He pauses and leans forward to whisper into Andy's ear. 'Only problem is,' he grins, 'I've already had three of the hosties on this flight.'

'Really?' says Andy, turning around.

'Yup. My only hope is that they haven't "shared" too much in the galley.' His fingers do the quotation-marks-in-the-air thing.

'Let's hope so,' agrees Andy.

'Looks like one of our bets might yet come to fruition,' I say.

'What's that?' asks Craig.

'Just a little something I've got going with Andy,' I say. 'That one day you'll have a whole plane of ex-shags to deal with.'

'Oh, right.' Craig smiles, enjoying the idea. 'Sadly it's just half of economy on this flight.'

'Keep at it,' I say, slapping him on the back as we turn left inside the plane.

'Now that's what I call an ambition,' he says.

'All right in there?' says Andy.

He is a few steps ahead of me and has paused by the galley curtain. He is giving someone the thumbs-up. I walk past and poke my head in to see who he is talking to. Sitting on a metal case, his face in an oxygen mask, is a handsome young bloke with straight blond hair and a straight long nose, who I presume to be Tom Raven. He takes another hit from the bottle, closing his eyes as he inhales, and gives me a thumbs-up.

'All right?' he says as he finally pulls the mask away.

'All right?'

'Thank God for this stuff,' he says, pointing to the oxygen bottle. 'I've got a fucking killer of a hangover.'

Oxygen steeling is a common hangover cure, especially on the early-morning flights. A couple of shots up the nose are usually enough to put any hostie who has spent a heavy night out on the tiles on the road to recovery. But it is rare for anyone to be using it this late in the day.

'Tom's clearly had a late one,' I say, sitting down next to Andy and fastening my seat belt.

'Yeah,' he says. 'I left him at about four a.m. this morning. I imagine he hasn't slept much either.'

Andy and I are sitting in two blue leather chairs in the middle of the front row of club class. To our right are Sue and Rachel, and to our left, sitting on his own, is some old bald bloke with an unfeasibly large stomach who appears to be half cut already.

'Evening, ladies,' says Andy, leaning across me to engage Rachel and Sue. 'Happy with your seats?'

'They're fine.' Sue smiles, her round face dimpling either side of her mouth.

'The normal space-available staff upgrade,' sniffs Rachel. 'You could've at least got us all into first.'

'There's simply no pleasing some people,' says Andy.

'Anyway,' Rachel continues, 'who else is coming on this little trip with us?'

'Well,' says Andy, putting his elbow on my armrest as he leans right over, 'there's Craig.'

'Yes,' says Rachel.

'You two.'

She smiles.

'Gareth, Loraine, Edith, and Tom, who has just recently decided to join us.'

'Oh.' She suddenly sounds a little more interested. 'Is Edith the one who . . . ?'

'Yes,' replies Andy.

'Right,' says Rachel, turning immediately to fill Susan in on the gossip.

And when it comes to Edith, there is plenty to gossip about. A sweet Essex girl in her late twenties, Edith somewhat usually had an affair with one of the pilots but made the mistake of getting pregnant, and the airline somewhat unusually flew her to Thailand for an abortion. There was quite a bit of pressure put on her to take the airline's option. It was explained to her that if she wanted a career with us, abortion was perhaps the best move. The pilot was a valuable and expensive captain and she was a hostess with potential. The airline has done this before – rather heavily suggested that pregnant, unmarried air hostesses have terminations in this Bangkok clinic where we seem to have some sort of deal. And we aren't the only outfit to do it. It's quite a common practice, particularly in the Middle Eastern airlines. The scandal is that Edith apparently hasn't handled it terribly well. Andy tells me that she has a bit of a temazepan problem. As you know, this is not unusual for a flight attendant, but when the accusation comes from Andy I suspect it's quite bad. In fact, I am surprised to hear that she is flying at all.

'All right there, Edith?' asks Andy as she comes through the cabin handing out the drinks.

'Fine.' She smiles weakly. Her face is pale beneath the trowel-load of make-up she's smeared on. Her thin, mousey hair is scraped back into a bun. You'd never guess, looking at her now, that she used to be the life and soul of the party. 'Champagne, orange juice or water?'

'Champagne, of course,' replies Andy. 'Looking forward to downroute?'

'Absolutely,' she says, with all the enthusiasm of a drowned rat. 'We're all very excited.'

'Champagne?' asks a male voice.

'Hello there!' I say, looking up to see Gareth.

Gareth's a tall, thin bloke in his late forties or early fifties with dark slap-down hair and an Adam's apple that slides up and down his throat as he speaks. He is the cabin services director – the bloke in charge of the whole plane. He's been with the company for years and has complained about it for years. Unfortunately his partner, both business and sexual, runs an import/export business and Gareth gets him free flights and free freight. Whether it's Triumph motorbikes from India or yards of silk from Thailand, Gareth's position means that the goods fly for nix, as does Larry, his partner. So Gareth is kind of stuck with his job for the sake of his partner, and is possibly a little bit bitter about it.

'So, how are you?' I ask as he hands me a glass of champagne and a small packet of brandless pretzels. We don't do nuts on our airline in case a passenger collapses with anaphylactic shock. Although the packet still does carry a 'might contain nuts' warning.

'Oh God, you know,' he says, with a small sniff. 'I think I might be getting a cold. You would have thought I'd be over all that by now, after nearly twenty years in the business. But apparently not.'

Rookie flight attendants are always struck down by every available illness when they start the job. Their close proximity to the general public and the constant circling of foul air means that they spend their first eight months or so with streaming colds and constant flu. Then, just when they think they can't take any more, they cross some sort of immune-system Rubicon, and they are never ill again. They develop the constitution of an ox. They wave snot and sneezes away for ever and can stay up all night, fly all day and still make happy hour when they land. I've always thought it's because they slowly replace their blood with alcohol, but apparently it's down to overexposure to germs and bottles of echinacea.

'Can't you take something for it?' I ask.

'No doubt Tom has some little pill I can have,' he says, rolling his eyes. 'Champagne?' he asks the man behind me.

I take a sip of my champagne. It is quite tart and acrid, and the bubbles go straight up my nose. It's not top-drawer stuff, but then again, we're not a top-drawer airline. However, I still can't believe that from all the champagnes our head of wine, Roger, had to choose from, he opted for this paint stripper. But then Roger has always had appalling taste.

I remember when he joined the airline about six years ago he changed all the wines and champagnes we were carrying overnight. There were rumours that he'd been given some sort of backhander. We'd always carried a rather nice Moët in first and a fizzy brut in club, and now we have some champagne that no-one has heard of and English white wine. He justified it by telling us it was the talk of the Cannes Duty Free Festival. But I can't say that I believe him. I've been to the Cannes Duty Free Festival myself and everyone gets so plastered there it's a wonder they can talk at all, let alone have a coherent conversation about champagne.

As freebie festivals go, Cannes Duty Free has to be one of the best. Anyone who is anyone in the food and drink business sets up shop on the Riviera for a couple of days in the summer in order to woo the airlines and any of the other carriers. They are so desperate to get their products on board planes, ferries and cruise ships that gin companies rent boats, vodka manufacturers hire speedboats, and they lay on an endless stream of tastings and parties. And when I tell you that a small company like Air Fayre churns out eighteen thousand meals a day for a small carrier like BMI, then you'll understand the sort of ten-million-plus volume the big boys like Gate Gourmet are producing for the likes of Virgin and British Airways. Get yourself in the first-class cabin of one of the big airlines and your profits go through the roof. I have heard of other airlines accepting envelopes stuffed with £2,000 in cash from alcohol suppliers desperate to get on the duty-free trolleys they wheel up and down the planes. It doesn't do to scrutinize Roger's alcohol choices too much, or indeed ask yourself too often how he can afford that air-conditioned conservatory.

Then again, our head of food, or development chef, Dennis, is just as bad. He gets flown all over the world to eat in the best restaurants, and all in the name of research. It's the most ridiculous thing I have ever heard. As if his eating at the Rock Pool restaurant in Sydney is going to make any difference to the sort of stuff they serve us on a flight. I know for a fact that he regularly dines at all of Gordon Ramsay's restaurants; he's also been to Jamie Oliver's Fifteen, the Ivy, Sheekey's, Zuma, all the gourmet hotspots, and he's had a stint at Mosimann's Academy, all in the name of following food fashion. He also flies on rival airlines just to sample the food and check out the competition, to see if we are up to date with the chicken chasseur we are serving. The extraordinary thing is that most of the food carried by other airlines comes out of the same place. So if you really want to see what the other teams are doing, all you need to do is get yourself down to the south perimeter fence and knock on the door. Yet somehow Dennis managed to justify a flight on Concorde in the name of research.

I knock back my champagne and put a dry pretzel in my mouth. It's far too salty. As I lean back in my seat I can hear some shouting. There seems to be something of an argument brewing in economy. Andy and I look at each other.

'What d'you think is going on?' he asks, his mouth full of pretzels.

'No idea,' I say, straining to look down the aisle.

Craig swishes out of first class and brushes past. 'Fight!' he says with a grin, rubbing his hands together.

'Over what?' I ask.

'Leg room,' he replies, turning round. 'Come and take a look.'

Both Andy and I look at each other again and immediately get out of our seats, making our way to the curtains that divide club from cattle class. In the galley to our left there are a couple of hosties taking their shoes off, exchanging heels for flats and putting their names on bottles of water.

'I don't know what his problem is,' says one to the other. 'Each of those seats is much like the other and they all give you DVT.'

'Maybe he's just one of those stressed-out bastards,' the other replies.

Andy and I poke our heads through and it appears that she is right. For standing about three rows back, in the middle of the middle section, and shouting his surly head off is the annoying stressed bastard Debbie and I conspired to put next to the fattest man on the plane.

'Oh shit,' I say.

'What?' asks Andy.

'That's the wanker Debbie and I deliberately placed next to the fat bastard because he was being so annoying.'

'Oh.'

'Yes, oh. I think perhaps I might keep a low profile. I'm going back to my seat. You coming?'

'You kidding? And miss this?'

The surly bloke is making so much noise that the whole of the back end of the plane is staring at him. One of the young economy-class flight attendants is trying to calm him down and he is shouting so close to her face that she has her eyes shut. Gareth moves in to see if he can do any better. Meanwhile, Craig has been despatched to phone the flight deck. He is muttering something down the telephone near the galley. As I walk back to my seat, I meet the first officer, with three stripes on his shoulder, marching towards me. This is serious stuff. For the first officer to leave the flight deck and abandon his cup of tea and pre-flight snacks, it takes some ruckus. Two minutes later he marches back, followed by Andy a few moments later.

'What happened?' I ask as he sits back down and fastens his seat belt.

'The first officer came down and threatened to kick him off the plane if he didn't sit down. He also pulled out some plastic handcuffs and said that he would use them without a moment's hesitation. Or he would have the man arrested. He looked bloody furious.'

'I bet. It takes a lot to get them out of their section.'

'He sure as hell meant business. I love it when a man gets all masterful,' he adds, draining his champagne glass.

Edith comes through to collect the glasses and the empty bags of pretzels. Meanwhile, Craig and a very young-looking attendant take their places at the front of each of the aisles for the safety demonstration.

'First day on the job,' whispers Craig, with a nod of his head in the girl's direction. 'Few little tricks up our sleeve.'

Craig and the young woman start the safety demonstration as the plane taxis off its stand. It always amazes me how few people pay attention to this bit. I know most people think that if the plane crashes their chances of survival are minimal, and to a certain extent that is true. It's often said that the reason you are told to adopt the brace position – head between your knees, arms either side of your head – in the event of a crash is so that you break your neck nice and cleanly and protect your dental records. That way you are unable to sue the airline and much easier to identify. The same goes for a water landing. The idea that a small yellow life jacket with a whistle will make any difference as the plane sinks into the sea, the cynics say, is risible. Yet in some cases, like when the skyjacked Ethiopian Airlines B-767 ditched in the sea off the Comoros Islands in 1996, it did. Despite instructions to the contrary from members of the cabin crew, several passengers had pre-inflated their life jackets and were unable to escape the rising water inside the fuselage, but others survived. It is also worth remembering that there have been several cases of planes overshooting runways at coastal airports and dropping into the sea. There have even been two cases since the late eighties of planes running out of runway at La Guardia airport and ending up in the bay. So perhaps a cursory glance at the flight attendant over your magazine is probably a good idea.

Although, looking up at the young woman in front of me, I kind of wish I hadn't bothered. As she places the oxygen mask over her mouth and nose and tugs on the imaginary line, I can see from the expression on her face that something is wrong. As she removes the mask, I and the rest of the cabin can see that her mouth and chin are covered in orange marmalade. The poor girl's cheeks turn bright red and she clenches her fists in embarrassment. Craig grins widely at the in-crew joke. The rookie attendant carries on. She places her yellow life jacket over her head, straps it around her waist and reaches into her top pocket for the whistle. While she blows valiantly away on the small white tampon that has hilariously replaced her whistle, Craig bites his cheeks to stop himself from laughing. This is an economy-class initiation that has been moved into club class for Andy's and my benefit. Only the sad thing is that Andy is reading *GQ* magazine and I'm a little bit too old to find it amusing.

As the girl skulks past back to economy, pointing out the emergency exits as she goes, Craig leans forward. 'We'll be sending her through to take a "long stand" with the captain later,' he shares, doing his quotation-mark thing again. 'I remember when I went through for my long stand, it took me twenty minutes of standing to realize that the joke was on me.' He giggles. 'I wonder how long she will last?'

'Let's see,' says Andy, not quite exuding the same level of enthusiasm as his flatmate.'

'Yeah,' says Craig as he goes to take his chair for take-off. 'See you in a sec,' he adds, leaning across the large stomach of the snoring man next to Andy to flip up his window blind.

The lights dim for take-off. Traditionally, we turn the lights off and open the blinds for take-off and landing so as to orientate the passengers inside the plane. In the event of a crash, it helps if your eyes are adjusted to the light outside, and the emergency path-lighting is more visible as you sprint up the aisle. There is, however, another much more sinister theory to which Craig subscribes: the plane blinds are raised so that in a crash situation – statistically much more likely to happen during take-off or landing – it is easier for the emergency services to count corpses through the windows, instead of having to board the plane.

We trundle up to the end of the runway and sit there. We've missed our slot due to our slight fog delay. There's a queue of some three or four planes ahead of us. This is a busy time of the night for the airport as they try to get all the planes into the air before the midnight deadline. I suspect they are all stacked up in a line behind us down the side of the runway.

The engines rev up. We turn the corner at the top of the runway and the captain increases the speed. We rattle along the tarmac, drips of water from the dodgy air-con falling on my head. An overhead locker bursts open and a giant doll falls into the aisle. Craig gets out of his seat and shoves it back in, slamming the door firmly shut.

'Christ, did you see that?' asks Andy as we are pushed back into our seats. 'That reminds me of that flight Craig went on when all those Japanese passengers got into pyjamas and climbed into the overheads.' He grins. 'Thought they were beds, do you remember?'

'Yeah.' I nod, my cheeks vibrating with the speed. 'That must have been such a strange flight.'

'Yeah,' he nods back. 'Imagine something like that happening here.'

9-10 PM

We lift off. I feel a surge in my stomach. I love it when a flight takes off. They say there's something about jet fuel that gets into your blood, and I think they're right. Almost as soon as I strap myself into a plane or feel it rattle down a runway, I get the sweet buzz of adventure. I sit back in my chair and smile.

We bank right and fly over the southern perimeter fields that are, by day, populated by camera-wielding plane-spotters (forced there since they closed the viewing gallery after 9/11), and by night by Special Branch officers on the lookout for sharp-shooting terrorists with handheld rocket launchers. Andy and I look through the fat man's window and the sickly smell of roast chicken fills the air. A couple of birds are cooking in the engines. That's another two Don hasn't managed to save, I think, as I sit in silence staring at the ever-diminishing lights below.

The plane turns to the left a bit and starts to flatten out. The captain rings a bell and both Edith and Craig get out of their seats. Our seat-belt signs are still lit as they disappear into the galley just in front of us to change into their serving jackets, and in Edith's case to change shoes. I can hear them rattling around in there, mumbling snatches of conversation. Another bell goes off. Edith pokes her head out of the galley. It's a blue light, which can only mean one of three things: a gin and tonic, a blanket or an extra pillow. A pink light in the galley is an alert or emergency call, and an amber is the toilet, which means that someone is either stuck in there, a child has switched it on, or a couple are having sex in there and have hit the button with their backsides. Edith walks past, attaching the Velcro sides of her navy tunic. She pauses to take something out of an overhead locker. She's betting, like I would, on some princess down the back wanting a blanket.

Talk to any number of flight attendants and they'll tell you that passengers divide up into easily definable groups. The worst, they say, are the princesses who always want a blanket or a little pillow immediately after take-off. They're always too cold or too hot, and invariably ask for the cabin temperature to be altered. They are fussy when it comes to food and ask if they can have everything fresh, and on the side. They drink obscure alcoholic drinks and continually demand bottles of water. They are loaded down with sprays, perfumes and unctions which they squirt around the cabin. They wear pashminas for comfort and DVT socks for their health and are full of questions. Why haven't we taken off yet? Why are we late? How long is the flight? Why aren't we there yet? And they are usually the first in line when it comes to the flight attendants spitting in their drinks or adding a bit of Dulcolax laxative to their meal.

Then again, the uptight control-freak man is just as bad. He always needs somewhere to hang his coat and somewhere extra special for his rather large briefcase he won't put into the hold and won't fit into the overhead locker. He resents turning off his computer and mobile phone and insists on using them right up until the last possible minute. He also resents taking orders from women or poofs, so basically he thinks that the normal plane rules don't apply to him. He is always first out of his seat before the seat-belt sign goes off, and first to the exit once the plane has taxied to its stand. He complains about the food and the choice of alcohol, and more often than not demands an extra bit of something, such as cheese, after all the food has been cleared away. He is not a popular passenger and a prime candidate for a face-fart halfway through the flight.

Other passengers are simpler to deal with: the trip-of-a-lifetime couple who want to fill you in on all the details of their itinerary; the loved-up holidaymakers who might try to make a sex-trip to the toilet during the flight; the horny businessman who tries to buy a hostie some duty-free perfume; and the harassed young couple with small child, who just need blankets and sympathy. There are, however, some uppity women who hand over their babies to the flight attendants for 'changing'. A mate of mine once took a white child down the end of the plane only to return with a black one, asking the woman if the baby was 'changed enough for her'. The pushy mother finally got the hint. But most of the time harassed parents just need a bit more wine than anyone else.

But it's the upgraders who really tuck in. Perhaps it's the fact that they haven't paid for their flight that makes them so greedy, or maybe they haven't seen such luxury before in their lives. Craig tells a story of a woman upgraded to first who ordered everything on the menu. She had the soup, the entrée, the focaccia, two main courses, dessert and cheese. Craig says that she sat there stuffing her face halfway to Sydney. By the end of the flight it was a wonder she was able to move at all. Upgraders also have a habit of getting quite drunk. There is a sensible drinking policy on all airlines, which means that we are not supposed to serve passengers once they start getting a little loud and leery, but there is also a school of thought that if you fill them with enough drink they will eventually fall asleep and give you no trouble at all. And as every flight attendant knows, a snoring plane is a happy plane – which is, of course, why we like to turn the heating up halfway through a flight.

The captain switches the seat-belt sign off. The man in the row behind me leaps out of his seat and grabs something terribly urgent from the locker above. Craig and Edith drag a trolley of drinks down my aisle, while Gareth and another friend of Andy's called Loraine do the other side.

In her early twenties, Loraine is one of those ambitious new recruits who will go a long way in the business. Her appearance is immaculate, her make-up is piled on, her nails and lips match, her dark hair is twisted into a bun, and she's wearing some old-school pearls. She is not the normal sort of friend for Andy to collect. Then again, I don't think he had much choice in the matter. Loraine soon worked out that Andy was a popular member of the airline and made sure that he became a friend.

'What would you like to drink, birthday boy?' she asks, all glossy lips and smooth hair.

'Champagne,' says Andy. 'And so will my mate.'

Loraine pops a couple of mini bottles of some unknown brand and pours a little into each glass.

'There you go.' She smiles. 'Enjoy,' she adds, before turning her attention to the fat bloke on Andy's right.

'Happy birthday, mate,' I say, clinking glasses with Andy.

'Thanks. I'm very glad you came.' He smiles. 'All right there, ladies?' he adds, leaning across me and raising his flute to Sue and Rachel.

They both raise their glasses back.

'Happy birthday,' says Sue.

'Thanks,' he replies.

'When are we doing presents?' she asks. 'Because I've got you something quite special.' Her eyes look up towards the overhead locker.

'You have?' Andy's cheeks flush under his tan.

'Just a little something,' she says.

'We bought it together,' says Rachel.

There is a slight pause before Sue agrees. 'Yes, we did.' She is not a very good liar.

'It's best to wait for the crew room in Dubai,' Andy says, taking a sip of champagne.

No sooner does he take the glass away from his lips than he spills it all the way down the front of his shirt. We have hit some turbulence and the whole plane is shaking. We are bouncing up and down like a boneshaker bicycle careering down a cobbled street. Sue spills her glass of champagne. I hold firmly on to mine. Suddenly the plane drops about twenty feet. All our buttocks part company with our seats. The 'fasten seat belt' sign springs back on. Gareth, Loraine, Edith and Craig struggle to get their trolleys back down the aisle. A small selection of Beefeater miniatures falls into my lap and a carton of Britvic Orange explodes onto the floor.

'Fuck!' says Edith as she rattles around in my trousers like a bargain hunter at a jumble sale. 'I'm sorry. Are you all right?'

'Fine,' I say. 'Just nearly lost my manhood!'

'Oh,' she says, rapidly withdrawing her hand, like she's only just realized where it's been. 'Sorry about that.'

The plane lurches to the left and then swings to the right. The woman behind me starts to whine like a small dog. I turn around to see one set of white knuckles gripping the seat; her other hand is squeezing her husband's thigh. She looks shit scared. The fat bloke next to Andy wakes up with a start and mutters something like 'Jesus Christ!' His voice is drowned out by the crash of bottles in the galley.

'Ladies and gentlemen,' comes the nasal, jaded voice of Gareth. 'As you can see, the captain has turned on the "fasten seat belt" sign. Would you please return to your seat and fasten your seat belts. We seem to have hit a bit of turbulence.'

'No shit, Sherlock,' says Andy as the whole plane continues to rattle and shake like it's going down the runway all over again.

The whining woman behind me is beginning to cry; she yelps each time we hit a large bump and her husband keeps shushing her like it's going to help. Craig and Edith strap themselves in just as the plane plummets another ten feet. There's a scream from the back of the plane, the giant doll escapes from the overhead locker again, and at least six oxygen masks fall out of the ceiling. Someone in economy shouts 'We're going to die, we're going to die!' The flat vowels penetrate all the way to first class. Someone to my left starts to mutter the Lord's Prayer.

'This is ba-a-d,' says Andy, growing pale beneath the orange. 'This is really ba-a-a-d.'

I have to admit that it doesn't feel good. Turbulence is never fun, and this really is quite full on. The plane shakes left and then right. We bounce along for a second, like we're falling down a hill, and then, suddenly, we stop. All is quiet. There's a moment of silence and then comes a collective sigh of relief from the whole of club class.

'Um, excuse me,' comes a loud voice from about five rows back. 'I think someone has been sick.'

I poke my head around the edge of my seat to see that the whole of the back of the cabin has been sprayed in vomit. The sides of the plane, the ceiling and the carpet are all covered in a virulent orange glow.

'Oh my God!' screams another, rather posh-sounding voice. 'They've been sick all over me!'

'And me!' adds someone else.

It seems that the whole of the back row is covered. It's extraordinary to think that one stomach could contain so much. It's everywhere. There are chunks of pretzel on the ceiling and half-digested crisps all over the floor. The warm, sweet smell of sick is beginning to creep down the cabin.

'Ladies and gentlemen,' come the handsome tones of Richard. 'This is your captain speaking. Sorry about it being a bit bouncy just then.'

'A bit?' says Andy, only just beginning to relax.

'We encountered a bit of turbulence on our way down to the Alps. It shouldn't be bothering us again. But just in case, I would suggest that when you are in your seats you keep your seat belt loosely fastened.'

As Richard drones on about the rest of the flight, mentioning altitude, speed and various landmarks we shall be flying over, Edith and Craig appear in blue plastic catering gloves with coffee jugs full of soapy water.

'It's all glamour in the world of flying,' says Craig as he walks towards the vomit.

Two minutes later, Edith comes back and collects a dustpan and brush.

'You OK?' I ask as she comes past again.

'Jesus Christ,' she says, shaking her pale face. 'The last time I saw this much puke we had to close down the toilet. It was the last Sydney flight I did and this girl came up to me and told me that she'd been a little bit sick in the basin. When I went in the whole thing was full to the brim and overflowing down the sides. You couldn't drain it so we had to bail the thing out, but we were handling food at the time, so we couldn't.' She shakes her head again. 'We closed the whole thing down for the entire flight.'

'God,' I say, recoiling slightly. 'That sounds disgusting.'

'Yeah, it was.'

'What are you doing with that?' I nod at the dustpan.

'Craig is sluicing down the back walls and I'm sweeping up the water and puke and putting it in the coffee jugs.'

'Right . . .'

'See you in a sec. We've got to get dinner out in a minute.'

'See you,' I say, making a mental note not to have tea or coffee later.

Gareth comes out of the galley and stands next to me in the aisle, supervising the vomit clear-up. He has his hands on his hips and his head cocked to one side. His long nose wrinkles as he sighs.

'It's always the fat kids who vomit,' he mutters out of the side of his mouth.

'Sorry?' I say.

'Take it from me,' he says, looking down. 'The fat kids always puke. I had one last week who managed to projectile over six passengers.'

'Really?'

'Mmm,' he says, looking up again. 'Although this little fucker hasn't done too badly.'

'Oh?'

'He's taken out his mother and two other people.' He walks up the cabin. 'Evening, everyone,' he says. 'Sorry about all the mess but we should get this cleared up in no time. In the meantime, can I offer anyone a bag to put their soiled clothes in? And some extra blankets? Sadly we don't have any clothes for you to change into. Unless of course you'd like a serving tunic?'

Ten minutes later, after numerous trips up and down the aisle with hot soapy water and dustpans of puke, the vomit is cleared up, the passengers are hosed down and the smell of sick begins to abate. Gareth continues to supervise from the far end of club and a couple of the attendants from first poke their heads through the curtain to see what all the stench is about.

'All right up at the front?' asks Andy as he spots an attendant called Belinda at the curtain. A brassy blonde with a bit of a reputation, Belinda has only recently been promoted to first class.

'Not bad.' She smiles. 'The boy band is being a bit frisky.'

'Really?' Andy squirms slightly in his seat. 'I think I might pop through and say hi.'

'Can you wait till after service?' asks Belinda. 'We're just about to hand out the warm rolls.'

'Oh, OK,' says Andy, slightly put out. It's not often that he gets put in his place. 'She's a bit of a stroppy bitch, don't you think?' he comments once Belinda has disappeared.

'Perhaps she just wants to keep the celebrities all to herself,' I suggest.

'You're right.' He nods. 'You're absolutely right.'

Andy sits and contemplates Belinda's celebrity-stealing capabilities while the crashing and clattering in the galley increases. The smell of hot food seeps down the plane, although what exactly this hot food is is anyone's guess. That's one of the main problems with airline food: it always looks and tastes the same, no matter how many swanky restaurants the food developers and celebrity chefs have been to. And that's all to do with the preparation and the quality of the ingredients.

All our meals are prepared on site, near the airport, by one of the large catering companies that is also used by most of the other airlines. These places are huge, cavernous warehouses where the rat-traps are regularly baited and the food is cook-chilled (i.e. cooked and then chilled to four degrees) or cook-frozen (cooked and then immediately frozen). The quality of the ingredients is not exactly top-drawer, but the main problem is the staff who cook it. None of them is a professionally trained chef. They are made up of locals recruited from the surrounding area whose criminal back-grounds can be checked as far back as five years, or they are loaders and baggage handlers with back problems who instead of being laid off sick end up stirring scrambled eggs for a living. There are some five hundred staff who work in the kitchens earning about £5 an hour, doing shifts that start at five a.m. and finish at midnight; between midnight and five a.m. the factory is hosed down ready for the place to start up again in the morning. The place used regularly to be raided by Immigration when half the staff would be taken away for ques-tioning, but the introduction of biometrics – fingerprint and retina scanning – has reduced the number of illegals and cut down the job sharing that inevitably used to go on.

However, according to my mate who works there, stealing is still rife. Anything that isn't nailed down goes. He says they'd take your shoe laces if you stood still long enough. The buttons go off the machines and the toilet seats disappear, as do the taps in the bathrooms, and half the stuff never makes it to the factory in the first place. The amount of chicken breasts, fish, meat and alcohol that is creamed off at the back has to be seen to be believed, and some of the scams are so brazen. There was a £60K bus service that supposedly collected staff from around the local area that never actually ran. How they kept that one running for a year is anyone's guess. But then these guys know how to keep everyone sweet. Come Christmas time, one of them is despatched to Baggage to fill up car boots with hampers and boxes of tricks for the festive season. The Baggage boys always pretend to refuse at first, before swiftly handing over their car keys. All you really need to do is check out the car park around the food area to see how much they are all making. There are just as many Jags and Mercs as you'd see over at Baggage.

When you learn how much money the airlines shell out for your food, it's a wonder anyone is making any cash at all. On a charter flight you can expect your meal to cost in the region of 90p. It goes up to £1.50 in a standard airline, rising to £2.50 in club and £5 in first, although there are some airlines who really do like to spoil you: Qantas spends up to £15 in first class, up to £10 in business and up to £5 in steerage. But it's all about volume. On our flight today we have a full plane of three hundred passengers who can expect two meals each: dinner, and then the breakfast they'll shove down their throats just before we land. We have three flights out of the airport today, and twenty flights out a week; most of them have up to three meals on board, so we have something like eighteen thousand meals a week leaving this airport alone. We don't back-cater (i.e. we don't stock up here for the return flight from Sydney) so we buy at least half that amount again in Australia. So if you are an airline it makes more sense to plump for the 30p dessert rather than the more extravagant 35p option.

And none of this includes crew meals. The crew eat different food from the passengers, or at least they are supposed to. And the captain and the first officer have to have different meals just in case one of them falls ill. On the whole the crew eat better than the passengers, and our lot can be quite spoilt, with chunky Kitkats, salads or lasagne that they heat up themselves. A lot of the time they bring their own food to cook in the oven in the galley, or they half-inch the passenger's food and pocket their crew rations to save themselves some cash. It's usually the rookie attendants who steal passenger food, but it doesn't take long for them to realize that passenger food makes you fat.

Packed with preservatives, washed in chemicals and high in salt and fat, passenger food is perhaps the only packaged food we eat these days that does not have the number of calories or a list of ingredients printed down the side. It's chosen for its reheating and reconstituting properties, and the recipes are put together so that the worst a hostie can do is burn, or drop, a meal. Fish and meat are usually covered in some sort of sauce to prevent drying out during the warming-up process. Food that flies well is food that can be roughly handled, left to sit for hours, and be reheated in less than eighteen minutes in ovens that reach 210 degrees. Passenger food is also designed to stop people caged in their seats for four to five hours from hitting the bottle and getting too drunk.

Airline food is supposed to look palatable, have at least two colours on the plate, and not make you ill. The last thing an airline wants is for any of its passengers to get food poisoning. So although it may not taste of anything, you can be sure that the food hygiene standards during preparation were second to none. In the catering industry, hats and gloves are worn at all times. Discover glass in your food or some sort of hair or bug and you will be showered with champagne by the airline, but your name and address will also be filed. Food scammers are the bane of the airlines. Some people deliberately bring glass or bugs with them to put into their food. Only a couple of weeks ago we had some bloke complain about a beetle that later turned out to be a native of South Africa when the meal itself had been prepared in London. Needless to say he was not compensated, and his name has been circulated.

Today, according to the menu in front of me, we've got salmon terrine as a starter, a choice of fish, chicken or lamb for main course, a chocolate parfait and fresh cream for dessert, and cheese and fruit and coffee and petits fours. None of it sounds too bad. If only I didn't know where it all came from, and that it's been reheated by the vomit-handed Craig and Edith, I might well be more keen to tuck in. Instead I stare at it all laid out in front of me, pick my way through the terrine, play with my lamb curry and take just a corner of the chocolate parfait, wondering if I might have another bottle of English white wine as compensation. I have to say that I am beginning to see the appeal of these new business lounges where you can have your meal before you fly. It's much easier for all concerned and probably a whole lot more pleasant.

'Don't you want that?' asks Andy, leaning over, his white plastic fork at the ready, eyeing my chocolate pudding.

'No, mate,' I reply. 'You have it.' I shove the white plastic dish over onto his table.

'You're not doing the no-carbs thing so your stomach doesn't bloat, are you? Just greens and protein for you?'

'No.' I shake my head. 'I just don't feel like it.'

'Great,' says Andy, piling in with his fork. 'I'm bloody starving.'

Craig rushes up all excited.

'Guess what?' he stage-whispers, squatting down by Andy's chair.

'What?' says Andy, his mouth full of chocolate.

'Tom's put Dulcolax in that mad nutter man's food!'

'Really?' asks Andy.

'He was going to wipe his steak around the toilet bowl, but it's too difficult to do if you're not in first or club. You know, everyone watches you and you can't disappear off for a second with the meal, and the teabag in the toilet was also too difficult as all the pots are communal, so he went for the laxative!' Craig almost squeals with delight. 'Loads of it!'

'Great,' says Andy, grinning widely and trying to look interested.

'I'll keep you informed,' says Craig, standing up and tapping the side of his nose. 'If there is any action, as it were.'

He disappears into the galley in front of us, and judging by the loud laughter and giggling that ensue gets a much more satisfactory reaction to his news. He pokes his head around, catches Andy's eye and makes a loud flatulent noise. The galley laughs again.

'That'll learn him,' says Craig, giving us both a wink.

10-11 PM

With this quality of entertainment on offer, I decide it might be more interesting to have a look at what the plane's in-flight system has in store. As we're not the most modern and up-to-date of airlines, we sadly still have the old tape system with the standard Hollywood-issue type of movies on offer. Some of the more luxurious airlines now offer fourteen-inch personal monitors, DVDs and AVOD (audio visual on demand), which means that you can choose your own film and pause if you fancy a chat, for a meal-break or a quick trip to the toilet; we, on the other hand, have a Hugh Grant film or *Shrek 2* for our delight and delectation. Both are suitably old and both are suitably banal.

But then, that is to be expected. Airlines are not allowed to show any Hollywood movies until three months after they have premiered in the US (although occasionally, because some films are so slow to progress across the pond, this can be before their UK release). The film packages on offer to the passenger vary from month to month, according to the time of year. During the school holidays, for example, we show more child-friendly material. The art-house stuff, although rare, does get shown during more low-season flights. Foreign films don't translate too well as there isn't much room for subtitles on small screens, but big hitters like *Amélie* do get a look-in. On the whole, the films chosen by those people who specialize in ordering in-flight entertainment for airlines are supposed to reflect the airline's image. BA would like to think that their in-flight entertainment is 'respectable, strong and intelligent'; Virgin, to go with their double-beds-in-upper-class image, might well have a slightly racier selection.

There are some films, however, that would never make it on to a plane. Anything that has too much sex and violence, for a start. Nudity and gambling are banned from Arab flights, and the film *Alive*, about a plane crash in South America where the survivors are reduced to eating one another, has never been shown anywhere. Neither, these days, are films about hijackings or terrorism, or films with scenes showing aircraft in 'extreme or distressing situations'. So you can see why it's so much easier for us to plump for a nice, simple, safe Hugh Grant movie.

The captive audience, sitting there for hours at a time, are an advertiser's dream. And with airlines operating at a 5 per cent profit margin, at the mercy of world markets, SARS and terrorist attacks, it's no wonder that more and more advertising is creeping on to planes. Spots either side of the news can go for as much as £1m a run, and when you consider that there are thirteen million flying BA a month and your average businessman works only for the first hour of the flight, you can see that it's worth it. Charge him up to five dollars a minute for the use of a mobile in the air, and one dollar per text, and sooner or later your skimpy 5 per cent profit margin starts to look a little more healthy.

I reach into the pocket in front of me searching for my earphones. I pull out the sick bag, a curled in-flight magazine with Billie Piper on the front, an old terry sock, and that's it. Not only are there no earphones, but my safety card is also missing. It's probably been nicked. Everything on board the plane that isn't actually bolted down gets pinched at some point. The earphones always go, which is why we try to collect them at the end of the flight, as do weird things like the safety cards, the antimacassars, the blankets and the pillows. And it's not always the passengers who do the pilfering. I remember a story about the mother of a mate of mine who was a hostie working the Concorde flights from London to New York. She was eventually fired for stealing the goose-down pillows they used to have on board. She was saving them up to make a duvet and was almost there when she was discovered. Then again, she'd always been quite naughty. I remember she had a Chinese chest in her living room that she used to call her 'retirement fund'. It was stuffed with fifteen thousand miniatures. At the end of every trip she ever made, she'd come home with her knickers and bra full of Gordon's and Teachers.

I ring the attendant bell. Gareth comes out of the galley.

'Yes, sir?' he says, exuding genuflecting sincerity.

'You don't seem to have handed out the earphones,' I say.

'Oh God,' he moans. 'All that puke has put everyone off their game tonight. I'll get Edith to hand them out right away. I wonder if they've done it in tourist,' he mumbles, walking off towards the back of the plane.

'Are you going to watch a film?' asks Andy, sounding mildly put out.

'Well . . .'

'Thanks a bunch,' he says. 'If I fancied watching a film, I'd have stayed at home.'

'Sorry, it's been a long day and I'm just a bit—'

'It's my birthday!' he moans. 'You can't watch a film. What are you going to watch?'

'It's a Hugh Grant movie.'

'Jesus Christ!' He starts to laugh. 'I'm being abandoned for a Hugh Grant movie. Fuck me, my conversational abilities must be bad.'

'No, it's just that I fancied—'

'Sue? Rachel?' he says, leaning across me again. 'He wants to watch a Hugh Grant movie!' Andy points an accusing finger at me. 'Can you believe it?' I can feel my face turning red as Sue and Rachel both turn around and look at me.

'Honestly,' says Rachel. 'It's his birthday.'

'My point exactly,' says Andy.

'Would you like some earphones?' asks Edith, walking past with a whole load hanging over her arm.

'Um.' I pause. 'No thanks.'

'Oh,' she replies. 'Earphones?' she asks Sue and Rachel. They both decline. Edith moves on.

'Thank you,' says Andy, leaning back into his chair. 'Now,' he adds, rubbing his hands together, 'd'you want another drink?'

'All right. But I can't take any more of that English white wine.'

'No,' he agrees, his face crumpling. 'How about a vodka?'

'Great.' I smile and push my tray to one side. 'You get me one while I just go into first for a sec for a piss and to stretch my legs.'

'You're on,' he says. 'And check out Fun Five for me while you're about it.'

Moving into first should be like moving into a different world. It should smell different, sound different and above all exude the luxury and comfort of a £5,000 ticket. Singapore Airlines' first-class passengers lounge around on seventy-six-inch seatbeds with down-filled duvets. Their cabin staff turn down their beds while the passengers slip into their Givenchy pyjamas. Virgin provide double beds, stand-up bars and an in-flight manicurist and masseuse. They also have fourteen different 'lighting moods' that can be adjusted by the crew. Swiss have Eames-style seating with a dining table and an extra seat so that the passenger could be 'joined' for dinner. BA have flatbeds, and Air Canada boasts sculpted sleepers with a massage function. We can only stretch to an extra-large leather seat that reclines to a twenty-five-degree angle. Even our goodie bag is a bit poor. While other airlines load their first-class passengers down with bottles of Molton Brown, shoes, lip balms and a rubber duck (if you're on Virgin), we hand out some red jogging pants, a pair of cloth flip-flops and a terry eyeshade.

At least it does smell a bit different from club. Here, the vomit seems to give way to a strong smell of aftershave, and the aroma of old lamb curry is replaced by the smell of truffle oil.

'All right there?' asks Belinda from the galley as she sees me come through the curtains.

'Fine,' I say. 'Just stretching the legs.'

'OK,' she says, adding some ineffectual-looking canapés to her tray of drinks. 'Gareth's on the flight deck,' she adds, pushing out in front of me.

'Oh, OK,' I say, following her.

Her hips develop a serious swagger as she approaches the boy band.

'Here you go, boys,' she purrs as she puts down the drinks.

'Wa-hey,' they all leer together.

She bends over in front of me. A hand covered in thick silver rings slips swiftly up the back of her skirt and cups her buttocks. She doesn't appear to be wearing any underwear or to feel the need to move in any way.

'Gin and tonic for you,' she trills, 'vodka on the rocks for you.' She leans over some more. The hand moves higher; she snakes her hips. 'Anything else for you two over there?'

'More champagne,' comes the reply. 'And you can forget the snacks.'

'OK,' she says, turning around to see me. 'Back in a sec,' she declares, looking me straight in the eye.

'Excuse me,' I say as I squeeze past her in the aisle.

'That's fine,' she says, brushing up against me. I swear she rubs her breasts against my back.

I walk through the rest of the cabin which is positively comatose compared to the reek of sexual tension at the back. There are a couple of businessmen in red jogging pants, sipping brandy or port, giggling along to the Hugh Grant movie. There's a young woman fast asleep with her eye mask on and her mouth wide open. An elderly man is reading *The Da Vinci Code* with his seat bolt upright and his shoes firmly on. There's a middle-aged couple going through a selection of property magazines – the holiday-home market is picking up in Dubai. There are the sheikh's two wives, still in their black chadors, reading brightly coloured magazines, and the sheikh himself is looking through some business papers in the row in front. And then, right at the end, leaning against the back wall, is Gareth. He is talking to Loraine.

'And then I said to her, "If you want to keep the baby, you should." But then she said . . . Evening,' says Gareth as he sees me approach.

'Oh, hello,' says Loraine, her glossy lips breaking into a smile. 'Had enough in steerage, have we?'

'Just stretching my legs.'

'Right,' says Gareth.

'It's all a bit hot and steamy up here,' I say, smiling and rubbing my hands together.

'Yeah,' says Loraine. 'Gareth and I were just discussing that. We think the band have dropped an E.'

'D'you think?'

'Yeah.' Gareth rolls his eyes. 'It's all we bloody need. A bloody boy band on bloody Ecstasy.'

'Are you sure?'

'Well,' says Loraine, 'they were perfectly normal to start with and then after a while they became like a group of octopuses, wandering hands everywhere. One of them even tried to dance along to the "fasten seat belt" bell.'

'It's hardly subtle, is it?' says Gareth.

'Belinda doesn't seem to mind,' I say.

'Yeah, well,' says Loraine, raising a finely plucked eyebrow. 'We all know about her.'

'Richard around?' I ask, sensing something I don't want to get into. 'Or is he having a sleep?'

'I was just about to give him this smoked salmon sandwich,' says Loraine. 'You can take it in if you like.'

'Great.'

Loraine picks up the intercom. 'The weather is good for this time of year. Would you like a pickled herring?'

'In you come,' comes the reply.

'The password is pickled herring,' whispers Loraine into my ear.

'Thanks. I would never have guessed.'

The flight-deck door opens. The first officer, Ashley, is standing there in his socks.

'Oh,' he says, sounding a tad disappointed, 'it's you.'

'Sorry, mate,' I say, handing over the smoked salmon sandwich. 'Is this for you?'

'No,' he says, turning back towards the controls. 'It's Richard's, but he's having a conversation with Air Traffic Control UK.'

'UK? Surely we must be out of UK airspace by now?'

'Miles away,' says Ashley, 'but someone's left a wheel behind on the runway at the airport and we're trying to work out if it's us.'

'A wheel?'

'Yup,' he says, turning around and picking up a crossword puzzle. 'Do you know the answer to this? Look with difficulty at Lords.'

'Sorry?' I say, still somewhat sidetracked by the wheel announcement.

'Peer!' says Richard, turning around, snapping his fingers and tugging one of his earphones away from his ear. 'Fucking peer,' he repeats. 'I knew if I thought about it for a second I'd get it. I'd have got it sooner had I not had to chat to bloody London. Of course, it's peer! How fucking thick of me.' He pauses. 'How are you, mate?' he asks me.

'Fine,' I say, sitting down in the jumpseat, taking in the rows of buttons, levers and screens glinting against the night sky.

'Roma, Roma, Roma,' comes a call down the radio.

'D'you want to take that, Ashley?' says Richard, picking up the crossword. 'I've spoken to them enough this evening.'

'Sure,' says Ashley, turning back to the controls. 'Roma, over?' he says, engaging Italian air traffic control.

'So, how's it going back there?' asks Richard, half talking to me, half doing the crossword, not at all flying the plane.

'Not too bad. Andy's on his third or fourth bottle of champagne . . .'

'Good lad.'

'Sue and Rachel are enjoying themselves . . .'

'Excellent.'

'And the boy band appear to have taken Ecstasy.'

'Right. I saw them coming in,' he says, looking up and indicating to the camera at the back of the flight deck from where he, the first officer and half the crew watch all the passengers board the plane, usually giving them marks out of ten. 'They looked like trouble. Loraine only gave them six. Was it six?' he asks Ashley. Ashley nods. 'But Belinda seems a bit more impressed. Are they being very leery?'

'Quite,' I say.

'Do you think I need to show my face?'

'No. I think Belinda has them under control.'

'Good.' He smiles. 'I can't believe you've got four down,' he says to Ashley. Ashley cocks an imaginary gun made from the first two fingers of his right hand. He shoots the windshield and then cools the barrel with a blow to his hand. 'Yeah, well,' says Richard. 'If I hadn't been on the blower to Swanwick I might have got it.'

'So what's this about someone losing a wheel?'

'It's not someone, it's us,' says Richard.

'Oh.'

'Yeah. Nothing we can do about it now.' He picks up his smoked salmon sandwich and takes a bite. 'Mmm, that's good.' He munches away. 'We'll have to wait until it gets light then I'll take a look outside the window to see if we can see which one it is. If not, we'll have to fly low over Dubai air traffic control to see if they can take a look at our undercarriage.'

'Right,' I say. 'It's not too bad?'

'If it's a side wheel, we're fine. If it's the front, we're fucked.'

'How likely is it that it's the front?' I smile, waiting for reassurance.

'One in three,' he says, looking down at the crossword. 'Jesus, Ashley,' he announces suddenly, 'have you just farted?'

The warm smell of wet egg and cheese and onion crisps engulfs the flight deck.

'Sorry, mate,' replies Ashley, taking his comms away from his mouth. 'I couldn't help myself.'

'Next time Loraine offers you some fucking egg sandwiches, you bloody say no,' says Richard. 'Honestly, it smells worse in here than travelling with old Dave Morris, and he used to smoke a bloody cigar all the way to Sydney. Or that other bloke James who still goes into the galley and smokes his Silk Cut, blowing the smoke down the plughole.'

Life inside the flight deck of a plane is a world unto itself. Sealed off from the outside world and only disturbed by the flight attendants every twenty minutes to see if they are in need of more food or refreshments, the captain and first officer can do more or less what they want. With autopilot able to land a plane in CAT 3 (thick fog with fifty feet visibility) and take off again at a moment's notice, the captain no longer has to fly the plane at all. This frees him up to read a newspaper, do a crossword, moan about his pay, terms and conditions, bitch about colleagues, eat, drink, fart, compare cars/houses/holidays/stereos/wives with his number two, whinge about getting up early, complain about the quality of the new flight attendants or, in the recent case of two pilots, strip off totally naked and have sex. To be fair, no-one actually saw them *in flagrante*, but they were discovered stark naked in the cockpit while supposedly flying the plane. Their excuse, before they were fired, was that one of them had spilt a drink. But other than sit there, calling in to various air traffic controls en route and listening out for alarm bells or for the American-voiced TCAAS (Traffic Collision Aviation Avoidance System) telling you to 'go down, go down', there is very little for the pilot actually to do.

I used to have a mate who flew short-haul flights for a budget airline who said that flying a plane was like driving a bus. They had ten destinations and the idea was to get the passengers there, get them out and get the next lot on as quickly as possible. He said they were the only airline to accelerate after they landed in order to get to their drop-off point as quickly as possible. He lived in London and commuted for sixteen hours a week to Stansted and back every day. The only place he did have a stopover of sorts was his Saturday-night flight to Ibiza and back, where he and the first officer had to sleep on the floor of the flight deck because there wasn't enough time to get to a hotel and back before the early-morning flight. He hated those Ibiza flights. He said that about ten minutes into the flight all the clubbers at the back would develop the 'Ibiza Cough'. They were so tired and dehydrated having come straight from the clubs, dressed in cropped tops and mini skirts and coming down off their drugs, that they couldn't cope with not smoking and the air-con. They'd cough their guts out all the way to Stansted. You can understand why after he made back the £80,000 he'd had to shell out to train himself (the airlines don't train pilots like they used to; instead, like many businesses these days, they rely on a fresh supply from

Eastern Europe) he sold up and bought a boat to sail around the world.

Long haul is slightly different. For a start there are a couple more officers on the flight deck. Known as second officers, they are there principally to rest while the captain takes off. They lie in the bunks behind the soundproof curtains eating, sleeping and reading until the captain and the first officer grow tired and want a lie down themselves. The second officers can fold maps and call in to air traffic controls, making sure that the airline has paid the 'navigation fee' for the plane to travel in that particular country's airspace, but as soon as an alarm bell rings the first thing they do is wake the captain.

As we are only flying to Dubai tonight the second-officer bunks are empty. Although these bunks have been used for purposes other than resting second officers before. I know of one of our captains who enjoyed a blow job from an over-enthusiastic hostie while the plane was taking off, only for a foursome to develop later on between the captain, the first officer and two hostesses. This *ménage à quatre* obviously made full use of the bunks provided.

Orgies and homosexual encounters notwithstanding, most of the time the captain and first officer are as bored as Richard and Ashley are now, and the only thing to inspire them is how much money they are earning. Cathay Pacific is supposedly the highest-paying airline, shelling out some £168K for a captain. We, on the other hand, pay our pilots £90K and our first officers £58K, but they make it up with flight pay which is another £10 an hour for every hour you are away from home. BA long haul are much better than that: on one trip to Cape Town you can add another £1.5K to your monthly salary. So you can begin to understand the appeal of long trips and time spent away from home.

But it's not all flatulence and quick fumbles with hosties. Pilots have to spend at least two days in a simulator every six months where every emergency under the sun is thrown at them, to help weed out those no longer capable of flying. They are also drug- and urine-tested as part of a six-monthly medical if they are over forty, and once a year if they're under. And they can be breathalysed on the flight deck, although plenty of pilots do fly with alcohol in their system, especially after a stopover where they have been drinking till five a.m. and have to fly at seven. A first officer mate of mine says that about 75 per cent of pilots fly with hangovers. But perhaps the most tricky thing of all for a pilot who sits on his arse, eats and talks all day is not putting on too much weight, because they also have to stay trim enough to make it through the small window in the cockpit. It has an escape rope curled above it that has to be scaled in emergencies. So there is such a thing as being too fat to fly. And judging by the gut that hangs over Richard's trousers as he tucks into his sandwich, he is heading that way.

'The stars are good tonight,' he says, his mouth full as he stares out of the window. 'There's no pollution up here. Apart from us, obviously.'

It's true. The stars through the heated windscreen do look

amazing, as if someone has sprayed a can of white paint across the sky.

'It's just a shame I know fuck all about them,' he adds, taking another bite.

'I had a St Elmo's Fire the other day,' says Ashley.

'Really?' I say. 'Is that when the windscreen changes colour?'

'That's right. The whole thing is lit up by static electricity. It went red, white and purple. Amazing.'

'I remember once we had a red football of electricity come through the windscreen and bounce around the cabin,' declares Richard. 'That was stunning.'

'That must be amazing,' I say, getting carried away. 'Have you ever seen a UFO?'

Richard looks at me like I'm a total moron. 'Fuck off,' he says, before taking another bite of his sandwich.

The intercom goes. 'We're thinking of having a party. Shall I get you some pickled herring?'

Ashley gets out of his seat to open the door.

'I'm bored of pickled herring,' says Richard. 'We've got to think of a better password.'

'Yeah,' Ashley agrees. 'And anyway, you've still got to say "Get your kit off" on the intercom before the end of the flight.'

'I know,' nods Richard. 'I'm working on that.'

Loraine walks into the cabin, carrying another tray. 'I've brought you some mineral water,' she says. 'Keep you nice and hydrated.'

'How many more times?' He sighs, leaning back into his chair and putting his feet up on the desk. 'We are not to have that stuff on flights any more. There are so many minerals in the water and when you're dehydrated like we are all the time it gives you kidney stones. American Airlines are supposed to be suing the company.'

'Sorry,' says Loraine, suitably chastened by Richard's tirade.

'Call yourself a flight attendant?' he says.

'What would you like, Captain?' she asks.

'Anything other than that shit.'

'Absolutely.'

'Everything else all right back there?'

'Fine.'

'The boy band?'

'Nothing we can't handle.'

'I'll put the heating up in a minute. That'll send everyone off.'

'Listen,' I say, 'I'm going for another drink, so I'll see you later?'

'Absolutely, mate,' sniffs Richard. 'The crew room in Dubai, it's a date.'

'Great.'

'Oh, one thing,' he says as I stand up to leave. 'Not a word about the lost wheel.'

'Oh, right.'

'I'll call Gareth in for a NITS briefing later on. No need to worry anyone for the moment.'

A NITS briefing usually follows six chimes, and it means there is an emergency. The number one gets called to the intercom and the captain discusses the Nature of the emergency, Intentions, Timings and Special instructions. The number one then has to repeat it all back to the captain just in case he or she is hysterical. If after the six bells and the NITS briefing all avenues have been covered and all else fails, the plane will issue a mayday call, which comes from the French *m'aidez* (help me). Although, this really is a last resort. Let's hope our missing wheel doesn't lead to that, I think, as I walk past the buzzing boy band on my way back to club.

11 PM – 12 AM

Back in club, the lights are low and the atmosphere is relatively quiet – all except the front row that is. Andy has moved into my seat and is drinking shots of vodka with Sue and Rachel. He turns around as I come through the curtain. His face is beginning to look slightly red and shiny beneath his orange tan.

'There you are!' he declares, as if I have been away for hours. 'Tell me,' he says, crossing one leg over the other, 'how are Fun Five?' He is slurring his words a little and his movements have become exaggerated. That old adage of one in the air equalling three on the ground is clearly taking its toll.

'Um,' I say, debating whether to tell him about their flying drug-assisted, 'they seem to be a little quiet.' The last thing Belinda needs is a drunk and flirtatious Andy trying to work it in first. She doesn't need the competition.

'Oh,' he says, sounding a bit disappointed. 'I knew they were lightweights.'

'Yes,' I say, sitting down in his seat. 'Did you get me a drink?'

'Here.' He shifts slightly in his seat to reveal a collection of some ten miniatures and a pack of small tonic tins. 'All sorted.' He grins. 'The only thing I don't have is ice.'

'Impressive,' I observe.

'We were just discussing the time when you scored Rachel on the staff bus,' he announces.

'Oh good,' I say, emptying the warm vodka miniature into my glass.

'Yeah,' continues Andy, oblivious to my growing discomfort, 'and Rachel was just telling us that you kissed like a lizard.' Rachel and Andy burst out laughing, Sue looks at the table in front of her, and I drain my drink in one. 'Apparently you are one of those sticking-it-in-and-out type of kissers.' He sticks his own tongue out and narrows it into a stiff probe, just to make his point.

'It was a long time ago,' I say, looking down, picking fluff off my trousers.

I can feel my ears growing red, and the embarrassment in Sue's eyes. This is not quite how I'd hoped the evening might pan out. I was supposed to be witty, charming and amusing, the sort of bloke a glamorous flight attendant might look twice at. But the idea that Sue feels anything for me other than pity is clearly careering out of the window.

'People change,' she says suddenly.

'What?' asks Andy, cracking open a tonic.

'People change,' Sue repeats, rather bravely. I look up and catch her eye. 'I used to be a terrible kisser. I once put my tongue up someone's nose.'

284

'But you were probably twelve,' declares Andy, 'not nearly forty.'

'It wasn't that long ago,' she mutters, taking a sip of champagne. We all know she is lying.

We sit in silence for a second. Andy pours himself another drink and opens a bag of pretzels, shoving a small fistful into his mouth. He turns towards me and, with a rather puzzled expression on his face, sniffs.

'Can you smell something?' he asks.

I nod. I didn't want to say anything before just in case it was him, but there really is quite a stench back here and it appears to be getting worse.

'I think it's coming from over there,' he continues, pointing at the fat bloke to my right.

'I agree,' I say. 'It smells like the toilets, doesn't it?'

'Yeah. It smells like shit.'

'It's not Tom's laxative man, is it?' asks Sue from the other side. 'Sometimes the smell of the toilets can come up this way.'

'No.' Andy shakes his head. 'It's him.'

'Do you think it will pass?' I ask, leaning back. The smell is beginning to get slightly overpowering.

'Not in my experience,' says Andy. 'Smells like this only tend to get worse.'

'I think we'd better do something about it before it takes over the whole cabin,' I say, getting out of my seat and walking towards the galley.

The place is empty. They must all be in economy. I turn and walk past the sleeping fat bloke and the turd smell is now very strong. My eyes water slightly and it's all I can do to stop myself retching. I walk towards the back of the plane and poke my head into the galley. There are about six flight attendants sitting in there. Some are squatting on silver food boxes, others are perched on the jumpseats and two are sitting on plastic bags on the floor. They are eating their supper. Some are polishing off what looks like the remains of the lamb curry, others are eating homemade-looking sandwiches and a couple are sharing a bag of crisps.

'Um, hi,' I say.

They all turn and look at me. I have clearly interrupted something.

'Can I help you?' asks Tom, who has a drink in one hand and the remains of a sandwich in the other.

'Um,' I say again, 'there's a bit of a stench in club and we think it's coming from the fat bloke sitting next to Andy at the front.'

'What do you want us to do about it?' asks a young blonde sitting on the floor. Her mouth hangs open at the end of the sentence, attitude seeping from every pore.

'What's your name?' I ask.

'What's it to you?' she replies, her head cocking to one side as she stares at me.

I recognize her as the girl who had marmalade on her face and who blew a tampon during the earlier safety display at the front of club. I'm not usually one to pull rank, but . . .

'I'm duty airport manager for the airline, so it's quite a lot to do with me.'

It's like someone has kicked one of Richard's red electric footballs into the area. Everyone suddenly sits up, puts down their drinks and metaphorically stubs out their fags. Sir's arrived, and he means business.

'Oh, right,' she says, pulling her skirt down towards her knees. 'I'm Angela and I'm new.'

'OK, Angela.' I smile. 'Has anyone got the PIL so that we can check to see if there is anything we need to know about him?'

'I'll do it,' says Tom, getting off his silver box and putting down what looks like a vodka-ed orange juice.

He pulls out the passenger information list from behind a tin container full of foil-covered dishes of half-cooked breakfasts and hands it over to me. Looking down the list I can see who has paid full price for their ticket, who is a gold-card upgrade and who has requested special meals, special assistance or special status for whatever reason. Even groups are marked as together. There seems to be a convention of doctors on board today. I run my finger down the list, looking for the seat next to Andy, 14E. I find him. His name is Graham Nutall and according to the list he has a kidney problem and a colostomy bag.

'He's got a colostomy bag,' I announce to the group.

'Jesus Christ,' declares Tom, helpfully holding his nose to illustrate his distaste. 'That sounds disgusting.'

'Yes, well, he clearly needs to be woken up and told that it needs emptying.' I look around the galley foolishly searching for volunteers. Everyone looks at the floor or suddenly becomes interested in their fingernails. 'Anyone?' I ask.

'I'll do it,' announces Edith, who appears to have been standing behind me throughout.

'Will you?' I ask, turning round.

'Yeah,' she says, looking so not bothered. Her eyes are half asleep, the expression on her face is mute. 'I don't see what the problem is.'

'Well, thank you. It is beginning to be a bit unpleasant up the front.'

'I can't smell anything,' she says as she turns to leave. 'But then I'm not feeling much these days.'

'Is she all right?' I ask Tom after she has gone.

'It's the abortion,' he says in front of the whole crew. No-one bats an eyelid. There are clearly no secrets here. 'She hasn't been the same since.'

'I think it's knocked her sideways,' agrees Angela from the floor. 'Not that I knew her before, but it's what everyone tells me. You know, by all accounts she used to be a right old laugh. Not any more. Mind you, if I was forced to have a termination in Thailand by the company I think I might go a bit crackers. Think how filthy the place must have been.' She pulls a face. 'It doesn't bear thinking about.'

There's a general murmur of agreement from the rest of the crew.

'Gillian went a bit odd after hers,' declares a brunette I haven't seen before.

'Did she?' says someone else.

'Oh yeah.'

'Which one's Gillian?' asks a blonde.

'You know, small, red hair, worked with us on the last Singapore run.'

'Oh, right, her. Who got her in trouble, so to speak?'

'Who's in trouble?' asks Edith as she comes back into the galley.

'No-one,' say Tom, Angela, the brunette and the blonde all at once. They could not look more guilty.

Fortunately, Edith is too off the ball to notice, or perhaps care. 'Oh,' she says. 'Well, Mr Nutall is refusing to change or empty his colostomy bag.'

'What?' asks Tom.

'Yup. And short of dragging him to the toilet myself and pulling his trousers down, there is very little I can do.'

'What do you mean, he's refusing?' asks Tom again.

'He said no,' says Edith.

'Can't he smell himself?' asks the brunette.

'Apparently not,' says Edith.

'That's disgusting,' says Tom.

'It's actually against flight regs, isn't it?' asks Angela. 'We stop people from flying if they smell, so . . .'

'In case you hadn't noticed,' says Tom, 'we're in the air already.'

'I know that,' she replies. 'But you know . . .'

'Are you suggesting that we put down to get the smelly bastard off the plane?'

'Well . . .' She looks embarrassed.

'Do we have any air fresheners?' I ask.

'Nothing that strong,' says Tom.

Everyone in the galley sits and thinks for a second.

'I know,' says the brunette, 'what about Poison?'

'What?' asks Tom. 'Poison him?'

'No, Poison the perfume,' she says. 'Christian Dior. It's the strongest-smelling stuff I know and we've got some on the duty-free trolley.

'Brilliant,' says Tom. 'Give it here. I'll go and spray the whole cabin and see how he likes that.'

The brunette rattles around in the duty-free tray and pulls out a dark green box. She opens it, hands over the purple bottle of perfume to Tom, and he sets off into club. Just as everyone is about to congratulate themselves on a job well done and a situation sorted, the amber toilet bell starts to turn on and off in an increasingly rhythmical fashion. The whole of the galley grinds to a halt and we all stare at the flashing light.

'Oh God,' says someone. Angela rolls her eyes. Edith sighs. 'Someone's in the toilets having sex.'

There isn't really any aviation policy on what to do when passengers are having sex in the toilet. Most of the time we choose to ignore them. It's a poky, filthy place, and if someone wants to have sex in such a tiny space they are clearly not going to stick around in there for long. So the flight attendants tend to hold off and hope for a swift one. But sometimes, if a queue's built up or a couple are being particularly loud, they have to interfere.

And you'd be amazed how often it happens. Passengers get a bit giddy, drink too much alcohol, think they're on holiday and then suddenly desire takes hold of them. It does make it slightly more palatable if they are actually a couple, but it's surprising how many aren't. My friend Shelly told me once about a whole load of travel agents leaving a conference in Frankfurt. She said there was this very large lady sitting in the second row of business next to her rather smaller husband. She got up and went into one of the toilets, and then Shelly noticed a man in the row in front get up and go into the same toilet. She thought she must have made a mistake, so she went and got a pen, tweaked the lock to one side and peeped through, as attendants do if they think someone might have passed out or just be locked in there, and saw them banging away. The woman was apparently so large, Shelly was astounded they were managing it at all. Anyway, five minutes later the large woman returned to her seat and sat down next to her husband who was still fast asleep, catching flies and obviously none the wiser.

But it's not just drunk or randy passengers who shag perfect strangers; off-duty cabin crew do the same. Shelly told me a story about a Qantas flight she was working a few years ago when she was asked to look after a passenger who'd fainted. She had to get his feet into the air to get the blood running back into his head, so she sent a hostie upstairs to the crew rest quarters to get some extra pillows. (On some long-haul flights the crew have bunks where they can rest in a container-size unit that has eight beds. It is usually situated up some stairs at the back of the plane.) The girl returned with only one pillow; she would have got more but for the couple having sex in the bunks. Shelly went upstairs to find a couple really going for it. She recognized the woman as an off-duty attendant from another airline who was travelling on a concession ticket. The man, however, was not the boyfriend she was travelling with but the stranger she was sat next to at the back of the plane. Shelly says that she brought the couple down and put them back in their seats. She says she told the woman, 'I should report you for this. I should also have your free travel rights revoked. But I think the fact that we are discussing this in front of your boyfriend is enough, don't you think?'

At least you could argue they got a room. Some passengers don't even bother to do that, particularly in first class. Kylie Minogue once famously got rather fruity with Michael Hutchence in the confines of first, and I know of one actor who woke up in the second row of the plane to find his producer's mouth latched onto the end of his cock. And it's not just the famous. Passengers are always fiddling and fondling each other underneath the blankets, thinking that if they are quiet enough they can get away with it. But no-one is fooled. There's a particularly gruesome tale of a fifty-year-old woman who drank so much that she was pawing every businessman in sight. An hour into the flight she was discovered with her tits out and a bloke on each nipple. She only brought herself under control when she was told she would be arrested at the other end. Blokes on their own can be just as bad, wanking away to Demi Moore in *Striptease* like their lives depended on it. I'm sure it's the combination of alcohol, lack of oxygen and boredom that makes some people so horny.

Our toilet lovers have been at it for ten minutes now and the chiming bell shows no signs of abating. A small queue is beginning to develop outside. Its most insistent member appears to be the surly, shouting businessman whose meal Tom laced with Dulcolax. It's obviously working because I have rarely seen a man more desperate. He is pacing up and down outside the door, occasionally pausing for breath as he appears to ride some form of contraction. His face is white and damp with sweat, and every now and then he hammers on the toilet door, urging them to get a move on.

'Does anyone know who the couple are?' asks Gareth, who has been called to the economy galley to deal with the situation.

'No,' says Tom, fresh from spraying club class with Poison, 'but I have a feeling it's that young couple near the front who were tucking into the brandy.'

'I think it's gone on long enough,' sighs Gareth, with the jaded air of someone who was last laid in the seventies. 'How long can a couple keep going for?'

'Well . . .' says Tom, who is sporting his recent handcuff marks with pride.

'Oh shut up,' says Gareth, leaving the galley and heading for the occupied toilet.

We all watch as he goes to the front of the queue and raps on the door.

'Excuse me,' he says, loudly. 'Could you hurry up in there? There are quite a few people waiting for the toilet.'

'Yes, we're desperate,' urges the surly laxative man, hunching forward.

Back in the galley, the amber light pauses for a second, as if trying to make up its mind what to do. But the silence is short-lived. The rhythm starts up again. But this time it's quicker, slicker and has more purpose.

'Jesus!' says Tom, whistling slightly through the back of his teeth. 'I want what he's on.'

At the toilet door, Gareth is undeterred. The laxative man is increasingly desperate.

'Excuse me!' Gareth raps harder this time. 'It's the cabin service director here. Will you stop what you are doing, vacate the toilet and let some other people use it, please!' What little sense of humour he has left is rapidly disappearing.

'Yes please,' adds the former nutter, rather weakly.

This time there is no pause to the quick-fire amber rhythm. If anything, it sounds all the more determined.

'Right,' announces Gareth with a determined clap, 'that's it.' He walks up to the intercom system. The plane's Tannoy springs to life. 'Ladies and gentlemen,' he says, 'I am terribly sorry to disturb you this late into your flight. But as some of you who are queuing here at the front for the toilet might be aware, the front right-hand toilet has been occupied for some time. This is not some sort of emergency, only a rather selfish couple having sex. They have been at it for some time now. I have asked them to leave the toilet but to no avail. So when they do eventually come out of the toilet, I would like the whole of the plane, if you can, to give them a round of applause. Thank you.'

The announcement plays out in the toilet too. The amber light stops. The whole galley stares, waiting for it to start up again.

Tom giggles. 'That's poured water on his ardour.' The light flashes again. 'Oh no, here we go . . .'

'No,' says Angela, 'I think that's just them moving around.'

We all stand and wait to see what the lovers are going to do next.

Gareth raps on the door again. 'Come on now,' he says. 'The show really is over.'

Then, slowly but surely, the toilet door is opened. The first to show, after much shoving and whispering, is the bloke. His red face and ravaged neck poke through the door.

'Um, hello,' he says to Gareth, sounding rather sheepish. 'Sorry about that.'

The girl follows swiftly behind. Her cheeks are flushed, her white blouse is unbuttoned and her suede skirt is covered in some unpleasant-looking stains. She says nothing; instead she tugs at her hair, looks at the floor and hunches her shoulders in embarrassment.

'Ladies and gentlemen,' says Gareth, 'I give you the toilet lovers!' He raises his hand in the air like some circus ring-master. A ripple of applause drifts down the plane. Someone wolf whistles.

'I hope they knew each other before they joined the toilet queue,' says Tom.

'Of course they did,' says Angela.

'Not necessarily,' says Tom. 'I had a couple just the other day who met in the queue, fucked, and went back to their seats ten minutes later. I don't think they even knew each other's names. She went into the toilet and he just followed her in.'

'Really?' says Angela.

'Yup. When you've been flying as long as I have, honey, nothing surprises you any more.'

The toilet couple walk back to their seats, which are fortunately together, and the lavatory is reopened. The laxative man is the first in. He is in no position to let the smell of sex and other people's bodily fluids bother him. He lets out a loud sigh almost as soon as he closes the door. Tom smiles; a couple of the other hosties giggle. The shared joke has gone down well. But they all quickly fall silent as soon as Gareth walks back onto the galley.

'Thank God that's over,' he says, leaning back against a trolley. 'I have no idea why anyone would want to shag in those toilets.' He shivers. 'They are so disgustingly filthy, especially after that man's emptied his bowels in there.' Gareth's been in the business long enough that nothing gets by him.

Just as I am thinking about wandering back to club to have another drink with Andy and brave the eau de Poison and colostomy that fills the air, the hugely fat man next to whom I had deliberately placed the laxative nutter man keels over in the toilet queue.

'Oh shit,' I say.

'Oh shit,' echoes Gareth, stepping away from the trolley. 'Here we fucking go.'

12-1 AM

All hell suddenly breaks loose. Gareth ushers the toilet queue to a facility up at the other end of the plane. Tom squats over the body and starts thumping the heart with his clasped hands, trying to administer mouth-to-mouth. Angela looks for the resuscitation machine. I call through to the captain to tell him what's going on. And Edith just stands there, arms stiffly by her sides, staring rather catatonically ahead, unable to do anything.

Richard seems quite unfazed when he hears of the drama. His first question is do I think the man will die. I'm afraid, I say, that due to my lack of medical training I'm not prepared to make that call. He is undeterred. He tells me to contact him if the situation deteriorates. I say I don't think it can get much worse. And then he tells me that whatever happens we are not going to land the plane. We have no landing light. We have no option but to carry on to Dubai. We will have to treat the fat bloke on the plane. He suggests I page a doctor. I pick up the Tannoy.

'Excuse me, ladies and gentlemen,' I say, trying to sound calm. 'We have a small situation at the front of the plane and we are looking for a doctor. If there is a doctor on board could they make themselves known to one of the cabin crew.'

I stand in the aisle, scanning economy, looking left and then right, searching for a raised hand. There's nothing. I return to the Tannoy.

'Sorry to bother you, ladies and gentlemen, but if there is a doctor on board, could they make themselves known to a member of the cabin crew.'

I look down the plane again. Out of the corner of my eye I can see the fat man flailing around and fitting on the floor. His face is turning blue. Tom looks panicked. Angela is fumbling with the resuscitation machine, unravelling the panels and the wires. Her unpractised hands are shaking. And still no-one in the body of the plane puts up a hand.

'Right,' I bark down the Tannoy. 'We have a suspected heart attack here. I know there's a group of doctors on the plane, headed for some sort of convention in Dubai. Will one of you bastards make yourselves known to a member of the cabin crew *now*!'

I put the Tannoy down and look up. Five hands are slowly raised. I march down the aisle and grab the nearest by the arm, practically dragging the bloke out of his seat towards the front of the plane.

'We're all ear, nose and throat,' mutters the doctor as he trots along behind me. 'Cardiac stuff is not our forte.'

'You know more than we do,' I say.

'Um, and I've had a few drinks,' he declares.

'Haven't we all,' I say, giving him a shove towards the body.

'Right,' says the doctor, standing above the body, rubbing his hands together, 'what seems to be the problem?'

Tom and Angela look up, their flustered pink faces exuding terror and confusion.

'Um,' says Tom, an electrical panel in each hand, 'the heart.'

'Good . . . right,' says the doctor, tweaking the legs of his suit trousers as he makes to squat down.

'Yeah,' agrees Angela. 'According to the first-aid course I did the other week he is displaying all the signs of a heart attack. The blue lips, the convulsions . . .'

'Good . . . right,' says the doctor, looking down at the man who is now just lying there, flat on his back with his mouth open, looking very blue and very dead.

The doctor leans in to check his pulse. Blood starts to ooze from the man's nose, ears and eyes.

'Oh dear,' says the doctor, releasing the man's hand, 'that doesn't look awfully good, does it? The heart has definitely stopped. I think we should use those panels right away. Are they charged?'

'They seem to be,' says Angela, looking at the machine.

'OK then. Stand back everyone.'

We all flatten ourselves against the wall as the doctor places the panels either side of the man's heart. There's a high-pitched squeal as the machine lurches into action.

'And, shock!' The fat man's body arches a millimetre off the floor. 'These things aren't terribly strong, are they? We need a bit more power. Can you turn them up?'

'Um, I think so,' says Angela, fiddling with a few buttons.

'Oh shit,' I say, looking down the plane. 'We seem to have an audience.'

There is a sea of faces staring up the plane. Rows of eyes and open mouths are all pointing in our direction.

'Jesus Christ,' mutters Gareth. 'Someone get a blanket.'

I walk straight through into club and find the comfort princess fast asleep on my right. Wearing an eye mask and ear plugs, and swaddled in a pashmina, she is covered in three blankets. I pull two off, muttering something about emergencies, and come straight back into economy. I stand between the body and the crowd and, in order to block their view, hold out the blankets like a matador waiting for a charging bull. I can hear the drama unfolding behind me. The doctor keeps asking for more power, Angela keeps turning up the machine, and still the man just lies there. After about another seven minutes of shocking with no result, the doctor decides to call it a day.

'I think that's it,' he says. 'I really do. I honestly don't think there is anything else we can do.'

'Right,' I hear Gareth saying.

'Do you want me to call time of death?'

'No, no, don't worry about that,' says Gareth, 'we'll sort all that out. Thank you for your help. Could you just return to your seat and not tell anyone what has happened. We can take it from here.'

'Oh, OK,' says the doctor, sounding uncertain. 'If you're sure . . .'

'We're sure,' says Gareth. 'We're quite used to this. There's a certain procedure to be followed.'

'Oh, OK,' says the doctor again, edging backwards towards me and the blanket.

'If you just slip through here,' I say, trying to shield the view of the corpse. 'Please don't tell anyone the full story.' I smile. 'We don't want panic to spread through the plane.'

'Oh Lord, no,' says the doctor. 'Absolutely.'

'Would you like a drink?' I suggest.

'Oh,' he replies, a little disorientated and confused. 'Um, a whisky would be nice.'

'Shall I make it a double?'

'Um, yes, right, that would be lovely.'

'I'll send a stewardess up with one right away.'

Edith seems relieved to be given an order, something to do that does not actually involve the corpse. She sets about getting the doctor his double whisky with a deliberate efficiency. Meanwhile, Gareth, Angela, Tom and I stand and stare at the dead fat bloke and wonder what to do. My arms are beginning to ache; holding the blankets across the aisle is becoming hard work.

'It's the first time I've seen a dead person,' says Angela, looking down. Her voice is quiet and her attitude distinctly muted.

'Plenty more where that came from, darling,' says Tom, pretending to be an old hand.

'What the fuck are we going to do with him?' sighs Gareth, absolutely an old hand. 'We can barely move him. He weighs

301

about thirty stone. He had to have a specially extended seat belt to fly in the first place. We could drag him up the aisle and put him back in his seat, but he's next to the psycho whose food you laced with laxative.'

'How do you know that?' asks Tom.

'Oh pur-lease,' says Gareth. 'D'you think I came down in the last fucking shower? I was poncing up and down the aisles of planes before you were born.' He rolls his eyes. 'There isn't a trick I haven't seen, or a scam I haven't pulled. You, my friend, are amateur hour.'

'Oh,' says Tom.

'Oh,' mimics Gareth.

We all look back down at the body. The man is dressed in a grey T-shirt and navy blue jogging pants, white trainers and grey zip-up top with 'fuck' misspelt across the front. For some reason, standing there, looking at him, still holding the blankets, I don't feel the same sort of sadness that I did for Mr Fletcher earlier this morning. Perhaps it's because there is no weeping wife with whom to empathize. Or maybe because it happened so quickly and in such a surreal place, just outside the toilet. But I have to admit I feel nothing. He is simply a big fat dead bloke who is causing us problems.

'Does anyone know if he is flying with anyone?' asks Gareth.

'No,' I say, numbly. 'I checked him in and he is on his own.'

'Right.' Gareth nods, his brain ticking over, trying to come up with a solution.

'What are we going to do with him?' asks Angela, stating the obvious.

'Shush,' says Gareth.

'What about first?' asks Tom. 'Are there some spare seats up there?'

'Yes,' says Gareth, pulling his bottom lip as he thinks. 'We could try and drag him there.'

'What, all the way through club?' I say.

'No, you're right. There's no way we could squeeze him through there.'

'I meant the other passengers,' I say.

'Ye-e-s,' says Gareth, staring at the body. 'Fuck it!' he declares suddenly.

'What?' I say.

'We'll put him here, in the galley.'

'Where?' asks Angela, sounding horrified.

'On the floor,' says Gareth.

'But we've got breakfast to get out.'

'Well, you'll just have to step over him, won't you?'

'That's disgusting.'

'That's the only solution.'

'Can't we put him somewhere else?' Angela is becoming somewhat hysterical at the idea of having to spend the rest of the flight sitting, working and eating next to a corpse.

'Angela,' says Gareth, rather slowly, 'there is nowhere else to put him, do you understand? The man is too fat to move. Short of picking him up by the legs and dragging him through club class on his arse, there is nothing else we can do. D'you get it?'

'Yes,' she whispers.

'OK then. On the count of three. Tom, you take the arms. Angela, you take a leg, I'll take the other leg and we'll drag him into the galley. You,' he says to me, 'keep going with the blanket thing so no-one can see this fiasco.'

'OK,' I say.

'Ready? One . . . two . . . three!'

They all take hold of a limb and with great difficulty drag the corpse across the corridor into the galley. I follow, shielding the body from view.

'Keep going, keep going . . . just a bit further. To me . . . to me . . . to me . . . And here . . . we . . . go!'

Tom, Angela and Gareth drop the body on the floor of the galley and all the other flight attendants look on in horror as they realize the full extent of the situation.

'Right, that will do,' says Gareth, exhaling with exhaustion, his hands clasping the small of his back. 'There's no way we could have dragged him any further.'

'No,' agrees Tom, wiping his forehead with the back of his hand. 'He's one heavy mother.'

'He's not staying there, is he?' asks a flight attendant.

'Certainly is,' confirms Gareth. 'You'll all just have to work around him. I'm off to tell the captain what has happened. Oh, by the way,' he adds with a wave of his hand as he leaves the galley, 'you'd better wrap the corpse in some bin-liners otherwise he'll only shit all over the floor.'

Angela spins round to face the sink and pukes all over her new uniform. It'll be a miracle, I think as I make my way back into club, if that girl ever flies again.

Back in club and the Poison perfume seems to have done the trick. The colostomy stench is not too overpowering. Or maybe I'm just so tired and worn out by my day that my senses are beginning to shut down. I am so goddamn numb that a man dying of a heart attack in front of me doesn't affect me any more. I slump back down in my seat. Andy has crawled back into his own chair and is fast asleep. His lips are slightly parted and he is still clutching a drink in his right hand.

'Are you OK?' comes a voice.

I look to my left and see that Sue is still awake.

'Fine,' I say. 'You?'

'I can't sleep. Rachel's passed out, but my body clock is all over the shop. That's what comes of flying all the time, I suppose.' She shrugs.

'Haven't you taken something?'

'I try not to. I don't think it's very good for you to be on pills all the time. All the girls are always on stuff. Uppers, downers, vicodin, temazepan, co-proxamol. It's a wonder none of us rattles when we get off the plane.' She smiles. 'Was it all OK back there?'

'Not really.'

'I heard the call for a doctor, so I presumed it wasn't good.'

'Heart attack.'

'Dead?'

'Yup.'

'D'you want a drink?'

'I wouldn't mind.'

'Here,' she says, handing over a vodka miniature, 'have one from Andy's collection. He doesn't look like he'll be needing it for a while.'

'No.' I look over at him and smile. 'He needs all the rest he can. He'll only get all over-excited again when he lands.'

'So, was he old? The man who died?'

'No, not really,' I reply, taking a sip of neat vodka. It burns the back of my throat as it goes down. My body shivers involuntarily. I'm really not feeling that good. 'He was quite fat.'

'Oh,' she nods. 'One of those. Was it quick?'

'Not terribly,' I say. 'And all this blood came out of his nose and mouth and ears.'

'Yuck.' She frowns. 'I've seen that before.'

'They've put him in the galley.'

'Really? That's happened to me before. It's a nightmare,' she adds. 'And they haven't done breakfast yet, have they?'

'No, I know. They don't seem very pleased.'

'That's awful. Those poor girls. I hate it when there are corpses on the plane. I remember doing a Middle East flight once when the whole of the back three rows of the plane were taken up with bodies, all wrapped in white sheets. It was terrifying. Their stiff toes were poking out.' She pulls a face. 'They were all members of some royal family or other – you know how many of those there are over there. And they refused to let them be put in coffins in the hold. I'll never forget it. It still haunts me.'

'Well, I have to say that this bloke might well stay with me for a bit,' I say, taking another sip of vodka.

I'm not sure if I'm lying. I'm not sure how I am going to react. But at this precise moment Sue is actually talking to me as if I am some sort of friend, so I would do well to sympathize.

'At least you haven't put him in the rubbish,' she says.

'What?'

'Well, when I flew seven-six-sevens, there's a place at the back where we used to store the rubbish and any dead body that came our way during the flights. It's terrible if you think about it too much. But what else are you supposed to do when you have a full flight and a corpse to deal with?' She makes it sound so reasonable, so practical, and so necessary.

'Exactly.' I nod. 'My point exactly.'

'Although,' she adds, leaning forward, her soft round face looking momentarily sad, 'there are some things that are truly shocking.'

'Oh yes?'

'I remember when I did the Abu Dhabi–Colombo run we used to find some awful things. Once, when we'd touched down in Sri Lanka, the cleaners noticed this trail of blood on the floor that went from one of the seats to the toilet. They opened the toilet door and saw more blood on the floor, then when they opened the litter chute they found a baby.' She winces. 'It wasn't making any noise or anything, it was tiny and naked, but it was still alive. The mother had apparently given birth in the toilet during the flight and bitten the umbilical cord with her teeth. She'd been raped by her boss in Abu Dhabi and didn't want to bring shame or disgrace on her family. We looked through the passenger list, found out who it was, and traced her back to her family just outside Colombo. The airline then delivered the baby back to the mother.'

'What happened then?'

'They offered all the flight attendants counselling.'

'No, I meant what happened to the mother and the baby?'

'Oh.' She shrugs. 'I've no idea.'

'Oh, right,' I say.

'But it used to happen quite a lot on those flights, because so many Sri Lankans work in the Middle East as servants. We'd get lots of pregnant girls crying on the flight, all the way to Colombo. Most of them had been attacked by their bosses. But I only saw one baby delivered in the toilet and thrown away.'

'Awful,' I say. 'How long ago was that?'

'About eight years ago now. But those were the days.' She smiles suddenly. 'Loads of rich sheikhs on the flights buying you Cartier watches and Boucheron jewellery. You had to be careful, though,' she continues. 'Abu Dhabi and Dubai are quite small places; you could get a reputation quite quickly. It wasn't always advisable to accept all their presents.'

'I didn't know you lived in the Middle East.'

'I didn't do it for very long,' she replies. 'There was one girl who worked with me who really knew how to work it. She dripped in gold and used to be collected straight off the plane on the tarmac by an air-conditioned limo. There was always some sort of fur waiting for her on the back seat. I wonder where she is now.' She smiles. 'What a strange place . . .' She looks perturbed. 'I can't believe I'm going back there. It'll be the first time since I left.'

I lean across the aisle and take her hand in mine. She doesn't withdraw it. I run my thumb gently across her soft skin.

'I am very glad you decided to come,' I say.

My mouth is smiling and my heart is pounding. I am touching her. I can't believe it. And she didn't recoil at the idea. Could Sue possibly feel the same way about me as I do about her? I feel a sudden rush of joy and adrenalin.

308

'Oh, I say!' comes the jaded nasal voice of Gareth. He is standing in the aisle looking down at our clasped hands. 'If I can tear you away,' he says, sarcastically.

I pull my hand back onto my lap.

'What?' I ask sharply.

'No need to be like that,' he says, pretending to be offended. 'I've got a problem at the back of the plane and I need your help.'

'Mine?' I ask. 'Why?'

'You're management. Craig's had a go, Tom's had a go, and I've been back and forth twice. I could go and get the captain, but seeing as we've already had the first officer through this evening, and what with the corpse and all that, I'd rather not. I don't want him to think I can't control the plane.'

'What is it?' I ask.

'Well, there are a couple of queens going for it on the back row of the plane and no matter how hard we complain or the people around them ask them to stop, they carry on,' he explains.

'What are they doing?'

'Blow jobs and . . . you know . . . the rest,' he says, his top lip curling in disgust. Or is it envy? I'm not quite sure.

'Do you really need me?' I ask. 'It's not the sort of thing I usually do.'

'I know,' says Gareth, 'but I'm sure you'd do it better than anyone else.'

Sue leans in. 'I could have a go if you want?'

'No, love,' says Gareth, patting the back of her hand, where my thumb has just been. 'You're off duty.'

'I don't mind,' she says.

'Don't worry,' I say, easing myself out of my seat. 'I'll go.'

I walk through rows and rows of sleeping passengers, all laid out as if they're at a contortionists' convention. Some are curled up in their seats, others have their feet in the air, propped up on the side of the plane. Some appear to have broken their necks, while others are folded up all over their next-door neighbours. Not one of them looks comfortable.

Towards the back of the plane, however, there are a few people who are not asleep. Rigid with irritation, they have their reading lights on as they sigh and whip their way through magazines. The scene in the back row to the left of the plane explains their annoyance. Three blokes are sitting in a line, half covered in a blanket, and even as I walk towards them I can tell they are up to no good. One appears to be bouncing up and down on another, while the third is moving both his hands briskly under a blanket. They are all obviously drunk. There is a collection of empty miniature bottles rattling around on the floor underneath them. They are either oblivious of my approach or don't seem to care.

'Excuse me.' I cough.

The one jigging up and down stops and the blanket wanker grinds to a halt. They all stare at me.

'Yes?' giggles the jigger.

'If you don't stop what you are doing right away,' I whisper, 'we will put the plane down and have you arrested in which-ever country we are flying over at the moment.' All three of them snigger. 'Which by my calculations right now would be Saudi Arabia.' I have no idea exactly where we are, but Saudi is the most frighteningly exotic country I can think of. They all continue to smile at me. 'Where they cut hands off for theft, stone people for adultery and, if I remember rightly, homosexuality is illegal.' That got their attention. The smirks slowly shrink off their faces – as I should imagine, does the rest of their anatomy. 'Think about it, because any more fun and games from you lot and that's where you're headed.'

As I turn to walk back up the other end of the plane, feeling slightly pleased with myself, I see Craig careering towards me.

'You shouldn't have any more problems with that lot,' I say, indicating over my shoulder with my thumb.

'Thanks, that's great,' he says, sounding flustered. 'We were at the end of our tether.'

'I just gave them a quick lesson in sharia law.' I smile.

'Great.' He's not really listening, just ushering me ahead of him. 'We need you up here. You won't believe what has just happened in first.'

1-2 AM

There seems to be quite a commotion going on in the galley back in club. I can hear raised voices that are trying to talk quietly. All hisses and spits, they sound like a pit of spatting snakes. Sue looks at me anxiously as I arrive. Andy is awake, sitting bolt upright and grinning from ear to ear. Even the colostomy man looks as if he has been stirred from his brandy-induced slumber.

'What's going on?' I ask Craig when he finally slows down long enough for me to talk to him.

'It's Belinda,' he says, trying to look shocked.

'Yes?'

'Well . . .' He pauses dramatically. 'Loraine's just caught her sitting on the face of one of the Fun Five boys.'

'What?' I say, so stunned by the information that it doesn't actually register. 'She was doing what?'

'She was sitting on the face of the lead singer of Fun Five,' he says, more slowly, adding more detail, just so that I can get the whole picture. 'Her skirt was hitched up around her waist, her thighs were either side of his head, and he was—'

'Yes, thank you,' I say, putting my hand out in front of me. 'I get it.'

'Isn't it fabulous!' declares Andy, practically clapping his hands in delight. 'I don't know how she thought she would get away with it!'

'Well, no,' I say, shaking my head. 'Quite extraordinary.'

'I heard some Qantas girl did the same thing all the way from Singapore to Sydney,' announces Rachel, who has also been woken up by the incident. 'I'm amazed a girl can keep her legs open that long.' She shrugs.

'Anyway,' I say, 'what has all this got to do with me?'

'Well,' says Craig, 'she's claiming that they slipped something into her drink and that you saw it happen as you came through the cabin a while back.'

'Oh?'

'Yeah. She says that you saw the boys and her interact and that they were overly friendly and that she was not, and that the only reason she did what she did was because she was drugged.'

'Oh,' I say again. 'Well, that's not really exactly what I saw . . . I don't think.'

'Well,' says Craig, 'they are all in there waiting for you.'

'Who?'

'Belinda, Loraine, Gareth . . .'

'And the lead singer?'

'Him? He's drinking champagne in first with the band,'

says Craig. 'Apparently they stopped making sense hours ago.'

'Right. And where did the incident take place?'

'In the back, in the corner, in first.'

'Did the other passengers report them?'

'No,' says Craig. 'Loraine noticed them on her way through to ask the captain what he might like for breakfast.'

'Right,' I say, nodding away.

'Hadn't you better get in there?'

'Are you sure they need me?'

'Yes,' confirms Andy, giving my leg a push from his seat. 'And I want every single gory detail.'

The hissing and spitting cease as soon as I enter the galley. Belinda is sitting down on one of the silver food boxes, Gareth and Loraine loom above her. Her smooth, swept-back blonde bun looks a little dishevelled, her navy uniform is creased and her red and white striped scarf is nowhere to be seen. Her cheeks are flushed, her lips plump and her eyes bright. In short, she looks like a girl who has just had a good seeing to.

'Thank God,' she says when she sees me, like I'm her knight in shining armour. 'Where have you been?'

'Up the back sorting out something,' I mumble. I don't quite understand why she is setting so much store by my help.

'Tell them,' Belinda announces, leaning back against the galley wall, thrusting her bosom out. The top three buttons on her white shirt are undone. 'Tell them what you saw.'

'Um,' I say, looking at both Gareth and Loraine who have turned to me expecting some sort of explanation. 'Well, what do you want me to say?'

'That you saw what they were doing. That you saw them

slip something in my drink. That I would not have done what I did otherwise.'

'So you do admit it, then?' asks Gareth.

'It wasn't as bad as Loraine makes out,' she says.

'Oh please,' says Loraine. 'You were right on top of him. The poor bloke could hardly breathe.'

'Poor bloke?' hisses Belinda. 'He spiked my drink!'

'When did he do that exactly?' asks Gareth. 'As you were serving him? I don't quite understand.'

'He asked me to join him and then he did it,' she says. 'You saw them, didn't you?'

She is looking at me again. I'm not really sure what to do. I don't really want to accuse her of lying, but then, sitting on a passenger's face while supposedly on duty is a serious offence. If only she had waited another couple of hours or so we would all probably be congratulating her on her splendid celebrity conquest. But somehow, in the back of first class, it doesn't seem right.

'Well, I'm sorry,' I say. 'I don't remember seeing anything that much. I remember seeing the boys behaving badly because I discussed it with you, didn't I?' I look at Gareth, who nods in agreement. 'And you.' I look at Loraine. 'But other than that, all I saw were some leery boys and you coping with them quite well, if I may say so.'

'So no drugs, then?' asks Gareth.

'Not that I could see.'

'You shit!' Belinda spits.

'Sorry?' I say, somewhat taken aback.

'If you hadn't been so bloody busy looking up my skirt or

copping a feel of my tits as you walked past, you might have noticed them spiking my drink.'

'I didn't feel your breasts,' I say, my heart beginning to race. 'I couldn't be less interested in your breasts. You rubbed them up against me as I walked past.'

'Yeah, right,' she says. 'As if.'

'Please yourself,' I reply.

'You sad old pervert.'

'That's enough!' says Gareth, raising his voice. 'You're in enough trouble as it is without accusing other people of things they patently haven't done. You came on this plane with a bit of a reputation, my young lady, and I'm afraid you have now added to it, and ended your career at the same time. I shall be reporting you when we land, and you won't be flying with us or any other airline again.'

'Picture me giving a shit,' says Belinda, her chin raised in defiance. 'They spiked my drink.'

'That's your story, love,' says Gareth, sounding deeply patronizing. 'But you're forgetting that I've been doing this for nearly twenty years and there is nothing I haven't seen before.'

'I'm a victim!' she yells.

'No,' says Gareth, as if he is talking to a small child, 'you're a little slut. And you are now officially off duty and you're to sit in here for the rest of the flight. Any trouble, and I'll have you arrested.'

'Wanker,' she says as he leaves the galley. 'And you're just as bad,' she adds as I follow him.

'What's her problem?' I ask Gareth as we stand in the aisle together.

'She knows she is in the wrong,' he shrugs. 'So she came out fighting.'

'Do you believe the drugs thing?'

'Not in the slightest,' says Gareth. 'For a start, people on Ecstasy are usually quite pleasant.'

'That's true.'

Gareth and I are joined in the aisle by a hassled-looking Craig, who rushes towards us from economy.

'Whatever it is, Craig, I don't want to hear it,' I say, about to put my hands to my ears.

'It doesn't concern you anyway,' says Craig. 'They have a loaves and fishes problem with breakfast in economy,' he says to Gareth. 'They are about ten short.'

'Ten?'

'I know,' says Craig. 'Angela is cooking the scrambled eggs at the moment. We are trying to thin it out with milk but we can only find the powdered stuff.'

'Right,' says Gareth. 'Let's go.'

Craig and Gareth go back down to economy to start halving sausages and dividing up hash browns, trying to make breakfast stretch for the whole of economy. It's not unusual for the catering company to serve us short. Sometimes we are to blame for not counting in the meals properly, and sometimes I think they are just pulling a fast one. Short-serving one plane doesn't make that much of a difference, but if you do it to a fleet for a week, think of all the money you could save. With any luck half the people passed out at the back won't actually fancy tucking into some par-cooked bacon and watered-down egg. It is, after all, only half past one in the morning. Most of them will want to carry on sleeping as much as possible before we touch down in Dubai.

'Off for the morning glory run,' says Loraine with a smile as she leaves the galley and makes her way up to the front.

One of the perks of serving breakfast for your average flight attendant is a bird's eye view of some of the male passengers' morning erections, often visible through their blankets or standing to attention in their trousers. This is usually Craig's favourite game, to go down the plane just before they get the trolleys out and point out the really large ones to the girls. Today, however, it seems that the food crisis has distracted him. Craig also says that there is one steward who always gets 'dawn horn' and has to have a wank in the loo before he goes out with the breakfasts. I wonder if it's Tom. He disappeared into the club-class toilet about five minutes ago and has yet to re-emerge.

'You all right there?' I ask Andy, who is looking a little rough around the edges to say the least.

'I'm a bit shagged.' He yawns, stretching his hands above his head, one still holding a drink. 'I'm waiting for Tom to come out of the loo, and then I should be all right.'

'Oh,' I say.

'He's got quite a few things to keep you awake, if you want anything.'

'No thanks.'

'Also,' continues Andy, 'there's a stash waiting for us at the hotel. Room two forty, or something like that. He knows where it is anyway.'

I have to say that I am not at all shocked. Crew smuggling

drugs is common enough, especially for personal consumption. There are secret stashes of coke and hash in hotel rooms all over the world. One lot takes them out, takes what they can and tapes the rest to the U bend of the hotel toilets, leaving it behind for a later date or for another visiting crew. It's relatively easy as no-one would suspect a band of hosties of carrying contraband, and they don't really go through Customs anyway.

Sometimes things are taken a little further. There's the story of the captain who was caught with half a million pounds' worth of heroin on him; the hostess in prison in the Middle East for four years, caught with a small amount of smack in the elastic of her shoes. There were also the girls who were smuggling heroin out of Thailand, Hong Kong and Bali. Their wheelie bags were full of the stuff, which had a street value of some £15m. They were nice middle-class girls devoid of problems, but they were earning something like £20,000 a drop, so you could kind of see the appeal. But the most audacious has to be the South America–Miami cocaine route where the caterers were lining the food trolleys with coke and the hosties were taking the trolleys off at the other end. Eventually the ring was busted, and now all food trolleys are weighed before and after they land and take off at the South American airport.

Tom comes out of the front right-hand toilet. His eyes are bright and his face alert. He comes past and squats down next to Andy.

'All right?' he asks me.

'Fine, thanks,' I say, looking the other way.

The last thing I want to do is witness the drug swap or even watch the gauche way they will try to pass the drugs from one to the other, thinking they are being subtle. Fortunately for all of us, Edith pops her head around the galley and announces in a quiet airline-crew-only voice that she has made some scones if I would care to join her up front. Belinda, she also shares, has been moved up to the first-class galley where Loraine can keep an eye on her to make sure that she doesn't get into any more trouble. So while Tom and Andy fumble about trying to look like they are up to nothing, I get up and join Rachel and Sue in the galley for some delicious homemade scones.

'Mmm, Edith, these look amazing,' I say as I lean against the lockers buttering a scone.

'I try to make them every trip,' she says. 'They make me feel better.'

'I can imagine,' says Sue, breaking a small amount off with her fingers. 'Rachel and I have made flapjacks a couple of times, haven't we?'

'Well, you did,' says Rachel, squatting next to Sue on a silver box. 'I just eat them all.'

'It does make all the difference on a long flight if you can have something homemade,' says Sue.

'I find it grounding,' says Edith.

'Well, I think they're delicious.'

I lean across to pick up what looks like a pot of tea.

'Don't!' says Edith, putting her hand out to try to stop me.

'Oh,' I say.

I pour out a bright orange drink that bears no resemblance to tea whatsoever. In fact, it stinks of alcohol.

'It's . . .' She stops.

'Not tea,' I say, helpfully.

'No. It's punch.'

'Oh, OK. Is it any good?'

'Not bad,' she replies. 'Tom made it. He always makes it. Every flight he is on, he rustles up a punch and leaves it hanging around for any member of the crew.'

'Jesus!' says Sue, taking a sniff. 'It smells lethal. What's in it?'

'I'm not sure,' says Edith. 'Tia Maria, vodka, orange juice, Cointreau. I don't know exactly. Everyone comes in and has a hit now and again.'

'Let's have a bit,' says Rachel, handing out a teacup.

'Don't tell Gareth,' says Edith, pouring Rachel a cup.

'I'm sure he knows already,' I suggest.

'He thinks we are drinking orange juice,' she says.

'Course he does.' I smile.

'It's certainly strong,' inhales Rachel. 'How many have you had?' she asks Edith.

'Two or three.'

'Slugs?' asks Rachel.

'No, cups.'

'I'm amazed you can stand.'

'It helps me get through.'

We all sit in silence for a few seconds, everyone aware of Edith's situation. And Edith is aware that everyone else is aware. Sue and Rachel shift uncomfortably on the silver box.

'So, how's Lizzie?' asks Sue, trying to clear the air and change the subject at the same time.

'She's broken her ankle,' replies Edith.

'No!' says Sue, eating some more scone. 'How?'

'She was on a tea tray and went slap bang into one of the toilets at the back of the plane. Really painful it was, poor thing. It took a while for her to think of a story for the insurance, but I think the company believed her.'

'Like hell they did,' I smile.

Tea-traying is a popular cabin pastime. Let a crew loose in an empty plane and it's the first thing they'll do to entertain themselves. Just before take-off a couple of hosties or stewards will grab a tray each and place themselves at the top of each of the aisles; then, as the plane takes off, they will sit on the trays and push themselves off, racing one another to the end of the plane. Then they will attempt to scale the aisle again, currently at about forty-five degrees, in order to repeat the process all over again. It's rather like tobogganing indoors, and accidents, as you can imagine, are common. Slamming into a toilet door or a row of seats is a surefire way to break your ankle. The worst accident I have heard of was when a crew was taking a forty-year-old decommissioned and stripped-out 747 that wasn't even fit for the haj or Lourdes over to RAF Lyneham so that it could be cut up for Coke cans. It was devoid of passengers and seats and light on fuel so when it took off, it tore off the tarmac like a bullet. There were two guys tea-traying inside and one of them broke his leg in three places as he was sent flying into the back wall. He came up with the lamest explanation – that he'd fallen out of the plane after it had landed – but everyone knew what had really happened.

'How long's she off work for?' asks Sue.

'I'm not sure,' says Edith. 'Six weeks or something?' She pauses. 'Talking of which, does anyone know what Gareth is doing? I should start getting the breakfasts out quite soon.'

'They've got a loaves and fishes problem at the back,' says Sue.

'Oh,' says Edith. 'Who's going to help me get the club breakfasts out?'

'Shall I go and get Craig and Gareth?' I ask.

'Would you?' she says, her white face looking all the more pallid. 'Otherwise I've no idea how I'll cope.'

2–3 AM

Before I can get anywhere near my white charger, Gareth and Craig make their way up the aisle to help Edith with the breakfasts. The loaves and fishes routine has apparently worked in economy and all those who wanted half a hash brown with some tepid bacon and a spoonful of milk-powdered-down scrambled egg have had their fill. So I sit back down in my seat and await some orange juice, coffee and a warm croissant.

'Are you going to have some breakfast?' I ask Andy as he comes back from the toilet.

'Jesus, no,' he replies, the idea of solids clearly making him gag. 'Are you sure you don't want a sharpener?' he offers, a clenched fist extended. 'It'll banish all thoughts of breakfast.'

'No thanks,' I say.

'Please yourself. I've got to go down the back to give this to Tom. Do you want to come?' he asks, as if it's the best invitation going. There's a clatter of plates and cutlery from the galley. 'Come on,' he says, 'before we get blocked in here.' He sees me hesitate. 'Honestly. Remember all the puke they cleaned up earlier? The last thing you need coming from that kitchen is a hot coffee and a roll.'

I have to say that the puke thing clinches it, as does a waft of something disgusting coming from the colostomy man. It's a while since anyone has been down the cabin spraying some Poison.

'OK,' I say, thinking that what I really want is my bed and a warm duvet. But as I am here I may as well join in.

As Andy and I walk towards the galley in economy, we can hear a strange sort of banging going on, as if someone is hitting something against a hard surface.

'What's that?' I ask.

Andy just smiles.

We pull back the curtain and find about six flight attendants sitting around on silver boxes slamming what look like small tequila shots on the floor. Behind them, pushed into a corner and currently being ignored by all of them, is a large black plastic bag in the shape of a curled-up corpse.

'Oh, hello,' says Tom as he looks up from the floor. His eyes are slightly rheumy. 'Landing drinks,' he declares. 'Do you want one?'

'You're a bit premature,' I say, trying to sound jovial. 'Doesn't the captain at least wait until the plane touches down?'

'Times change.' He grins.

Actually, indeed they do, because in the good old days when the flight deck was open to all and there wasn't a pistol locked in a box at the front, the captain and the first officer used to be given a nice cool beer or a gin and tonic after they landed. Just as they were circling above the airport, the chief hostie would be cracking open the ice and serving the nuts so that as soon as the chocks were on the captain could have something to take the edge off his long day. But now that they are breath- and drug-tested, such civilized perks are no more. Equally, the crew used to pocket a load of miniatures and finish up what was left over before the wheels hit the tarmac. However, slammers before the duty free has gone out is a new one on me.

'Budge up,' says Andy to Angela, who is sitting on a silver box.

'Take it,' she says. 'I've got to do the duty-free trolley.'

As Andy sits down, Angela starts rootling around in the cupboards above his head, looking for her perfume samplers. As the most junior member of the crew it is her job to carry the samplers on and off the plane. She also gets to take them home with her, for safekeeping. This is not a popular job. It is a bore and a pain, and the samples themselves are surprisingly heavy.

'You look a little light on samples there,' says Tom.

'What?' says Angela, looking down at him as she rearranges her trolley. 'What are you saying?'

'You're just looking a little low.' He grins.

'Well, the Poison has gone, if that's what you're asking.'

'And the rest?'

'Are you accusing me of selling them on?' she asks.

'You wouldn't be the first, love,' he says. 'Or indeed the last.'

Tom's right. Juniors are always flogging on their samples at car boot sales or to friends and pocketing the cash. It's one of the first things they learn when they join the airline. They then ring up the perfume companies and ask for more. It's not exactly rocket science. But then there are the clever duty-free scams. For example, I would be quite careful if you were thinking of buying a watch off a duty-free trolley, particularly if it is expensive and designer: another old trick is to replace the real Gucci watch that the passenger gets to touch and feel before purchase with a fake picked up in Thailand. Flight attendants have been known to replace whole trolleys with a load of fakes and quietly pocket the difference.

Despite all the cons and fakes, cabin crew do actually make money off the duty-free trolley anyway. The person pushing the trolley gets 5 per cent on all goods sold, and 2½ per cent is shared with the rest of the crew. Some attendants can take the whole thing very seriously indeed, dressing up their trolleys with toys and tinsel at Christmas and spraying dashes of perfume ahead of them like someone out of a department store. On some flights, such as Lagos and Moscow, you can make quite a lot off the trolley, pocketing up to £400 a trip. If you're on £18K a year, that goes some way towards helping you clear the £30K target you're after.

'Well, maybe just a few bottles have gone walkabout,' admits Angela, finally. 'But it has nothing to do with me. I've only just qualified.'

'Aha,' says Tom. 'Good point. How about you, Katie?' he asks, looking across at the other quiet-looking mousey girl putting together a trolley on the other side.

'I've got the full complement,' she replies.

'Course you have, love.' He grins. 'Haven't we all?'

As the girls set off down the aisles to try to flog a few old teddy bears, some silver tie pins and the odd bottle of Anais Anais to the sleeping passengers, Tom gets out the tequila.

'One more shot each?' he asks. 'It is Andy's birthday after all.'

He and Andy line up another four shots for the two of them and the two other girls remaining in the galley.

'Looking forward to seeing your boyfriend?' one of them asks the other.

'Oh, don't tell me you have an MMD here in Dubai,' says Tom, his shot poised by his lips.

'A what?' asks Andy.

'A "My Mohammed is Different",' he says.

'But he is,' wails the girl.

'Yeah, right,' says Tom, exuding sarcasm as he downs his shot. 'He treats you "right and proper", not like the other guys.'

'He really is different,' she insists.

'Bev banging on about her MMD?' asks Craig, as he pops in behind the curtain.

'Yeah,' says Tom. 'There's no changing her record.'

'You're just jealous,' she says.

'Oh, green,' agrees Tom.

'Tom's just the sort of man who is dying to settle down and go steady,' says Craig, leaning forward, trying to get his hands on some tequila.

'Rather like you,' says the other hostie. She looks sour and hurt, definitely like one of his downroute conquests.

'I haven't heard you complaining,' Craig replies tartly.

'Children, children,' says Tom.

329

'I'm going,' she says. 'It's suddenly a whole lot less enter-taining in here.'

'Good,' says Craig. 'It is a bit of a squash in here, especially with that fucking corpse.'

'Jesus,' says Andy, recoiling his legs and looking over in the corner for the first time. 'I didn't see that was there. When did that happen?'

'While you were asleep, mate,' says Tom.

Craig squats down on the floor and starts to talk Andy step by step through the heart attack he didn't witness. He adds and embellishes as he goes along, making the whole thing all the more dramatic and disgusting. I lean against the galley wall, thinking about going back up to club and talking to Susan.

'Did you hear that Dee was got for prostitution last week?' Craig suddenly announces.

Bev chokes on her tequila in total shock. 'What, our Dee?'

'Yup,' says Craig. 'Apparently she was working out of a hotel in Bangkok on her stopovers, slipping the concierge ten per cent. He was organizing all her bookings and she spent her weekends flat on her back supplementing her income.'

'That's a bit like taking coals to Newcastle, isn't it?' says Tom. 'Whoring in the Far East?'

'I knew loads of Asian hostesses who doubled up as call girls over in the UK,' I say. 'I remember the story of one airline that lost its whole crew and eventually found them working in a massage parlour in Birmingham. But I didn't know it went on the other way around.'

'Apparently so,' confirms Craig. 'She had a thing going in Singapore and Sydney as well.'

'God,' says Bev, her voice full of awe. 'I always wondered why she had such nice stuff, so many handbags and things. I always thought they were fakes she picked up in Thailand.'

'She certainly picked them up in Thailand,' says Tom.

'How did she get found out?' I ask.

'Unfortunately, the concierge booked her with a pilot from our airline,' replies Craig.

'And he reported her?' I ask, slightly incredulous.

'They're such wankers, those boys, they'll report you for stealing a Kitkat,' says Craig.

He is right. Some pilots can be very unpleasant indeed. One of them did actually report a hostie for nicking a Kitkat once and she lost her job. I suspect this bloke was so embarrassed at being caught whoring in Thailand he thought that he'd get in there before Dee did.

'So has Dee been fired?' asks Bev.

'Yup,' says Craig. 'Her and a bloke called John, who I don't think you know, who tried to smuggle his ladyboy lover into Australia.'

'That's common enough,' says Tom, sounding jaded. 'I've heard that a few times. There's something very alluring about those Thai boys.' He smiles. 'Makes you want to bring one home.'

'I think it's them who are more keen,' says Craig. 'This one had stowed away on the flight and cut up his passport. John was apparently going to try to smuggle him through in a crew uniform.'

'Sounds very Bonnie and Clyde to me,' says Tom.

'Sounds bloody illegal to me,' says Bev. 'I don't know why

331

people would want to compromise their position and job like that,' she says, finishing off her tequila shot.

'We can't *all* be lucky enough to have an MMD,' laughs Tom.

A blue light goes off in the galley.

'I'll go,' says Bev. 'Anything to get away from you lot.'

Bev leaves the galley and we all sit in silence. Andy stares at the corpse in the corner and Tom plays with the half-empty tequila bottle.

'Does anyone fancy racing toilet rolls?' asks Craig.

'The flight's far too full and grumpy,' says Tom. 'That's a day-flight thing when everyone's bored and awake and up for a laugh.'

Toilet-roll racing ranks up there with tea-traying as a game peculiar to inflight entertainment. Each attendant picks up a roll of toilet paper, places one end down the toilet and takes the other end as far up the plane along the aisle as he or she can. Then two fellow attendants are instructed to flush the toilets at the same time and their immense suction pulls all the paper back along the plane. The toilet with the quickest paper suckback wins.

'Anyway,' continues Tom, 'aren't we landing in a bit?'

'You're right, not far off now,' says Craig, looking at his watch. 'All right there, Edith?' he asks as she walks behind me down the aisle.

She does not reply. She is looking straight ahead, as if in a trance. I turn and watch her walk slowly towards the back. There's something odd about her behaviour. Her body is rigid; her arms are stiff by her sides. Someone tries to engage her as she walks past. She doesn't pause.

'What's wrong with Edith?' I ask as I step into the aisle.

'What?' asks Craig, poking his head out of the galley. 'Jesus Christ!'

We both stand and stare as Edith, who is halfway down the plane, starts slowly but surely taking off her clothes. First she undoes her skirt and steps out of it. Staring straight ahead in her girdle and American tan tights, she then slowly takes off her scarf, removes her jacket and unbuttons her blouse. None of us knows what to do. The passengers start to whisper and nudge one another as they realize what is going on. Edith starts moving again, walking towards the back of the plane.

'Shit!' I say. 'I think she's lost it. Shall I go down there?'

'Good idea,' says Craig. 'And I'll . . .' He stands there flummoxed.

'Go and get Sue in club,' I say. 'I know she'll be good at this sort of thing.'

Craig rushes off to club and I slowly walk towards Edith, not wanting to scare her but wanting to reach her before she is totally naked in front of the whole plane. Either she hears me coming or the growing sniggers coming from passengers perturb her, because she suddenly marches off to the small galley at the back of the plane and opens a cupboard. By the time I get there, she's locked herself in.

'Edith! Edith!' I say, knocking on the door.

'Go away,' she replies.

'Let me in.' I'm having flashbacks of the paracetamol boy this afternoon, and it's scaring me. 'What are you doing? Are you OK? Can I help?'

'Leave me alone,' she says.

'How can I get into the cupboard?' I ask a rather shocked-looking flight attendant who is standing at the back of the plane.

'You can't,' she replies. 'Once it's locked, it's locked.'

'Shit!'

'What's going on?' asks Sue, appearing with Gareth behind me. I fill them both in and watch the concern grow on their faces. 'I think you should leave me to deal with this,' says Sue, finally.

'Do you think?' asks Gareth.

'Well, I couldn't do any worse,' she smiles. 'There's nothing in this cupboard, is there?' she asks the flight attendant.

'No.'

'So she can't harm herself,' says Sue, talking more to herself than anyone else. 'That's a good thing. Edith?' she says, gently tapping on the door.

'What?'

'It's Sue.'

'Hello.'

'Are you OK?'

'Not really.'

'Is it all a bit much?'

'Mmm.'

'D'you want to come out and tell me about it?'

'Not really.'

'Do you want to talk to me about it here?'

'Not really.'

'Are you cold in there?'

'A bit.'

'Do you want a blanket?'

'Not really.'

Gareth taps me on the shoulder. 'I think we should leave her to it,' he mouths.

I nod. I give Sue's shoulder a squeeze before I turn and walk away.

'What the hell is that all about?' asks Gareth when we are halfway up the aisle.

'We all know what it's about,' I say. 'The question is, what brought it on?'

'All those Temazers she's been taking and Tom's little cocktail, I should imagine.'

'You knew about that?'

'Yeah. You'd better get back to your seat. The plane's landing in about a quarter of an hour.'

I make my way back to club. Andy's yet to return. The smell from the colostomy man has dissipated somewhat. Someone must have been through with the perfume bottle again; either that or I've got used to it. The captain switches on the seat-belt sign and announces to the cabin crew that we have fifteen minutes to landing. The woman behind me whimpers – clearly turbulence and landing are not her thing. If she knew we were a landing light short and had a bloody wheel missing, she might well want to bail the aircraft altogether. Although a parachute at ten thousand feet is useless, and anyone leaping from this plane would end up in the engines smelling of roast chicken in a matter of seconds.

The cabin crew go through the plane raising all the blinds, letting the daylight in. It's a rude awakening, bearing in mind it's nearly three a.m. for the passengers on the flight, though the local time is nearly six a.m.

'Weird,' says Andy as he sits back down beside me, fastening his seat belt. 'I have been queuing for the toilet and I have had to give up. There's someone locked in there and they're not coming out.'

'Maybe it's the bloke who had his food laced with laxative.'

'No, I saw him in his seat,' says Andy. 'I've told Gareth but he doesn't seem to care. He says we're landing anyway.'

'He's got a lot on,' I say. 'Any news from Edith and Sue?'

'Sue's got her out of the cupboard; they're sitting at the back. Edith's wrapped in a blanket.'

'Good.'

Gareth comes through to check that all the seats are upright and our tables are put away.

'Apparently there is still someone in one of the toilets,' I say.

'It's probably stuck,' he remarks dismissively as he walks on through.

'Told you,' says Andy.

'Cabin crew, take your seats for landing,' says Richard over the Tannoy.

Only Craig comes to the front to strap himself in the seat in front of us. Edith and Belinda are missing. I close my eyes and pray that it is not the front wheel we're missing.

3-4 AM

Ten minutes later we are still circling over Dubai airport. And it's not the normal sort of gentle horizontal circling that happens as you stack up over London; this is swooping circling, presumably as we buzz air traffic control in the hope that they can spot which one of our wheels is no more. We have gone over about five or six times already so they can't be getting much of a look.

'What the fuck is going on?' asks Andy, looking pasty and sweaty in his seat.

'I have no idea,' I lie.

'It's not as if we're approaching fucking London,' he says. 'London, you expect this sort of thing. It's first come first served, but here . . .'

The first come, first served philosophy is one of the pilots' big irritations about the London approach, particularly if you are coming across the Atlantic. Instead of being able to slow

337

down as you near Ireland, talk to Shannon air traffic control and find out the state of traffic over London, you have to belt it across the pond to ensure your place in the queue, keeping enough fuel on board to be able to circle over the south coast for up to ninety minutes. Land any sooner, and on your last sortie over the south you end up having to dump fuel in order to be light enough to make the runway. The thousands of tons of fuel burnt over London and dumped over the south coast every day is a crime in itself. And it wouldn't take much to sort it out.

However, the situation we find ourselves in this morning is slightly more urgent. All I can say is that I'm glad we're not on a 777. The 777 has a camera mounted on the front so the passengers can see take-off and landing. The last time I flew one we developed an engine fire and someone forgot to turn off the camera, so as we came in to land all the passengers got to see the ten fire engines waiting for us on the tarmac. At least this time we are all flying in blissful ignorance. Or at least some of us are.

The plane lurches around again and swoops down over the airport. The woman behind me is whimpering again. Her husband is trying to shut her up. This time I don't really blame her. I think the whole plane is sensing that something is not quite right. Even Craig is starting to look quizzical.

'Do you have any idea what is going on?' asks Rachel from across the aisle. 'It's never difficult to get into Dubai. I can't feel a crosswind or anything.'

'I'm sure we'll be fine,' I lie again. There really is nothing else to say.

The plane goes around again. It stutters slightly. Everyone looks at one another.

'I'm not liking this at all,' says Andy. The coke and the alcohol are clearly getting the better of him. 'My heart is going ten to the fucking dozen and I'm feeling sick.'

'Try and breathe slowly,' I say. 'Calm down, you don't want to hyperventilate.'

'I think I'm having a heart attack,' he says. 'I feel like I'm fucking dying.'

'You're not. It's the cocktail you've taken and the fact that you're a bit tense and tired.'

'A *bit* tense?' he says. 'I'm fucking shitting it.'

The woman behind starts mumbling 'Oh my God, oh my God' over and over again as we descend towards the runway. It seems that Richard has decided to go for it. Maybe the tower has identified which wheel we have missing, maybe they haven't. The faster and lower we descend, the more I grip my chair, the more I hope and pray it's not the front wheel.

'Hold on,' I turn and whisper to Andy.

'What?' he says, his white face turning towards me.

'When we hit the ground,' I say, 'just hold on tight.'

'I knew it! There *is* something wrong!' He closes his eyes. 'Jesus Christ . . .'

I look out of the colostomy man's window and see the radar tower and the ground rapidly approaching. I think of Sue and hope that she is well strapped in at the back, or that she is, by some slim chance, over the wings somewhere – the safest part of a plane.

The plane hits the ground. The woman behind me screams.

Andy yelps. I grit my teeth and wait for the screech of metal, the crash, the bumps, the swerving fuselage, the smell of burning and the yell of sirens. Instead, there is nothing. In fact, the plane lands so beautifully it's as if it has floated down and ended up gently skating on ice. There is no bounce, no swerve, no leaving of the tarmac at all. We have one of the smoothest rides in I've ever experienced.

'Oh,' says Andy, looking surprised and relieved.

'Thank God,' exhales the woman behind me.

A ripple of applause flows up from the back of the plane.

'Ladies and gentlemen, this is your captain speaking. Welcome to Dubai where the local time is twenty past six in the morning and the temperature is already twenty-eight degrees. Due to the tailwind we encountered coming over the desert we are a little early but we shall be taxiing up to the terminal in the next few minutes, where we will disembark the plane. I hope that you have enjoyed your flight with us today, and rest assured we will endeavour to get your kit off as soon as we can so you won't have to hang around the airport.'

I can't believe it. Having just averted what could possibly have been a disaster Richard has the bravado to remember the 'get your kit off' bet that he has with the crew.

Craig gets out of his seat, giving me the thumbs up. 'Nice one.' He grins, nodding his head. 'A quick CPA and we're off!'

The plane finally grinds to a halt and the bloke behind me is straight out of his seat and rootling around in the overhead locker. The captain has yet to turn off the 'fasten seat belt' sign, but no-one seems to care. Craig is too busy checking his personal appearance, Edith is up at the back of the plane, and Belinda is obviously detained elsewhere.

Finally, the bell sounds and we are all released. We are hit by a cacophony of clicking belts, snapping lockers and bleeping of reactivated mobile phones.

'I think we should sit here and wait for the whole plane to leave,' I suggest to Andy, 'and get the crew bus.'

'What?' he exhales, turning to look at me like a man who has just been to the brink and back.

'Wait and get the crew bus?'

'Oh, yeah. Absolutely.'

Doors are switched to manual, the steps arrive, and Craig opens the plane door. A surreal bright light pours into the plane, as does a cleansing blast of fresh air. All the passengers are standing, clutching their hand luggage and duty-free bags, queuing down the right aisle, jostling slightly, all eager to get off.

Craig stands to one side, indicating that they are now allowed to disembark. The first-class passengers come through ahead of the others. The sheikh and his wives look untouched by the flight; by contrast, the boy band look as if they have all been run over. The lead singer says goodbye to Craig and has the decency to look slightly sheepish. He looks down the plane but Andy doesn't even bother to flirt. He must be feeling terrible.

Next to leave is club. The agitated businessman is the first out, having managed to make it to the front of the queue without anyone noticing. He is rapidly followed by the whimpering woman and her exhausted husband. The colostomy man also shuffles past, as does the princess, the child puker and his unfortunate victims, both of whom, rather amazingly, say thank you to Craig.

The passengers in economy then start pouring forth from all sides. They come up Andy's aisle and cut across through the galley in their attempt to exit the plane more quickly. The irate laxative bloke is so exhausted by his flight he doesn't even have the energy to be rude to Craig as he leaves the plane. I see Andy's ex-shag who he downgraded, plus the doctor who tried to save the fat cardiac patient's life, and the couple who shagged across most of Europe. Eventually it's just the last dribs and drabs who are weaving their way up the aisle. The active homosexuals are the last to leave. They appear a lot quieter and more respectable then they did in the drunken half light at the back of the plane. They all walk out with their faces down, avoiding eye contact with anyone, obviously feeling a whole lot less witty at this hour of the morning.

'That it?' asks Craig.

'Yup,' calls Tom from the other end of the plane.

'Thank fuck for that.' Craig yawns expansively and stretches his arms above his head. 'What a fucking flight!'

'Yes, well,' says Gareth, walking down the aisle, 'it's not over yet. There's something blocking that toilet at the back of club.'

'Do you want me to try to get it open?' I offer.

'Would you?' asks Gareth, sounding hassled for the first time on the flight. 'There's so much to do, to clear up here; there's the corpse to get out, and I'm not sure if Angela has bonded the bar correctly. The last thing I need is a whole load of alcohol to go missing from the plane.'

I understand his anxiety. Bonding the bar, or sealing it all back up again in the correct order with the right numbered seals and documents, is a vital part of the flight attendant's job and it is all supposed to be done before the plane touches down. Since no duty has been paid on any of the alcohol, it has to be under lock and key as soon as it's no longer in the air. It comes from a bonded warehouse and must remain bonded when it is not flying. Every bar is the same size and they all slot into the drinks trolleys. There can be as many as forty bonded blocks on a long-distance flight.

Just as I get up to go and check the toilet, the captain comes through, looking pleased with himself.

'Good landing,' I say to him. 'So it wasn't our wheel after all?'

'Oh, it was,' he says. 'Just one of those at the side.'

'Oh, right. So they spotted it from the tower, then?'

'No, they couldn't see a thing, but we had to come down eventually.' He smiles. 'Couldn't stay up there all day, now could we?'

'Um, no,' I say as the magnitude of the gamble he's just taken hits home. 'I suppose not.'

'So, right,' says Richard, nice and loudly, rubbing his hands together, 'where's the party?'

'We've got a few things to sort first,' says Gareth from the other end of the plane.

'Right behind you, Gareth, right behind you,' declares Richard, walking off the other way.

I walk towards the toilet and try to push the door open. It appears to be locked from the inside. I take a pen out of my pocket and slide it in next to the lock. Pushing the metal panel to one side, I peer through the gap. Inside there appears to be a man sitting slumped on the toilet.

'Gareth!' I yell. 'There seems to be someone in here.'

'Oh shit, no,' he says, walking towards me. 'Here,' he says, rattling around in his pocket and producing a passkey. He turns the lock and together we kick open the door. We both stand back. 'Oh shit,' he says. 'Not another one.'

Sitting on the toilet with his trousers round his ankles and a syringe stuck in his groin is a young man. His white face lolls to one side, his eyes are nearly closed, his mouth is hanging open, one of his tattooed arms hangs limply to one side, and the other is holding the needle.

'D'you think he's dead?' I ask.

'I would imagine so,' says Gareth, leaning over to check the man's pulse. 'He's dead,' he announces. 'Jesus! What a mess.'

'I can't believe one of us didn't notice him going in,' I say.

'I can,' replies Gareth. 'We had quite a lot going on.'

'I suppose. Who do you think it is?'

'No idea,' says Gareth, shaking his head. 'D'you know, in the twenty years I have been doing this, this is only the second smack death I've had.'

'Really?'

'I once caught two queens sharing a crack pipe in the toilets, but I thought that smack thing was over, an eighties thing – Boy George and all that. Didn't he take heroin on a plane?'

'I don't know,' I say. 'There was some journalist who took it on Tony Blair's plane, wasn't there?'

'Oh yeah, I vaguely remember that. So,' Gareth says, trying

344

to get some sort of a grip, 'two corpses to deal with. Oh well,' he says, slowly turning to smile at me. 'Looks like I'm going to be a bit late for the party.'

'I could stay behind and help if you like.'

'Nah,' he says. 'You're not on duty, and anyway, I know all the guys here at the airport. It will be much quicker if I do it on my own.'

'If you're sure?'

'I'm very sure. You haven't travelled all this way to work, and you're the best mate of the birthday boy. We wouldn't want to ruin his day, now would we?'

'OK then.'

'Listen, you lot,' says Gareth, talking to the whole plane. 'The crew bus should be here by now. Leave me to deal with all this shit and I'll join you later.' A loud whoop of joy and a round of applause ring out around the plane. 'Off you go then,' he says. 'Except you, Angela. You can stay and learn something. Your baptism of fire may as well continue.'

Like rats leaving a sinking ship, Andy, Craig, Rachel, Tom, me and the rest of the crew hotfoot it off the plane and into the waiting minibus. It's early morning but the sun is out and the air is warming up. I wish I had thought to bring my sunglasses. I also wish I didn't feel so tired, disorientated and really rather sick.

The driver starts up his engine and a rattle of glass miniature bottles comes from at least two of the wheelie suitcases above my head.

'Are we not going to wait for Belinda, Sue and Edith?' asks Rachel, looking around the bus.

'No,' says Craig. 'They're getting that car.' He points to a Mercedes on the tarmac.

The bus door closes, and as we head off I see Sue and Edith coming down the steps of the plane. Edith is hunched over and covered in a blanket; Sue has an arm wrapped around her. Belinda walks slowly behind.

'Is Sue coming along later?' I ask.

'Woooo,' says Andy, leaning over the back of his chair like a teenager. 'Don't worry, she'll be along in a bit.'

I sit back in my chair and stare out of the window. I am too old and too tired for this.

'OK,' says Tom, getting out of his chair, standing in the aisle and shaking a mineral water bottle full of orange liquid above his head. 'Who's for some Bus?'

A lethal mixture of champagne, Cointreau, brandy and orange juice, a Bus is a cocktail specifically mixed for the journey from the plane to the terminal. It's almost guaranteed to get you wasted before you disembark.

'Wicked!' says Andy. 'When did you mix that?'

'On the flight,' grins Tom. 'Want some?'

'Is the Pope Catholic?' he replies.

The bottle of Bus is handed around and everyone takes a swig. By the time it gets to me it is warm and full of crew spittle, but I can't refuse. I take a mouthful to a round of applause. My eyes water as I struggle to get it down. Jesus Christ it's strong. I cough, wipe my mouth with the back of my hand and look up. The world is suddenly a brighter-looking place.

'All right there, mate?' asks Tom, patting my knee.

'Fine,' I say, finally inhaling. 'Happy birthday, Andy.'

'Yeah,' says Tom. 'Happy birthday, Andy.'

The bus pulls up outside the terminal to a terrible bleating rendition of 'Happy Birthday', and the crew tumble out. We collect our bags, carriers and rucksacks and make our way through the building. All the female flight attendants have changed back into their high-heeled shoes and are giving it some swagger as they weave their way through the airport. None of our passports or bags is checked; in fact, as we go through, Customs could not seem less interested. Their only reaction is to smile when one of the girls gives them a wave. I follow the group out of the airport and into the sunshine. We walk out to the left across some tarmac and file like a school party into another waiting vehicle. On the short ten-minute journey to the five-star hotel we finish off the cocktail.

Once inside the hotel, no-one bothers to check in. Instead we follow Tom, in a well-behaved crocodile. He is, after all, a man who looks like he knows where he's going. He stops and knocks loudly on a door towards the back of reception. A high-pitched collective scream replies. He knocks loudly again. The door is flung open. The smell of cigarettes and alcohol is overpowering, as is the sound of Britney Spears.

'Welcome to Sodom and Gomorrah!' Tom grins, waving us through the door. 'Have a nice day.'

4-5 AM

Walking into the crew room at our Dubai hotel is a bit like entering Dante's first circle. Given entirely over to bad behaviour, this small lounge on the ground floor is the hotel's way of discouraging the crew from holding parties in their bedrooms. It's always full of anyone who is up for it. It doesn't matter what time of day or night it is, there's always a hardcore gang of party animals passing through on their way to or from Australia, Singapore or Bangkok, and there are always enough of them to make sure that the blinds are drawn, the music is shoutingly loud, the air stinks of fag smoke and there are empty booze bottles spinning all over the floor.

Today, there are some seven or eight flight attendants who have flown in from various destinations all over the world, and who have obviously been caning it for some time.

'Andy!' screams one blonde as she rushes over and wraps herself around him. She has a cigarette in one hand and a cocktail in the other. Her white shirt is unbuttoned, and she has tied her red and white striped scarf around her head like a bandanna and hitched up her navy blue uniform skirt. 'Hello there, birthday boy!' she purrs as she rubs herself up against him and kisses him on the lips with a wet, glossy, open mouth. 'Welcome to Dubai.'

'Thanks, mate,' says Andy, wiping her saliva off his mouth with the back of his hand.

'Who the hell is that?' I whisper in his ear.

'No fucking idea,' he says, a large grin on his face.

'Right! Cocktail time!' yells Craig, waving a bottle of rum in the air. 'Who's brought the rest, as requested?'

'I've got the pineapple juice,' says Tom, hauling six cartons of the stuff, obviously lifted from the plane, out of his suitcase.

'Coconut milk!' declares some bloke from the earlier arrivals.

'And cream!' shouts another.

'Pina coladas, here we come!' shouts Craig, pulling out a plastic water bottle to double as a cocktail shaker. 'I love it when a plan comes together.'

'Here, love,' says the half-undressed blonde girl, pulling out a large bowl from under the desk, 'why don't you mix it in here?'

Craig sets about his brewing like a scientist on the verge of a discovery while Andy and Tom merge with the rest of the group. Rachel is hanging back slightly. She comes and stands next to me.

'Jesus,' she says, 'where have all this lot come from?'

'I have no idea, but they certainly mean business.'

'You can say that again.'

She and I stand on the sidelines, clearly contemplating our next moves. Craig pours the whole bottle of rum into the bowl plus the cream, coconut milk and pineapple, and looks up.

'Shit,' he says, trying to shout above the music. 'I've got nothing to stir this with.'

'Hang on,' yells the blonde. 'Back in a sec.'

She disappears off to the other side of the room and opens up her suitcase. After a few minutes she returns with an enormous red dildo which, when she switches it on, starts to curl around in a circular motion and vibrate.

'How about this?' she suggests to Craig, who looks momentarily floored. 'It's clean,' she adds. 'Scrubbed it myself.'

Craig hesitates. 'Hang on there!' shouts some bloke, putting both his hands in the air. The whole party slowly grinds to a halt and turns to stare at Craig as he makes his decision. Then, to rapturous and raucous applause, he takes the large red vibrator and thrusts it straight into the cocktail. It seems to work quite nicely. After a few turns with it around the bowl, Craig loses his inhibitions.

'Can you make it go faster?' he enquires. 'It would be good to get some foam.'

'Foam is good,' purrs the girl, taking hold of the big red cock and giving it an expert tug.

'Foam is always good,' confirms Craig, maintaining eye contact with the blonde as he dips his finger into the cocktail and sucks it. She smiles. 'Do you want some?' She smiles more broadly as he repeats the dipping process and offers her his finger to suck instead. The blonde obliges. She looks like an obliging kind of girl.

Suddenly, there's a loud screeching noise coming from a nearby room. The glass fire door bangs open and two girls, half naked, wet and covered in bubbles, tumble into the middle of the room. They are chased by a totally naked man, also covered in bubbles, who appears to be rather excited by the game. They collapse on top of one another and roll around on the floor, covering the grey carpet tiles in water and frothed-up bath gel.

'Get off, get off, get off!' shouts one girl, laughing and patting her naked bosom, trying to remove the man's groping hands.

'Help! Help!' screams the other woman as the bloke attempts to pull off her soaking wet skirt.

'For Christsake, someone help me!' the naked man says as he collapses onto the floor, spent after all this horseplay.

'Who's that?' I ask a steward who is standing next to me, swigging a small bottle of Baileys.

'Our first officer,' says the attendant. 'He's married with two children. But I think he's just pulled off a threesome in the shower.'

'Oh,' I say.

'Not bad going for a man who'd sworn off hosties two months ago.'

'No,' I agree. 'Not bad going at all.'

The lounge door opens and Susan walks in. She looks exhausted as she stands in the entrance, taking in the naked man frotting the hosties and Craig stirring his cocktail with a vibrator. I am about to go over and take hold of her hand to escort her out of the room to somewhere altogether quieter and more salubrious when she smiles, claps her hands and walks over to Craig to demand a drink. I look at Rachel and she looks at me. We walk up to the bowl and do the same.

'You OK?' I ask Susan as I take a sip of my drink. It tastes sweet, creamy, very alcoholic and vaguely rubbery.

'Not too bad,' she says. 'Edith's in a terrible state. I've left Gareth to look after her. Apparently there's some crew liaison officer over here who knows Edith and who wants to help.'

'Well, that's good,' I say, taking another sip of my cocktail. It doesn't taste so bad second time around.

'I'm just glad she's got a mate here to look after her,' says Susan, knocking back half the contents of her plastic beaker. 'I really need a few drinks.'

'This isn't too bad,' says Rachel, waving her beaker in Sue's face. 'Bearing in mind it has been mixed with a sex toy.'

'I think it makes it taste better,' replies Sue. She finishes her drink and turns to me. 'Who are all these people?'

I talk her through what little I know of the crew, including the few intimate facts about the first officer on the floor.

'I think I know him,' she says, turning her head to one side to take a closer look. 'I might have flown with him before. Although it's hard to tell without his uniform.'

Someone changes the music from Britney to a dance album and a few of the early arrivals take to the chairs and a table to express themselves fully. Andy and Tom go into the back room together to, I presume, take more drugs.

'Have you been to this crew room before?' I ask Sue.

'Once,' she says, 'about six months ago. But I normally stop over in Abu Dhabi if I'm coming this way. Or I'm straight through to Singapore.'

'How about you?' I ask the Baileys-drinking steward next to me, who introduces himself as Mark.

'All the bloody time,' he says. 'But you know, if you're in a place for twelve or twenty-four hours and you've seen all it has to offer over a hundred times already, what else is there left to do but play stupid drinking games?'

'I suppose so. What else *is* there to do here other than shop and tan and maybe take a trip into the desert?'

'Oh God,' he says, finishing his Baileys and scrabbling around on the long table of miniatures behind me for another. 'Don't mention the bloody desert. Been there twice, got stuck in the sand twice. You only come back looking like her.' He points across the room at a girl with a scarlet face and virulent pink stripes down her legs. She appears to be having great difficulty moving both her arms. 'She fell asleep in the desert yesterday, and now not even a bloody skin graft can save her. I don't know how she's going to work the flight tomorrow. She can't bend down to pick anything up her legs are so burnt.' He laughs and cracks open another bottle of Baileys. 'Oh no,' he adds, turning conspiratorially towards me, 'here comes trouble.'

I face the door to see Richard, the captain, walk in. Dressed in an orange Hawaiian shirt and khaki shorts, he appears to have gone up to his room to shower and change before coming in here.

'Trouble?' I ask Mark. 'Richard?'

'Fuck yeah,' he says. 'Last time I flew with him he shagged three hosties on a four-night stopover.'

'Richard?'

'Yeah. He did two of them in one night. We had some party in his room and they both stayed behind at the end. He didn't know which one to choose so he did both of them while watching Robert Palmer Night on MTV.'

'He's a dark horse,' I say.

'He's not the worst by any means,' says Mark, taking out a cigarette and sparking it up. 'Do you want one?'

'Thanks,' I say, tucking in.

'The last week-long stopover I did the captain had five,' says Mark. 'I think that takes some beating. But we did sort of get our revenge.'

'Oh yeah?'

'We got him so pissed that he passed out. We put him on a room-service trolley, stark naked, tied a luggage label around his cock, put him in the lift and pressed the button for ground-floor reception. He went up and down a few times before the hotel staff got so pissed off that they woke him and sent him to his room. He had to fly the plane the next day. Somehow he did it. He must have had the hangover from hell. I imagine he was on autopilot the whole way home.'

The music grows louder and the table dancing gets more and more frenetic, some people leaping from chair to chair. Craig shouts something along the lines that the pina colada needs replenishing and two girls walk across the room with their wheelie bags and start filling the bowl with their collection of randomly stolen spirits. The half-dressed blonde stirs the mixture with the red dildo while Craig puts his hand up her skirt. His cocktail is ruined but no-one is sober enough to care, least of all Craig, who at the last count was two tequila shots, one Bus and three pina coladas in.

'All right?' says Andy, shaking his shoulders at me in some weird dance move, then pausing for a second to belch. 'Tom's going to try to get together a small group to go skinny-dipping.'

'What, now?' I ask, finishing my drink and pouring myself a slops cocktail. 'It's far too early, surely?'

'Is it?' He hiccups. 'Oh well, we may as well give the neighbours something to complain about.'

'Mmm,' I mumble.

I've just taken a swig of my drink and am now trying to work out how to get it down me. It is foul, fetid and burning my mouth. I want to spit it out. But Sue walks past so I hold my breath and swallow. My eyes start to fill with water and a tear rolls down my cheek.

'Jesus Christ,' says Mark.

'What?'

'Over there.'

As the water slowly clears from my eyes, I can see over by the door two stewards who have just walked into the room. The first is wearing leather chaps, a black leather codpiece, black boots, a leather-studded cap and a sort of buckled harness across his naked and waxed chest; the other is on all fours, wearing a spiked dog collar, and has, quite simply, come as his bitch.

'Are they with you?' I ask Mark.

'No, they came in from Bangkok some time last night.'

'Do you know them?'

'Yeah.' He snorts. 'They're a couple of exhibitionists. They're always dressing up like this. One of them has got some pretty dodgy piercings that are always getting him into bloody trouble if we ever go through the metal detectors at Customs. They're not my cup of tea.'

'No?'

'No.' He grins at me, finishing his Bailey's. 'My addiction is passengers. The straighter the better. You'd be amazed how many you can turn on a long-haul flight. I've done it on a plane, in the toilet and in the galley, but I usually like to wait until we land and get it back at the hotel room.'

'Did you manage to pick up anyone on the last flight?'

'No,' he replies, making a sad face. 'But I did manage to bag some bloke who sells mobile phones on the last trip out to Sydney. I filled him full of free champagne and he took me for a weekend spa in the Blue Mountains.'

'Sounds great.'

'It was.'

Mark and I stand in silence. He stares at the leather-clad master and dog while I watch Richard doing the rounds. He greets every woman in turn with the same wide smile and the same once-over with the eyes. The half-naked girls covered in bubbles appear to hold his attention the most. Their naked first officer in crime seems to have disappeared so they are happy flirting with Richard. He is, after all, a higher rank.

Andy has hooked up with the leather boys and is playing with his blond hair for all he is worth. He throws his body around with laughter, and it seems to be doing the trick. Tom's disappeared. Sue is talking to another hostie. Craig is still mixing cocktails with his hand up the blonde's skirt, and Rachel seems to be chatting up a slim, dark-haired steward in the corner. There are fewer dancers than earlier and the music seems to have slowed somewhat. The frantic boozing and bonding pace has abated a bit.

'Let's play truth or dare!' suggests one of the half-naked girls as she clambers onto a table and claps her hands to get everyone's attention. 'Come on,' she slurs. 'I promise to be the first person to strip totally naked and cover myself in soap.'

Just as it looks as if she might have the room's attention, the nude first officer bursts through the door in a pair of Burberry swimming trunks, a large yellow Garfield cartoon tattooed on his chest.

'Skinny-dipping!' he yells at the top of his voice, his arms outstretched like Jesus. 'Come on, the pool is empty, there's no-one about, let's get our kit off!'

'I'll show you mine if you'll show me yours,' says Richard to one of the bubble girls, who giggles loudly.

'I'll come with you!' says one of the girls still dancing on a chair.

'Me too!' shouts someone else.

'Doesn't anyone want to play truth or dare?' queries the topless girl on the table, looking oddly confused. 'I thought that's what we were playing.'

'I'll play truth or dare,' declares Andy, banking on the two leather boys not being swimmers.

'I'll join you,' says the man in the cap.

Relief is writ large on Andy's face.

The party is beginning to divide up into those who want to drink and swim and those who want to drink and hand out forfeits. Someone turns the music down a bit. Not that Craig notices as he has his tongue down the throat of the blonde. She is sitting on the table, her legs wrapped around his waist, her backside in a pile of empties.

'What are you going to do?' asks Mark.

'Not totally sure yet,' I say, taking a step away. 'How about you?'

'I thought I might go skinny-dipping,' he says, looking at me straight in the eyes.

'Good,' I say. 'That sounds good. I think I might play truth or dare. I'm not a great one for swimming.'

'Is that really your thing?' asks Susan, slipping her arms around my waist and leaning up against me. Her timing is excellent. 'I can think of much more pleasant ways of passing the time.'

'Oh, right,' mutters Mark, looking quickly at the floor. 'Um, fine,' he adds, moving slowly away. 'I'll leave you two to it.'

Sue turns to face me, a wide smile on her expectant face, her dimples showing. Her breath smells sweetly of alcohol.

'Thanks for that.'

'For what?'

'For seeing him off. I think he was after me . . .' My voice fades as the expression on her face grows ever more confused.

'After you?' she asks. 'What?'

'Nothing.' My heart is beginning to race, my chest to tighten.

'Why don't we go somewhere else?' she asks softly, starting to play with the edge of my suit jacket.

'Um . . .' I swallow. My mouth has gone dry.

'Alcohol!' yells Tom from the doorway, waving what looks like bottles of Asti spumante. The whole room erupts into cheers and a round of applause. 'Don't ask me where I got it,' he declares. 'A true barman never reveals his sources.'

'Come on,' Sue whispers in my ear, 'let's go somewhere a little quieter.'

Hand in hand we make our way towards the door. Everyone is too crucified by tiredness and jet lag and too distracted by the sight of fresh alcohol to notice.

'Flying!' says Tom, as Susan and I slip past him. 'A champagne lifestyle on lemonade money. Don't you just love it?'